Going to Pieces

Going to Pieces

The Rise and Fall of the Slasher Film, 1978–1986

ADAM ROCKOFF

McFarland & Company, Inc., Publishers

Jefferson, North Carolina, and London

Library of Congress Cataloguing-in-Publication Data

Rockoff, Adam, 1974–
Going to pieces : the rise and fall of the slasher film, 1978–1986 /
Adam Rockoff.
p.   cm.
Includes bibliographical references and index.
ISBN 0-7864-1227-5 (illustrated case binding : 50# alkaline paper) ∞
1. Horror films—United States—History and criticism. I. Title.
PN1995.9.H6R63   2002   791.43'6164—dc21   2002000543

British Library cataloguing data are available

Cover photograph: Michael Myers (George Wilbur) in
Halloween 6: The Curse of Michael Myers (1995).

Manufactured in the United States of America

McFarland & Company, Inc., Publishers
Box 611, Jefferson, North Carolina 28640
www.mcfarlandpub.com

For Lori,
who likes romantic comedies

Acknowledgments

Contrary to popular belief, writing a book is never an individual effort. The prevailing image of a solitary writer hunched over his keyboard, pounding on the keys in a monotonous rhythm, subsisting on copious amounts of coffee, is only part of the story. The reality is that a book relies on the efforts of many individuals. In this case, there are more than a few people to whom I am forever indebted for their time, assistance, support and, most of all, enthusiasm.

First and foremost, I would like to thank the directors, producers and writers of these slasher films who took time out of their busy schedules to speak with me: Ruth Avergon, Danilo Bach, John Carpenter, Sean Cunningham, Tom DeSimone, John Dunning, Herb Freed, Bill Lustig, Paul Lynch, Armand Mastroianni, John McCarty, Jack Sholder, Roger Spottiswoode, Fred Walton, Irwin Yablans and Joe Zito. While their recollections and anecdotes were indispensable to this book, more importantly, I know I speak for horror fans everywhere when I say *thank you*

for your films. They are part of the reason I still check under the bed before going to sleep.

I would also like to thank the various individuals and companies who were kind enough to supply me with the stills from these slasher films: Eric Caidin and Hollywood Book & Poster, Jerry Ohlinger's Movie Material Store, Inc., Gene Massimo, Buddy Barnett and Collectors Book Store. *The New York Ripper* ain't *Star Wars*, and to say that there is a dearth of material on some of the more obscure slashers is a gross understatement. Luckily, these people had the foresight to preserve this memorabilia and were kind enough to share it with me.

Finally, words cannot express how grateful I am to my wife Lori, whose unwavering support throughout the course of this project was instrumental to its completion. For over a year and a half, she fell asleep to the soothing hum of a chainsaw as I stayed up well into the night screening hundreds of slashers. That's what a good woman will do for you.

Table of Contents

Introduction

People are generally intrigued when they find out I am writing a book about film. When I tell them it's about horror films, they often raise their eyebrows and shake their head in consternation. When I tell them, somewhat sheepishly, it's specifically about slashers—that especially violent breed of films which proliferated in the early 1980s—they quickly gather their children and hurry off in the opposite direction, usually throwing a nervous glance over their shoulder.

If there is something commendable about writing a book on cinema, then there is something less than noble about writing a book on horror films, and something downright perverse about writing a book about slasher movies. These brutal and gory films which came of age during the late 1970s were the bastard children of the horror film, too gleefully violent and graphic to be embraced by the mainstream, but far too popular and successful to achieve true cult status. They hovered somewhere in a cinematic netherworld—between popular and counterculture—taunting critics who found them indicative of the decline of Western civilization while enthralling millions of dedicated fans who flocked to every new release.

Critics often dismiss the slasher film

without acknowledging the indelible mark it left on American culture. To parents, Michael, Jason and Freddy were the all–American kids down the block, but to teenagers—whose fear and devotion (not to mention their money) gave these boogeymen life—they were a new breed of hero. Comic books and trading cards detailed their adventures. Miniature action figures, complete with plastic knives, axes and machetes, filled toy stores where once upon a time Luke Skywalker and Han Solo held court. Nintendo released video games based on both *Friday the 13th* and *A Nightmare on Elm Street*. On Halloween, what self-respecting kid would want to be a ballplayer, or even a vampire for that matter, when for only $19.95 he could brandish a plastic replica of Freddy's glove? The slasher film hadn't just entered our nightmares, it had entered our national consciousness.

After I'm asked what my book is about, if people aren't immediately turned off by its subject, the next question is inevitably along the lines of, "Why slasher films?" Few can comprehend how I can both enjoy and admire these films, and even fewer understand how I could have devoted hundreds of hours to researching, watching and writing about them. They seem baffled that any normal well-adjusted adult could possibly immerse himself in such a disagreeable subject for so long.

Unlike most of the authors who have written on the horror film, I was not weaned on the Universal Classics. I didn't collect EC horror comics or sprint to the corner newsstand each month eagerly awaiting the new issue of *Famous Monsters of Filmland*. I was far too young to sneak into the now infamous "drive-in double feature." Instead, I read *Fangoria* and *Gorezone*, viewed horror films mostly in the comfort of my living room, and terrified my babysitting girlfriends with taunts of, "Have you checked the children?" I was a child of the slasher film.

In the early 1980s, cable television was still in its infancy. Viewers were not yet bombarded with 500 channels, 498 of which they cared little about. In those days, the cable guide was a slim full color pamphlet printed on glossy paper, not the flimsy newsprint booklet of today. The films were listed alphabetically with a short blurb describing each one, followed by any of the four words or phrases used to describe potentially objectionable content: adult themes, nudity, profanity, violence.

I was drawn to the ones which warned of violence. Even their names were terrifying: *Halloween, Friday the 13th, He Knows You're Alone, Terror Train, The Burning, Hell Night*. What unspeakable horrors could possibly be contained within a film that had the temerity to call itself *My Bloody Valentine*? What terrors lurked under such innocuous sounding titles as *Prom Night, Graduation Day, Night School* and *Happy Birthday to Me*? Was *To All a Goodnight* really an uplifting drama about holiday cheer. I didn't think so.

If cable television was theater industry's Scylla, then home video was its Charybdis. Renting a video, making some popcorn and plopping down in the con-

fines of the home was both cheaper and more convenient than trekking to a movie theater. The video store squared off against the multiplex for the eyes and ears of America. Although the traditional movie theater never became obsolete, as the traditionalists predicated, its monopoly on theatrical exhibition was forever shattered.

While the birth of cable television and home video sent shock waves through the industry, for me, and thousands of kids like me, it meant one thing—films which in a million years our parents would never have allowed us to go see were now readily available. What's more, since I was the only one in the house who knew how to use the record feature on our VCR—not to mention the only one who knew that such a feature existed—I could record *Visiting Hours* at 3 A.M. right under the noses of my sleeping parents. But you could only amass a modest library by recording the few generally mainstream offerings which the movie channels would air in the dead of night. For the rest, you had to go to the video store.

Back in the early days, before Blockbuster, Hollywood Video and West Coast Video monopolized the industry and purged all things subversive from their shelves, for the horror aficionado, the video store was a sight to behold. Endless rows of clamshell boxes released by companies such as Key, Vestron, Media, Continental, Wizard and Gorgon proudly offered a smorgasbord of gore. Many times, the artwork and photographs on the video box were more compelling than the films they advertised. For example, anybody who plucked *Class Reunion Massacre* (the video release of *The Redeemer*) from the shelf, thinking the scenes of carnage shown on the back of the box were indicative of the film itself, was no doubt sorely disappointed.

As I got older, I began to take an interest in the more intellectual aspects of the slasher film (an amusing oxymoron to some). What was their lasting impact on the film industry? What were their mechanisms of production? Distribution? Exhibition? Were they nothing more than harmless entertainment, or shrewd social commentaries on society's mores? It didn't take long for me to realize that there was a conspicuous lack of literature on the subject. Most books about horror films barely mentioned the slasher, and if they did, it was only to attack it. To make matters worse, those which did devote substantial time to the subject were highly problematic. John McCarty's seminal and influential *Splatter Movies* was too broad, as was William Schoell's earlier *Stay Out of the Shower: 25 Years of Shocker Films Beginning with* Psycho. Kim Newman's *Nightmare Movies* has absolutely no respect for the slasher and Vera Dika's *Games of Terror: Halloween, Friday the 13th and The Films of the Stalker Cycle*, while often brilliant, is sometimes contradictory and a bit too plodding for casual fans of the genre.

My goal then became clear—to write a book about slasher films for *fans* of the slasher film. Rather than compile a text which simply regurgitates the plots of these films, like so many other books have done, I wanted to create a work which examines, critiques and, above all, celebrates all aspects of the slasher. I wanted to hear all the compelling behind-the-scenes production stories from the directors, writers and producers themselves. I wanted to give fair, insightful and accessible reviews of the films. And finally, I wanted to bring some historical perspective to the slasher phenomenon, to show how a group of films—which, by all sensible logic, should have been dead on arrival—altered the landscape of American cinema.

People are often under the impression that the hardest part of writing a book is the actual writing. Nothing could be further from the truth. For a writer, to write about a subject about which he or she feels passionate is the easy part. The challenge, especially for a subject as esoteric as the slasher film, is the research and preparation. Source materials on these films are, to say the least, scarce. There was a lack of articles, essays and reviews about these films upon their release, and now, over 20 years later in some cases, the original documents are nearly impossible to track down. Many of the people who played an integral role in the creation of these films are now deceased. Sadly, they passed away leaving no memoirs about the films they helped create; and, even more tragically, no one ever thought to ask. But the hardest part, by far, was finding the films themselves. I can only say, thank God for the few independent video stores who are not afraid to carry the likes of *The New York Ripper*, rent-by-mail video companies such as Video Wasteland and the many individuals I've met who long ago recognized the value of these forgotten films and were shrewd enough to keep pristine copies.

Before you embark upon the remarkable tumultuous history of the slasher film, there are a few points I would like to make about the nature of this book. I should first say that this is not an exhaustive study of every slasher film ever made. Such a Herculean task is beyond the scope of this work and would be nearly impossible if one takes into account every obscure slasher and all the straight-to-video nonsense which has been released since the heyday of the genre. I have made every attempt, however, to examine in great detail the major offenders and create the most comprehensive and thorough history of the slasher film to date. That said, there are still inevitably some lesser-known films—some which may have even received theatrical distribution—that I may have neglected.

The date listed for each film generally

refers to the year in which it was released in its country of origin. Quite often, quality foreign horror films languish in obscurity before receiving a stateside release. It is not uncommon for these films to be found floating around in bastardized bootleg versions years before they are properly released theatrically. In addition, some of the most successful domestic slasher films were given limited releases before opening wide. Since the same film was sometimes released in different forms and at varying times, I've tried to choose the date of both its earliest and widest release.

The most problematic aspect of this book was deciding which of a film's titles to use. It is not uncommon for a film, especially a horror film, to go through several different title changes before its release. Nor is it unheard of for a film to be released, pulled from theaters and later re-released under a different title. For example, Wes Craven's *The Last House on the Left*, was called—at various times during its saga from script to screen—*Sex Crime of the Century*, *Krug and Company* and *Night of Vengeance*, before finally settling on the title by which it is known today. Home video has further muddied the issue. These distributors, usually with no good reason, often rename a film once they acquire its rights. This is why *The Redeemer*, also known as *The Redeemer ... Son of Satan!*, is found in video stores as *Class Reunion Massacre*.

Sometimes a film's multiple titles will be so similar that one wonders why anybody took the trouble to alter them at all, as is the case with *Don't Go in the Woods ... Alone*, also known more concisely as *Don't Go in the Woods*. Other times they couldn't be more dissimilar; *The Prowler* is sometimes called *Rosemary's Killer* or *The Graduation*, while Mario Bava's ultra-violent *Twitch of the Death Nerve* is called anything from *Bloodbath*, to *Bay of Blood*, to one of its Italian titles, *Ecologia del Delitto*.

In an effort to clarify the issue, I have tried to consistently refer to the film by its best-known title. While I realize that this itself may be a matter of opinion, almost all films—even those with multiple titles—have one by which it is universally known. This is why I refer to Dario Argento's first film as *The Bird with the Crystal Plumage*, rather than by its Italian title, *L'Uccello dalle Piume di Cristallo*. For those who are either sticklers for accuracy or simply curious to see what creative appellations were once bestowed upon a film, I have included an appendix which lists all the films contained within, along with most of their alternative titles.

But enough preliminaries. The fact that you're holding this book right now and have read this far means one thing—you're a fan of the slasher. So sit back, relax and welcome to a world where cars never start, a wrong number is never just a wrong number, and the creaky door in the next room is not just your imagination.

CHAPTER 1

What Is a Slasher Film?

When I told John Dunning, producer of both *My Bloody Valentine* and *Happy Birthday to Me*, that I was writing a book about slasher films, his response shocked me. "What's a slasher film?" he asked. Completely taken aback, I managed to stammer out some official sounding definition about how slasher films were a subgenre of horror movies which share similar formal and stylistic elements and adhere to a fairly rigid paradigm. There was a moment of awkward silence. "Hmm, okay," he finally said, sounding no more convinced than I that the makeshift definition I had just given was an accurate description of the films he made.

Then it occurred to me: If John Dunning, the man responsible for two of the most successful and well-known slasher films, didn't know what one was, and I, a person who is writing a book on the subject, couldn't immediately give an accurate definition, there must be some confusion about this type of film.

So what is a slasher? We've all seen them, or are at least familiar with their *modus operandi*. Ironically, detractors of the slasher film have no problem giving what they feel is an accurate depiction—a maniac with a knife slaughtering a group of young, good-looking teenagers in a myriad of gruesome ways. Clean and simple, but too easy. Both *The Thing* (1982) and *The Evil Dead* (1982) are exceptionally gruesome, bloody and violent, yet they're not slasher films. Both *Cobra* (1986) and *Kalifornia* (1993) involve a knife-wielding maniac, yet they're not slashers either.

The fact is, unlike *film noir*, the Western and the musical, the slasher is not easily defined. It is a rogue genre, and like the films it encompasses it is tough, problematic and fiercely individualistic. However, there are some distinctive and consistent elements which are prevalent in enough films that a workable, however malleable, definition of the slasher can be formed.

The Killer

There is a prevailing misconception, due in part to the enormous popularity of *The Texas Chainsaw Massacre*, *Halloween* and *Friday the 13th*, that the killer in slasher films is always a supernatural boogeyman who wears a battered hockey mask and wields a machete. However, in the majority of slasher films, the killer is an ordinary person who has suffered some terrible—and sometimes not so terrible—

trauma (humiliation, the death of a loved one, rape, psychological abuse). It is because of this past injustice that he (or in a few cases, she) seeks vengeance—and the bloodier the better.

It seems logical that the best-known villains are vaguely supernatural—not in a spectral way like ghosts and angels, but as being impervious to ordinarily mortal wounds—since their nature was determined by economics, not narrative. That is, their indestructibility was less a thematic choice than a practical measure. To maximize the profitability of their series, producers had to ensure that their killers—on whom the success of their series hinged—were immortal. In both the *Halloween* and *Friday the 13th* series, the two franchises which best illustrate this phenomenon, neither Michael Myers nor Jason Voorhees became "unkillable" until producers realized that there would indeed be sequels. In fact, in *Friday the 13th*, the killer is not even Jason, but his mother. This forced a rather unbelievable scenario for *Friday the 13th Part 2* in which the boy returns decades after drowning in a lake. Realism, it seemed, was obviously a minor casualty in return for box office profit.

With few exceptions, the killer in slasher films is overtly asexual, aside from the brief bouts of voyeurism which tend to precede the murders, and his/her gender is left ambiguous.[1] However, even though the nature of the slasher usually dictates that the killer's identity remain unknown until the film's final scene, it is implicit throughout that he is male, and not just an ordinary male, but one who epitomizes masculinity to ludicrous extremes. He is not only tough, he is immortal. He is not only strong, but powerful enough to string his victims up as human booby traps for their horrified friends to find. He is not only aggressive, he is psychotic. Surprisingly, a few of the earliest and most suc-

cessful slashers had a woman killer. The murderer in both *Happy Birthday to Me* and *Night School* is female, as is the killer in *Friday the 13th*, the archetypal slasher. Of course, these films, with the exception of *Happy Birthday to Me*, take great pains to make sure the visual cues point indisputably to a male killer. In *Friday the 13th*, the killer drives a beat-up pickup truck, wears work boots and a flannel shirt, is adept with both a knife and ax, and has the strength to toss the corpse of a full grown woman through a glass window. When we finally see the killer—a rather small middle-aged woman—the film avoids having to answer any questions regarding the plausibility of her actions by distracting the audience with a wild finale.

For the most part, these killers are homicidal maniacs, not sadistic tormentors. Contrary to popular belief, their killings are usually quick and relatively painless; swift decapitations and throat-slitting, while not pleasant, are infinitely more humane than fingernail extraction, branding and other medieval tortures in films such as *The Pit and the Pendulum* (1961), *Witchfinder General* (1968) and *Mark of the Devil* (1970). Slasher films don't linger too long on the victim's agony. Prolonged scenes of misery and suffering quickly turn off mainstream audiences and are more appropriate for hard-core cult films like *Ilsa: She Wolf of the SS* (1974) and *In a Glass Cage* (1986). There are few scenes of extreme brutality, such as in the low-budget hit *Reservoir Dogs* (1992), in which Michael Madsen slices off a police officer's ear and then attempts to burn him alive. Nor do the villains conjure up some elaborate diabolical plan, *à la* the James Bond films, to ensnare their victim. They simply go about their duty, which is killing, with systematic precision, uncaring, emotionless and unmerciful, which may be the chief reason why many people find these films so objectionable.

Freddy Krueger (Robert Englund), a hideously burned child murderer (shown here in *Freddy's Dead: The Final Nightmare* [1991]), first appeared in Wes Craven's *A Nightmare on Elm Street* (1984). He went on to become one of the slasher film's most popular killers, appearing in six sequels as well as his own short-lived television series.

Weapons of Choice

If there is one constant of the slasher which has remained unchanged throughout the entire cycle, it is the consistency of the killer's weapons of choice. In slasher films, never does the terror-stricken victim run blindly through the woods only to be gunned down in a hail of bullets. Never does she start the car's engine—which invariably fails to turn over anyway—to be blown to smithereens in some elaborately constructed booby trap.

The slasher film—which was not named erroneously—is defined by the method by which its characters are killed. The victims are usually slain by a knife, although any sharp metal object seems to be sufficient. Killings by swords, razors, axes, machetes, arrows, chain saws, powerdrills, hammers, swords, spears, saws, scythes, hatchets, darts, sickles and pitchforks are commonplace. The killer, in a burst of creativity, may even use such innocuous household items as a corkscrew or road flares. Sometimes a specific weapon is reserved for a specific villain (Freddy Krueger's finger knives), sometimes it is used as a plot device (*The Toolbox Murders*, *The Driller Killer*), and often it is the only convenient instrument lying around.

The slasher film is not, as many would assume, defined by the brutality, explicitness or frequency of its murders. If this was the case, then a typical action film would be far more contentious. If slasher films are nothing more than "a series of executions," then the frenetic action films which were released around the same time are orchestrated massacres. The early slasher films averaged about four to six killings per film. As the cycle wore on, the body count rose steadily in an effort to keep a rapidly desensitized audience stimulated. Still, this is far less than a film such as *Commando* (1985) or *Rambo: First Blood*

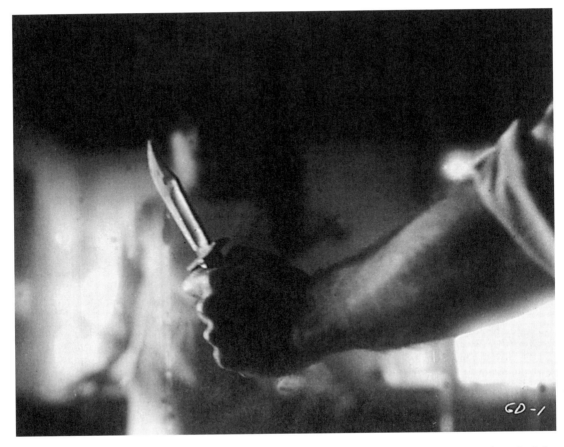

In slasher films, the knife is the weapon of choice as seen here in *Graduation Day* (1981). Of course, psychotic maniacs generally aren't too picky and, in lieu of cutlery, any sharp object that can penetrate a victim seems to do the trick.

Part II (1985) in which people are slain by the dozen. The victims in these action films are spared no indignity, nor are their demises any less graphic. In one five-minute stretch in *Commando*, Matrix (Arnold Schwarzenegger) scalps one adversary with a saw blade, hacks off another one's forearm with a machete, and buries an ax into another one's crotch. And this doesn't include the 50 or so mercenaries he shoots, stabs or blows to camouflage-patterned confetti. In a carefully staged scene from *Rambo*, our sociopathic hero (Sylvester Stallone) covers himself entirely in mud to surprise an unsuspecting quarry. As soon as the man is within striking dis-

tance, Stallone lunges from his hiding spot and buries his wicked serrated hunting knife into the victim's chest. He exhibits far more brutality than Michael Myers does when impaling a victim to a closet door with one quick thrust of his knife.

So why are the slasher-like killings of our testosterone-soaked heroes cheered, admired or discounted as harmless entertainment? Most likely, it is because these killings don't require the same amount of identification and role-play as those in a slasher. To paraphrase the old saying, if you kill a few men you're a murderer, if you kill thousands you're a conqueror. In action films, the killings—while bloody and brutal—are quick and indiscriminate. Our hero barely has time to remove his knife from the chest of a wounded adversary before taking off the head of a rapidly approaching reinforcement. Everyone except the hero is a villain who deserves to die. They're not people, they're set pieces, whose sole job is to be easily eliminated in a variety of fashions.

On the other hand, the killings in slasher films *are* personal. We usually know the victim and although we often don't like them—think the shrill teenage harpy who whines to her boyfriend to hurry back to bed—we can still identify with them. We are also intimately familiar with the weapon, having seen it used in a previous scene or displayed in glorious full color on the film's one-sheet. There is, however, nothing more personal than the morbid fascination between the audience, the weapon and the victim's body. The promise of disfigurement provides an illicit thrill. While the weapons themselves provide the most convenient tool for this disfigurement, it is the act, not the method, which piques the audience's curiosity. There isn't much disappointment when Jason Voorhees crushes his victim's head, or tears out their heart, instead of offing them with a slice of his machete.

Pundits of the slasher, most of whom undertake a gender-based reading of these films, emphasize the physical act of the knife (weapon) penetrating the flesh. To them, the knife's phallic blade becomes a symbol of violation, entering the victim's body in a painful, bloody and unnatural way. As Carol Clover states, "all phallic symbols are not equal," demonstrating that the symbolic nature of a knife is far more powerful than that of a gun, rope or any other tool of death. What this theory fails to take into account is that in slasher films both men and women are killed indiscriminately. The knife, as many have proposed, is not a surrogate penis. Much

has been written on the difference between the deaths of the sexes, how men are killed quickly while the women are forced to suffer. However, it is certainly a stretch to propose that this was ever a conscious choice on the part of the filmmaker. I refuse to believe that, for example, Herschell Gordon Lewis and David Friedman sat around discussing psychosexual paradigms before making *The Wizard of Gore*. In slasher films, death is not gender-biased. It is a unisex curiosity whose realism was enhanced by trends in special effects which were coming into their own.

Special Effects and the Dawn of Savini

By the 1980s, special effects were no longer dictated by what could be *done*, but what could be *shown* on screen. An argument can be made that it was not the themes or plots of these films which ignited the fury of its critics, but advancements in the field of special effects. It was not the fact that somebody was stabbed—people had been killed in far more gruesome ways since the early days of cinema—but now, instead of seeing them crumple to the ground in a quick bloodless death, audiences could actually watch the knife enter the body. To many, these slashers were less traditional thrillers than surgical documentary.

The art had come a long way since the days when makeup legend Jack Pierce transformed Lon Chaney, Jr., into the Wolf Man through a five-hour painstaking process in which strips of yak fur were meticulously applied to his face in 21 stages. It had reached such a level of frightening realism that its effectiveness and the talent (some would say genius) necessary to accomplish these jaw-dropping effects could no longer be overlooked. In 1981, Rick Baker won the inaugural

Best Makeup Academy Award for his work on *An American Werewolf in London*.[2] Even today, the film's werewolf transformation scenes are still the benchmark for such effects. Then in 1982, Rob Bottin raised the bar a notch higher with his groundbreaking work in John Carpenter's remake of the sci-fi classic *The Thing*, proving that whatever the writers could conceive, the effects men could create. In fact, special effects took on such importance that they often supplanted the writer, director and even the actors. The makeup men became stars in their own right, and for the slasher film, one name stood out above all others—Tom Savini.

As a child growing up in Pittsburgh, Savini saw *Man of a Thousand Faces* (1957), the biography of silent scream great Lon Chaney, and instantly realized his true calling. While in college at Carnegie Mellon University, he ran into another Pittsburgh native, George Romero, who was then busy making *Night of the Living Dead*. Savini tried to get a job on Romero's classic film, but he was called into service as a combat photographer in the Vietnam War. One can only guess how the American horror film would be different had two of the genre's greatest artists collaborated on their first project. After returning from Vietnam, Savini met the art director of Bob Clark's *Children Shouldn't Play With Dead Things* (1972), which subsequently landed him work on Clark's 1972 film *Deathdream*, and then on the Ed Gein—inspired cannibal film *Deranged* (1974).

Although Savini achieved his first major success with Romero's *Dawn of the Dead* (1979), *Night of the Living Dead's* sequel, it was his work on *Friday the 13th* which had the greatest impact on the history of the slasher. From the moment an arrow shoots up through the neck of Jack (Kevin Bacon) as he lies in bed smoking a joint, the horror film was never the same.

This one effect, more than any other, done in plain view of an unsuspecting audience without the safety of a cutaway, ushered in a new era of spectacularly bloody and graphic special effects.

Since *Friday the 13th*, which also contains other such memorable effects as an ax to the face, a throat-slitting and one of the most realistic decapitations ever caught on film, Savini has left his bloody mark on many of the most successful and important slasher films ever made. His work reads like a highlight reel of the genre's greatest moments: the exploding head from *Maniac*, the raft scene in *The Burning*, *The Prowler*'s brutal bayoneting and, maybe the most impressive of all, Jason's demise at the end of *Friday the 13th—The Final Chapter*, in which his recently unmasked face slides down the blade of a machete. Savini has been christened the Gore Guru, the King of Splatter and the Gore Maestro—wearing each moniker as a badge of honor—and was instrumental in creating the essence of the slasher film, those horribly realistic and bloody deaths which were alternately loved, hated, admired, feared and reviled by fans and critics alike.

Setting

Slasher films take place in a variety of different settings. Because the audience for these films is predominately teenage, as are the characters with whom they identify, the location is often a universally recognized place associated with adolescence: summer camp (*Friday the 13th*, *The Burning*, *Sleepaway Camp*), high school (*Prom Night*, *Graduation Day*), college (*Night School*, *Black Christmas*, *Hell Night*) or even the comforting streets of suburbia (*Halloween*, *Slumber Party Massacre*, *A Nightmare on Elm Street*). Even if the film isn't specifically set in this milieu, its characters have come from there. For example, *Terror*

Train takes place on a train which a group of collegians have rented for their graduation party. Sometimes the characters are intimately familiar with the location, giving them a presumed, however fleeting, advantage over the killer. They know where the darkened corridors lead, in which cabinet Daddy keeps his gun, and which neighbor's house is always unlocked. This knowledge, however, is possessed in vain, for the killer always prevails in the end. Other times it is the killer who has the edge, and the terrified teenagers who stumble into his domain find themselves incapable of coping with the hostile unfamiliar environment. When night falls, as it invariably does in every slasher film, the characters are at a further disadvantage for the darkness never seems to hamper the killer's effectiveness.

These locations are all similar in their isolation. This isolation functions to separate the characters from society at large and negates the possibility of a rescue. However, it is interesting to note that with very few exceptions (*April Fool's Day, Hell Night*), there is nothing physically preventing the characters' escape. In a life-or-death situation, as is always the case in these films, any normal person in control of their faculties would be able to get away. In fact, this is one of the most problematic areas for those who question the slasher film's plausibility. This isolation also symbolically separates the characters from the adult community. Slasher films are notoriously devoid of grown-ups, and the few who are present tend to play three general roles: (1) the killer him or herself (*Friday the 13th, A Nightmare on Elm Street*); (2) the wise "seer" or "elder" who offers advice on how to defeat the killer (*Halloween*); or

A bunch of young, good-looking teenagers left alone in the woods is a sure recipe for disaster. Take for instance these teens in *Friday the 13th–The Final Chapter* (1984).

(3) the ineffectual authority figure who refuses to believe or acknowledge the danger at hand (*Hell Night, Don't Go in the Woods … Alone*).

Since isolation is of paramount importance, the city would seem to be a poor place to set a slasher. However, with their impersonal antiseptic nature, vast urban sprawls can sometimes appear more isolated than a campsite or abandoned mansion. In these films—*The Driller Killer, Maniac, The New York Ripper*—the killer, as well as his victims, is usually an adult, and his madness is often seen as a byproduct of the city's desolation and decay. These are also among the most controversial, albeit intelligent, slasher films. Instead of attributing the killing sprees to random madness, they bring up tough social, economic and philosophical questions—although often obscured by eye-gouging, throat-slitting, and mutilating—about society's responsibility for the actions of violent criminals.

Past Event

Slasher films often begin with a prologue which takes place years before the events in the film. In it, the killer either witnesses a traumatic event, usually to a family member (*Friday the 13th, Prom Night, Happy Birthday to Me, My Bloody Valentine*), or is the victim of a devastating, humiliating or harmful accident, prank or tragedy (*The Burning, Terror Train*). On the anniversary of this horrible event, usually designated by a holiday or traditional celebration (Christmas, New Year's Eve, Thanksgiving, April Fool's Day, birthday, graduation, prom), the killer

Holidays in slasher films are never cause for celebration, especially Halloween (as seen here in *Halloween: H₂0* (1998). Instead, they signify the return of some traumatized psychopath who is out for vengeance.

returns to the scene to claim his revenge. If that exact location is no longer available, or is deserted, any place in close proximity will do. For example, in *The Burning*, Camp Blackfoot, where the original tragedy took place, is now closed, so the killer moves on to the nearby Camp Stonewater. During the rest of the film, the killer sets out to punish the guilty. This may include the ones directly responsible for his misery (*Terror Train*), a symbolic representation (*Friday the 13th*), those related to the guilty (*A Nightmare on Elm Street*) or any person unlucky enough to get in his way (*Halloween*).

There are two reasons these slasher films typically employ this prologue, which tends to condense the expository elements of the film into a brief scene. The first is a practical reason, to grab the audience's attention from the beginning and whet their appetite for the carnage to come. After all, it's not the complex characters and lush cinematography of these films which tide them over until the bloody entrée. The second is to give the audience an explanation for the killer's fury, no matter how implausible, ridiculous or unlikely that explanation may be. It is interesting to note that this explanation rarely makes the killer a more sympathetic figure, most likely because it is hardly sufficient to explain the level of psychosis these villains display. Only a few films, *Halloween* being the prime example, operate under the supposition that the killer was born bad, or is inherently evil, for congenital pathology is far less interesting than the timeless theme of revenge.

The Final Girl

One of the most enduring images of the slasher film is that of the beautiful heroine screaming in abject terror—her eyes wide with fear—as the killer rapidly approaches. These postmodern damsels in distress, who have been collectively referred to as the "Final Girl," are usually the lone survivors of the killer's rampage. Unlike the helpless schoolmarm of the Western, who is rescued at the last minute by the valiant gunslinger, the headstrong ladies of the slasher film do not rely on their inefficient heroes to pluck them from the jaws (or rather blades) of death. From the outset of the film, the Final Girl is defined by her toughness, resourcefulness, determination and perseverance. In contrast to her friends—whom she finds carved up in variety of places—she survives to fight the killer in the film's climactic sequence.

Much has been made of the masculinity of the Final Girl, which, in the case of the slasher film, is used as a euphemism for strength and competence, not as a reference to sexuality or gender. However, in her marvelous study on gender in the horror film, *Men, Women, and Chain Saws*, Carol Clover writes:

> The Final Girl, is on reflection, a congenial double for the adolescent male. She is feminine enough to act out in a gratifying way, a way unapproved for adult males, the terms and masochistic pleasures of the underlying fantasy, but not so feminine as to disturb the structure of male competence and sexuality.

This theory, which has merit, cannot apply to every slasher. For if the travails of the Final Girl are a face-saving way for the predominately male audience to vicariously enjoy the victim role, what can account for those slashers in which there are two survivors, both a man and a woman? Or the few slashers in which a man is the lone survivor? Some writers have even pointed out that the names of the Final Girls themselves are purposely ambiguous. This is, however, a gross overanalysis. For every androgynous name like

Marti, Stevie or Bobbi, there are two gender specific ones such as Alice, Ginny, Laurie or Nancy.

Those who find the morality of slasher films distasteful generally hold as evidence what they take to be these films' prevailing mantra: good girls don't die, but loose ones do. To simplify it further, the girls who refrain from having sex survive, the ones who indulge in their passions die. As Jamie Lee Curtis, the prominent scream queen of the time, said, "There's usually a sexual factor, yes. They kill the loose girls and save the virgins in most of these movies." The slasher antecedent of this theme—whose literary roots are an-

cient—is *Psycho*, in which the thieving, licentious Marion is murdered before she can return the stolen money and marry Sam. The theme was continued most famously in *Halloween*—where the virginal Laurie thwarts the killer while her promiscuous friends are murdered—and from there in later films such as *Terror Train*, *Hell Night* and *A Nightmare on Elm Street*. The truth is that in the slasher film, both "good" girls and "bad" girls are killed with equal gusto. The fact that this usually occurs after sex is less a comment on morality than a simple exploitation technique used to titillate the audience by giving them a liberal, and much appreciated, dose

Final Girl par excellence, Jamie Lee Curtis (here with Donald Pleasence in *Halloween II*) was the lone survivor of four slashers: *Halloween* (1978), *Prom Night* (1980), *Terror Train* (1980) and *Halloween II* (1981).

of nudity. There are, in fact, just as many "bad" girls who survive. In both *He Knows You're Alone* and *My Bloody Valentine*, the Final Girl not only vacillates between two rival lovers, but tacitly leads both of them on. While both girls are extremely likable characters and hardly malicious, by the stringent definition of slasher morality they are certainly immoral and deserved to be punished (murdered). Yet both of them survive.[3] Films like *Happy Birthday to Me* and *Sleepaway Camp* further turn this theory on its head; not only does the "pure" Final Girl survive, she turns out to be the killer.

Eyes of the Killer— Subjective Point of View

One of the most problematic, controversial and misunderstood formal aspects of the slasher film is its persistent use of a subjective camera. There are numerous stylistic techniques used to designate subjectivity: a hand-held or shaky camera; an uneasy tracking shot; strange, awkward or unnatural camera angles. Music is almost always used as an audio cue to warn the audience—but obviously never the characters—of the killer's presence or approach. An absence of reaction shots—employed mainly to hide the killer's identity—also functions to preserve subjectivity and suspense.

The prevailing theory states that a subjective camera, by its very nature, represents the point of view of something. In the case of the slasher film, that something is the killer, thereby making the audience vicarious participants in the murders and forcing them to identify with the villain, not the victim. This defines an uneasy and uncomfortable relationship between the audience—who has been conditioned to always root for the hero—and the killer, whose "view" they are adopting.

Professor Bruce Kawin writes:

As Roger Ebert observed in a fine article on *I Spit on Your Grave*, the crucial influence of *Jaws* and *Halloween* has been to validate the use of subjective camera for the visual viewpoint of the horror object; whereas in earlier decades the audience tended to share the viewpoint of the victim and to see the monster, in the 1970s it became commonplace for the audience to share the viewpoint of the killer or monster, and with this came an emphasis on the isolated female as primary victim.[4]

This is not, however, the only, or even the main function of the technique. Even in *Halloween*'s opening murder, the most famous example of slasher subjectivity, the audience never really feels as if they are the killer. Rather, Carpenter is just showing the murder from a different, albeit more personal perspective.

As Dika says in *Games of Terror*, the purpose of this technique is not to become the "eyes" of the killer, but to "fragment the visual field and make the killer's exact position within the film's space unidentifiable." This subjective view allows audiences to feel involved in the "game" of the slasher—the major points of which are figuring out just *who* and *where* the killer is, and *when* and *how* he will strike—heightening both their enjoyment and excitement. Slasher films, contrary to what many believe, are not a nasty breed; they are far more interested in providing thrills and fun rather than a first-hand look into the minds of those on-screen psychos who kill for pleasure.

The Slasher Question

No book on the history of slasher films can be complete without discussing the persistent controversy which surrounds the subject. Moreso than in any other genre, both popular opinion and establishment ruling have had a profound effect on the success, marketing, booking and distribution of these films. It is hardly a secret that the slasher film is loathed by many individuals and is, as a rule, not looked upon too fondly by the power elite.

Every controversial art form, however, usually has its own group of staunch supporters. Even hard-core pornography, which I don't think anybody ever mistook for art—despite those pre-film disclaimers which assure audiences that the purpose of the following program is only to educate viewers about sexual practices—is vigorously defended by civil libertarians. Yet as much as Americans enjoy rallying around the issue of censorship, decrying government intervention, championing the First

Amendment and vilifying Big Brother, you'll be hard-pressed to find many defenders of the slasher film. It is almost as if there are a few subjects unworthy of the protection afforded in the Bill of Rights.

Even authors who write exclusively on the horror film, and often tread in the murky waters around the slasher, treat these films with a certain degree of contempt. In *Stay Out of the Shower*, William Schoell writes of the slasher film (which he calls the "stalk-and-slash"), "A few of these pictures exhibit a modicum of style and some imagination—at least in the violent death sequences—but most are just dreadful, far below even the level of the films that inspired them." In *Nightmare Movies*, Kim Newman devotes an entire chapter to what he calls "psycho movies," only to rip apart every aspect of them,

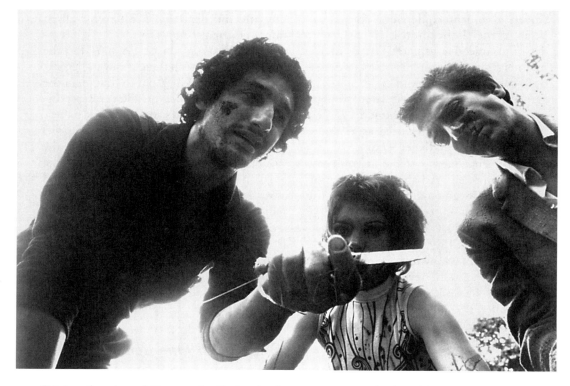

Critics oftentimes fail to see the distinction between movies which utilize realistic violence to stir up philosophical debate, such as *The Last House on the Left* (1972), and those which wallow in cartoonish violence for the sake of entertainment.

from the stock players whom he characterizes as "a parade of dumb American kids, marked for death by predilections for drink, soft drugs, stupid practical jokes and giggly making-out," to the film's narrative, which he refers to as the "Idiot Plot." Even John McCarty, whose book *Splatter Movies* brought the slasher film a great deal of attention, looks derisively at almost all of these films and is one of the few knowledgeable critics who doesn't consider *Halloween* a classic of the genre. Nor are the filmmakers themselves oblivious to the way in which their work is viewed. In the June 2000 issue of *Fangoria*, John Carpenter admits, "[I]f you direct my kind of pictures, you are kind of a ghettoized guy anyway. Horror directors are a little above pornographers. Just a hair."

This fear of horrific entertainment is hardly a modern phenomenon. In the 1950s, EC horror comics—with their violent tales and gruesome graphics—became the scapegoat for a rise in juvenile delinquency. By today's standards, these comics seem rather tame, even quaint, but 50 years ago the country was in a tizzy over them. Psychologist Dr. Fredric Wertham, the Joe McCarthy of comics, even wrote a book, *Seduction of the Innocent* (1954), which exploited the unfounded correlation between comic books and juvenile violence. His work, however, was instrumental in bringing down the horror comic industry.

The public's knee-jerk reaction to the dangers of the slasher film was first played out in January 1976, when theaters which planned to show a reputed snuff film, appropriately titled *Snuff*, were besieged by protesters, picketers and furious feminists. A few theaters even received bomb threats. Of course, *Snuff* was no snuff film. It was the 1975 (filmed in 1971) Argentinean production *Slaughter*, repackaged and released by research engineer turned exploitation film producer, Allan Shackleton. What is most

remarkable about this story is that even after *Snuff*'s phoniness was proven beyond a shadow of a doubt—the film was eventually forced to carry a disclaimer which exposed its inauthenticity—the furor over it refused to die down. People were hellbent on finding a genuine snuff film, and if one wasn't in existence, they were prepared to invent one. Rumors abounded that wealthy perverts were paying astronomical fees for private viewings of these films. The scare reached such extremes that the Los Angeles Police Department was forced to launch an investigation. Naturally, they didn't find a single shred of evidence for the existence of an actual snuff film.

The slasher controversy was thrust into the mainstream on October 23, 1980, on the PBS show *Sneak Previews* when America's best-known film critics, Gene Siskel and Roger Ebert, launched an attack on what they called "a disturbing new trend in today's movies." That trend, of course, was slasher films. Siskel, in a bout of self-importance, took it upon himself to not only berate Paramount executives for releasing a film as reprehensible as *Friday the 13th*, but actually implored the faithful readers of the *Chicago Tribune* to boycott *all* Paramount releases.

Ebert, while no apologist for the slasher film, was a bit more restrained in his rhetoric, as his record on such films had hardly been consistent. He not only championed *Halloween* but was one of the first critics to appreciate the brutal genius of Wes Craven's *The Last House on the Left*. In fact, his favorable review of the film was instrumental to its success. The contempt he has for the slasher film is even more interesting considering he scripted Russ Meyer's ultra-sleazy exploiter *Beyond the Valley of the Dolls* (1970). Apparently, a sleeping woman performing mock fellatio on the barrel of a gun—only one of the many gems from the film—is in better taste than the cartoonish violence of the slasher film.

Forget the blood, gore and rather explicit sexual violence in *Silent Night, Deadly Night* (1984). Just the idea of a murderous Santa Claus didn't sit well with America.

Most of Siskel and Ebert's colleagues, while not as zealous, felt the same way. Describing the slasher film in her November 21, 1982, article, "Bloodbaths Debase Movies and Audiences," *New York Times* film critic Janet Maslin wrote:

> Campers, stewardesses or sorority girls with no distinguishing characteristics are slaughtered one after another, by a killer whose motives are explained only in the most laughably cursory manner. He's identified either as an escaped lunatic, or perhaps as someone who has been horribly injured and now wants revenge. Since no one in any of these films ever has the brains to lock a door, to stay near the campfire, to head away from the direction from which those funny sounds are emanating, there is absolutely no hope that the killer will be outwitted. At the end of the film, he will simply run out of steam and be stopped—only temporarily—by

the lone survivor. That way they're both around for a sequel, should anyone want to see one.

At least Maslin, and Siskel and Ebert for that matter, have watched the films they despise. In fact, Maslin seems to get a cheap thrill from them; if a horror film comes out, no matter how bad, she critiques it. Her condescending reviews, while seldom positive, reveal someone who is baffled, rather than truly offended, by the slasher phenomenon.

Then there are critics such as John Corry who have the audacity to criticize a film without having ever seen it. In a review of *Friday the 13th Part 2*, from *The New York Times*, Corry, who obviously thinks he's being far more witty than he actually is, says that in the original *Friday the 13th*, "a crazy momma's boy killed a lot of counselors." As anybody who has seen the film knows, Jason, the aforementioned "momma's boy," doesn't kill anybody, his mother does. Unfortunately, critics like Corry are hardly the exception. If I had a dollar for every time someone referred to Jason as the "hockey masked—killer of *Friday the 13th*," I'd have a sum larger than the budget of most slashers.[5]

This condemnation, however, was not reserved for critics. The most famous and effective war on the slasher film was waged by government officials. It happened in England and become known as the "video nasties" controversy. What made this crusade especially unsettling was that it was spearheaded by people who had never even seen the films in question.

In England, where government censorship had always been extremely harsh, *Friday the 13th* was released on June 13, 1980. At this time, the Yorkshire Ripper was still at large. The Ripper was a mysterious killer who, between 1975–80, committed over a dozen murders so brutal that they made the best of Savini look benign by comparison. The terror finally ended in 1981 with the capture of Peter William Sutcliffe, a psychotic truck driver who confessed to the murders. Needless to say, this wasn't the most hospitable climate for the slasher film.

Meanwhile, the home video market was expanding. The boom in affordable video cassette recorders created a demand for product. Low-budget horror and exploitation films, many of which had very little chance of ever being seen again, found a new life on video. At the beginning, there was no official legislation regulating their release. Almost any type of film could be distributed on home video.

Once the ultra-conservative English press got wind that many of the films which were finding their way into the public's living room were, shall we say, less than wholesome, the Department of Public Prosecutions (DPP) created a list of 52 films which they felt warranted prosecution under the Obscene Publications Act.[6] These nortorious films, which included *Anthropophagus* (1980), *Blood Feast* (1963), *The House on the Edge of the Park* (1980), *I Spit on Your Grave* (1978) and *Mardi Gras Massacre* (1978), became known as the fabled "video nasties." The video witch hunt continued and reached such laughable extremes that films like *The Best Little Whorehouse in Texas* (1982), a harmless Dolly Parton musical, and *The Big Red One* (1980), a dramatic war movie, were included based solely on the suggestiveness of their titles. Apparently, the watchdogs were too busy stomping out sleaze—not to mention civil rights—to actually view the films they were banning. The movement's greatest achievement came in 1984 with the introduction of the Video Recordings Act (VRA) which required that all films intended for video release be classified by the British Board of Film Classification (BBFC). The VRA effectively allowed the government to decide which films were suitable for public consumption. It was a dark day for both civil liberties and the slasher film.

Opponents of the slasher film are sometimes under the mistaken impression that these films have some nefarious antisocial agenda, created to subvert the status quo and plunge contemporary society into chaos. On the contrary, the reason for their production is almost always economic. The 1982 slasher spoof *Student Bodies* opens with the following statement: "Last year 26 horror films were released.... None of them lost money." Whether or not the numbers are accurate is immaterial; the fact remains, slasher films make money. And they make money for one reason—because people enjoy them.

There have been countless books written, and even more hypotheses proposed, about the allure of horror. If the audience for horror is predominately adolescent males, as James Twitchell proposes in his book *Dreadful Pleasures*, then these movies might act as a barometer for teenagers to measure and affirm their manhood. Or maybe our own morbid curiosity—the exact same force which compels us to crane our necks to search out the carnage in a traffic accident—prompts us to seek out the most depraved, gruesome and antisocial sights and sounds we can imagine.

Catharsis has always been a favorite explanation of the psychological community. The theory supposes that by vicariously experiencing all things horrible, we sate and purge our own violent impulses in a healthy internal manner. The flip side of this, of course, is that we're all proverbial time bombs, ready to maim, kill and torture should we find no release for our pent-up hostilities.

A less exhilarating, but equally legitimate theory is proposed by Vera Dika in *Games of Terror*. She attributes the slasher film's popularity to its formulaic structure, archetypal characters and familiar themes; it fulfills audience's expectations in the same way as the Western or screwball comedy.

There is no shortage of people willing to explain why the slasher film is dangerous. In this chapter's section on the Final Girl, I've already touched upon the theory that these films propagate violence against women. Because the victims are

While one of the most prevalent criticisms of the slasher film is that it demeans women and propagates violence against them, postmodern readings of these films have begun to acknowledge a measurable degree of female empowerment in the representation of the heroine as in this scene from *Friday the 13th Part 3* (1982).

often female, and even more often scantily dressed, slasher films have been accused of an anti-female bias. This theory, however, fails to take into account both the films directed and written by women—*Slumber Party Massacre*, directed by Amy Jones and written by feminist author Rita Mae Brown, is the best example—and those films such as *I Spit on Your Grave* and *Ms. 45* which detail the violent, though not unwarranted, revenge which the female victims take against their male attackers.

Desensitization, the belief that overexposure to violence will render one immune to its negative effects, is another popular theory. Says Maslin:

> To say that these films aren't very frightening is not to say that they don't have a profound effect on those who watch them.... Lurid headlines in the tabloids will seem positively realistic; after watching a dozen young vacationers being garroted, the news of, say, a gunman on the loose in a hospital ward will sound comparatively harmless. Violence in the real world becomes much more acceptable after you've seen infinitely greater violence on the screen.

The truth is that although desensitization has as much validity as any other theory, there has never been a single reputable study which proves a correlation between the amount of fictional violence watched and the subsequent psychological, emotional and physiological response to real violence.

The most prevalent, and certainly the most disturbing claim is that violence in the movies causes violence in real life. This theory supposes that the average theatergoer is unable to distinguish between fantasy and reality and will blindly emulate whatever he or she sees on screen. Even if movies were able to have this profound effect on viewers, why would the mechanism be specific to violent films? Nobody has ever proposed that the screwball comedies from the 1930s were responsible for a funnier nation. Nor were we besieged by troupes of singing and dancing gangs in well-choreographed routines after the release of *West Side Story* (1961) and *Grease* (1978).

Nevertheless, slasher films continue to come under attack from those who propose that fictional violence is responsible for many of society's ills. In "Watch and Learn: Yes the Media Do Make Us More Violent," from the September 1, 1999, issue of *The Saturday Evening Post*, Gregg Easterbrook writes:

> For in cinema's never-ending quest to up the ante on violence, murder as sport is the latest frontier. Slasher flicks began this trend; most portray carnage from a killer's point of view, showing the victim cowering, begging, screaming as the blade goes in, treating each death as a moment of festivity for the killer. (Many killers seek feelings of power over their victims, criminology finds; by reveling in the pleas of their victims, slasher movies promote this base emotion.)

This convenient and careless bit of pop psychology is far more dangerous than the films to which Easterbrook is referring. In the very same article he flippantly lays the blame for the Columbine massacre squarely on the movies, as if there were no question where the responsibility lies: "Two Colorado high schoolers have murdered 12 classmates and a teacher—often, it appears, first taunting their pleading victims, just like celebrity stars do in the movies...."

Recently, however, there have been some seriously disturbing crimes which have had an eerie relationship to horror films. On February 9, 2000, a nine-year-old Brazilian boy stabbed a neighborhood girl 25 times three days after watching *Child's Play 2* (1990), a film in which a demonic toy doll, Chucky, does the same. Two months later, in Paris, a teenager wearing the "Ghostface" mask from *Scream* stabbed his father and stepmother. The most bizarre case, however, is that of horror film director Eric Red, best-known as the writer of the 1986 film *The Hitcher*. In early June 2000, Red rear-ended a car at a red light, then inexplicably drove across three lanes of traffic, jumped a curb and smashed through the window of a billiard parlor. He killed two patrons and injured several others. After asking whether he had hurt anyone, Red picked up a piece of shattered glass and began slashing his own throat until other patrons finally restrained him. The strangest aspect of the case is its similarity to parts of Red's 1991 film *Body Parts*.

Naturally, opportunistic critics have laid the blame for these tragedies directly on the slasher film. Finding a convenient scapegoat, especially one which has few defenders, is far easier than examining the true root of this violence. While it may be tough to argue for the redeeming qualities of a film in which a drooling psychopath hacks naked women to bits, it is equally tough to propose that this fictitious violence, however objectionable, is in any way responsible for anything more than a few disgusted theatergoers.

CHAPTER 2

The Pre-History of the Slasher Film

Mankind's appetite for violence is as old as mankind itself. Throughout history we have always been intrigued by the specter of pain, torture and death. The ingenuity of ancient Rome was only eclipsed by its brutality. Thousands flocked to the Coliseum to witness countless atrocities. Mock battles were held in which thousands of "warriors" were systematically slaughtered, much to the delight of the screaming hoards. Gladiators fought to their bloody deaths. Prisoners and criminals were tied to stakes and mutilated by wild animals. Grown men dressed as satyrs would sodomize young boys. Exotic animals from all corners of the globe (giraffes, elephants, hippopotami, ostriches, and pumas) were exhibited only to be killed in a number of gory ways. When it seemed that darkness would temporarily halt the day's festivities, Christians could always be dipped in pitch and set aflame to keep the games alive well into the night.

In the Middle Ages, nothing attracted a larger crowd than public executions and torture. Criminals, enemies of the state, heretics and witches were subjected to every conceivable indignity and torment. During the Spanish Inquisition, which elevated torture to an art form, men were pulled apart on wooden racks, boiled alive, drawn and quartered and dismembered in a variety of ways. Women had their breasts torn off, their eyes gouged out and their flesh mutilated and flayed. It seemed that no amount of burnings, beatings, whippings, drownings, stonings or beheadings could satisfy the masses. Humanity called for blood, and in one form or another, she always delivered.

There is a pervasive false assumption that dramatic violence is exclusively a modern institution, the result of a civilized society vicariously indulging in its more primitive fantasies under the guise of entertainment. But our bloodlust did not wane, it just took on a different incarnation. In France, a little more than a century after the Reign of Terror had relieved hundreds of Parisians of their heads, a new and lurid form of drama was born. On the same streets which once ran red with the blood of their countrymen, patrons flocked to a small theater at 20 rue Chaptal to watch their darkest nightmares brought to life.

The Theater of the Grand Guignol was the earliest modern antecedent of the slasher film. It was one of the first venues to recreate fictional atrocities for their own sake on a grand scale. At different times during its 65-year history, it was both the sanctuary of the lower class and the curiosity of the elite. The Grand Guignol was like nothing the world had ever seen, a theater which embraced not the beauty and sanctity of life, but the horror, fear and agony of death.

The Industrial Revolution brought with it not just a new breed of workers who came in droves to the urban centers of Europe, but a fresh and gritty type of entertainment—the melodrama. Melodrama plays, which generally ended happily, sated the people's craving for grim crime stories and whet their appetite for even more grisly fare. *Fait divers,* short news items which gave graphic accounts of actual crimes, usually with a perverse undertone and bizarre twist, were also devoured by the public.

The first to recognize and exploit this demand for morbid art was a Frenchman named Andre Antoine. In 1887, Antoine founded the Theater Libre. His theater embraced naturalism, a realism movement espoused by proponents like Emile Zola. The highlight of the Theater Libre was its *rosse* plays which revealed the dark underbelly of Parisian life, focusing on such depressing topics as rape, spousal abuse and prostitution.

The *rosse* play's greatest writer was the Theater Libre's co-founder, Oscar Méténier. Méténier was a former secretary to the Police Commissioner and his intimate knowledge of the criminal underworld added an element of authenticity. As vile as his characters were, Metenier often cast them in a sympathetic light.

In 1893, Antoine's Theater Libre, which had begun to distance itself from Metenier's *rosse* plays, went out of business. The novelty had worn off but its dark themes still piqued the interest of theatergoers eager for a new type of thrill. On April 13, 1897, Metenier opened the 285-seat Theater of the Grand Guignol. In order to distinguish itself from the Theater Libre, the Grand Guignol alternated short comedies with *rosse* plays. Metenier divided his *rosse* plays into two distinct categories. "Plays of Popular Manners" were dramas which discreetly ridiculed the upper class, while "Newspapers Items" dramatized actual criminal exploits which were documented by the police. In the beginning, Parisians flocked to the Grand Guignol, entranced by its violence, but just like the Theater Libre, it eventually lost its luster. In 1898, after just four seasons, Metenier sold his interest in the theater to a mysterious showman named Max Maurey.

Maurey harbored few artistic ambitions. His knowledge of the theater was negligible and he displayed little concern for the preservation of legitimate dramatic art. Maurey's interest in the Grand Guignol was purely financial. As an astute observer of the human condition and a public relations genius, Maurey realized the one surefire way to lure patrons to his theater was to make the Grand Guignol as bloody, sickening and depraved as possible. Murder, rape, torture and other unspeakable deeds were no longer incorporated into the act, they *became* the act, gory stunts designed only to shock and disgust the audience. In *The Grand Guignol: Theater of Fear and Terror*, Prof. Mel Gordon encapsulates the base essence of the attraction:

> Here was a theater genre that was predicated on the stimulation of the rawest and most adolescent of human interactions and desires: incest and patricide; blood lust; sexual anxiety and conflict; morbid fascination with bodily mutilation and death; loathing of authority; fear

of insanity; an overall disgust for the human condition and its imperfect institutions.

Maurey's nihilistic view of humanity did not extend to his craft. He was a perfectionist who constantly angered his performers by obsessively rewriting scenes and tinkering with their line-readings. He was a meticulous planner who took great pains to insure that the stage effects were properly prepared. Most of all, Maurey was an unequaled salesman and promoter. There is a famous story about the Grand Guignol in which a man, whose wife had fainted from fright, called for a doctor. Maurey, standing in the theater's foyer, gleefully declared that the doctor too had passed out. It was this kind of black humor which endeared Maurey to the Guignolers. He was the P.T. Barnum of the macabre, who proved that in early twentieth century Paris, a sadist, not a sucker, is born every minute.

While Maurey took—and rightly deserved—much of the credit for the early success of his theater, the Grand Guignol never could have thrived without the unwavering dedication of its performers. The best of them viewed their commitment to the theater as more of a calling than a job. According to Gordon, "If anyone was responsible for the Grand Guignol's ascension from a local Parisian sensation to international success, it was the playwright and essayist André de Lorde, known in his lifetime as 'the Prince of Terror.'" From 1901–26, de Lorde wrote over 100 horrific plays. His ultimate goal was to write a play so suspenseful that the audience would flee from the theater in sheer terror.

If there was a ever a man perfectly suited for a career in the Grand Guignol it, was de Lorde. His father had been a surgeon and as a child de Lorde would camp outside his office, listening to the agonized shrieks of the patients, all the time conjuring up fantastic images of the most horrific torments imaginable. In an effort to purge him of this fascination with death, de Lorde's father made him stand vigil over the body of his deceased grandmother. The ploy only fueled the young de Lorde's obsession. For the rest of his life he would be consumed by the prospect of death, and like his idol, Edgar Allan Poe, de Lorde projected his anxieties onto a public which willingly devoured them.

Among the most famous contributors to the Grand Guignol was Dr. Alfred Binet, a close collaborator of de Lorde's, as well as his therapist and the director of the Psychological-Physiological Laboratory of the Sorbonne. Although Binet was one of the most successful authors of the Grand Guignol and co-author of "A Crime in the Madhouse"—one of the theater's most popular plays in which a beautiful young woman has her eye gouged out by a delusional mental patient—he is best-known as the creator of the Binet Intelligence Test. The Grand Guignol's influence can be seen in the original examination which asked such questions as, "What is the first thing that you would do, if you came home after school and found your mother strangled and mutilated?" Needless to say, these types of questions were deleted in the American version.

The Grand Guignol was also blessed with colorful personalities like Camille Choisy, a flashy innovator who expanded the possibilities of theatrical death to include such modern horrors as poisonous gas, explosives and electrocution. Maxa, a prolific performer the newspapers coined "The High Priestess of the Temple of Horror," was murdered more than 10,000 times in 60 different ways. She was also raped over 3,000 times. Some of her more creative ends included being cut into tiny pieces and then glued back together, flattened by a roller-compressor, and disemboweled by a salesman who covets her intestines. Jack Jouvin, a playwright-actor-producer who acquired a financial interest in the Grand Guignol in 1926, forced both Choisy and Maxa out. He toned down the physical violence in the traditional plays in favor of more psycho-sexual fare. Among the last of the performers who called the Grand Guignol home was Eva Berkson, a British-born actress who bought out Jouvin in 1937. She brought back Maxa—who ended up permanently damaging her vocal cords during a performance—and managed to keep the Grand Guignol running through the wartime occupation. The postwar years were tough for the theater. As the Nazi atrocities surfaced, the fictional horrors of the Grand Guignol seemed tame by comparison, not to mention somewhat inappropriate. After valiantly attempting several new formulas, including adaptations of foreign novels, Berkson retired in 1951.

The Grand Guignol managed to remain afloat for a few more insignificant years, catering almost exclusively to the foreign tourists and French students who were drawn to the theater for its reputation rather than for the performances themselves. In November 1962, the doors at 20 rue Chaptal closed forever. After 65 years, the Grand Guignol had run its course. Gore for the sake of gore, even under the guise of a morality play, no longer shocked a generation weaned on the real life horrors of World War II. While the most violent, gruesome and depraved artistic spectacle in the history of civilization was no more, other forms of entertainment were more than willing to accept the torch.

It is almost poetic that the birth of the modern slasher coincided with the death of the Grand Guignol. For years, the horror film had been flirting with, without ever fully embracing, the conventions of the slasher film. Horror cinema at the dawn of the century was dominated by silent films such as *The Cabinet of Dr. Caligari* (1919) and *The Golem* (1920) which relied on visual terror. German Expressionism was at its height and the madness of the films' *mise-en-scene* mirrored the insanity of their plots and characters. Later, with the advent of sound, Universal's monsters dominated the horror landscape, as Dracula, Frankenstein, the Mummy and the Wolf Man bit, groped, skulked and howled their way in the public consciousness. In the 1950s, the public's paranoia over Communism and atomic energy was manifested in countless science fiction films about alien invaders and mutant creatures. Then, in 1960, the world was rocked by a new kind of screen terror.

If anybody was qualified to carry on the tradition of the Grand Guignol, it was Alfred Hitchcock, the British-born cinematic genius who, by the time of the Guignol's fall, had secured his reputation as the master of suspense. By 1960, Hitchcock had reached a turning point in his career. Although he was revered by some contemporaries, especially those of the French New Wave (Jean-Luc Godard, Francois Truffaut, Claude Chabrol), Hitchcock was far from content. He was still bitter over his loss for Best Director at the 1940 Academy Awards to John Ford for *The Grapes of Wrath* (1940), even though his *Rebecca* had netted the Oscar for Best Picture. While he hobnobbed with Tinseltown's elite—to be invited to dine at the Hitchcocks' home was the mark of having "made it" in Hollywood—his growing obsession with his leading ladies, and its inevitable futility, was taking its toll. He characteristically dealt with his problems the only way he knew how—on screen. It was as if he condensed all of his anxieties, anger and frustration into a single film, his masterpiece and the first true slasher film—*Psycho*.

Psycho is loosely based on the 1957 case of Ed Gein, one of the grisliest mass

Norman Bates (Anthony Perkins) comes to grips with what "Mother" has just done in the most famous scene from Alfred Hitchcock's *Psycho* (1960).

murderers in American history, who was also a cannibal, transvestite and necrophiliac. When police finally investigated Gein's dilapidated farmhouse they found, among other things, clothes fashioned from human skin, a half-skull used as a bowl, two pairs of human lips on a string, a headless disemboweled corpse and a freezer stocked with human organs.

Both Robert Bloch, the author of *Psycho* (the novel), and Joseph Stefano, the screenwriter, took great liberties with the story and the actual details of the Gein case. In the film, Marion Crane (Janet Leigh), a Phoenix secretary, steals $40,000 from her boss and heads off into the California desert. She stops for the night at the Bates Motel, where proprietor Norman Bates (Anthony Perkins), a nervous young man, lives with his elderly mother. That night while showering, Marion is brutally murdered by a knife-wielding woman.

Lila Crane (Vera Miles), Marion's sister, and Arbogast (Martin Balsam), a private investigator who has been hired to recover the $40,000, finally track Marion to the Bates Motel. As Arbogast investigates the house adjacent to the motel, he is stabbed to death by the same woman. Lila runs into the fruit cellar and finds Mrs. Bates—an eyeless stuffed corpse. The real murderer is Norman, who for years has been dressing up as his dead mother and offing unsuspecting guests.

Psycho is Hitchcock's most daring and influential work. Although agonizingly suspenseful—especially the scene in which Marion is trailed by a curious policeman—it was the perception of *Psycho*'s excessive violence which secured its notoriety. Like any good showman, Hitchcock subscribed to the idea that what an audience could conjure up was far more horrible than what could actually be shown on screen. Secrecy was of paramount importance. It was rumored that Hitchcock even bought as many copies of the novel as he could find

in an effort to conceal the ending. Theater employees were warned not to admit anyone after the picture began. Of course, many people were still shocked at what they saw. Walt Disney was so offended at the film's gratuitous violence that he forbid the director to ever use his theme park for any of his future projects.

The most controversial aspect of *Psycho* is the infamous "shower scene," at the time viewed as the single most heinous act of murder ever captured on celluloid. Taking over a week to shoot, this 45-second scene, which contained an unprecedented 75 camera setups, is a stirring visual composition of calculated violence. It is perfectly augmented by Bernard Herrmann's unforgettable "shrieking violins." While today it may be impossible to imagine the scene without this musical accompaniment, the composer actually had to persuade Hitchcock to use it. The genius of this scene, however, lies in its ability to give the impression of extreme bloody violence, when in reality, very little graphic detail is shown. Ironically, not only did a model double for Janet Leigh in some of the shots, but during the week the scene was filmed, Anthony Perkins was in New York rehearsing for a part in an upcoming play.

Released in England at approximately the same time as *Psycho*, *Peeping Tom* (1960) has the dubious distinction of effectively ending the career of Britain's greatest director after Hitchcock, Michael Powell. Powell had been previously lauded for such well-respected films as *Black Narcissus* (1947) and *The Red Shoes* (1948), but after *Peeping Tom*, the notoriously narrow-minded British press turned on him with a vengeance. They completely misinterpreted his brilliant study of voyeurism and its relation to the cinematic medium as offensive schlock.

The film involves a handsome photographer, Mark Lewis (Carl Boehm), who was intentionally traumatized as a child so that his scientist father could study the effects of fear on the boy's nervous system. As expected, these heinous experiments have left a deep scar on Mark's psyche, turning him into a homicidal sadist whose lone source of sexual gratification is slaying young women. The diabolical contraption he uses to perform the murders is fiendishly ingenious: a camera equipped with a razor-sharp dagger which photographs the victims at the exact moment of their death.

Nearly two decades before the slasher film began to use the subjective point of view shot to signify the presence of the killer, *Peeping Tom* was already toying with this convention. Powell's camera was not only symbolic of the killer, but an active participant itself, with the capacity for murder. It is obvious that this self-reflexive device was far too complex for most critics to grasp, just as the film's themes of child abuse, sadomasochism and fetishism were far too controversial for the time. Powell, who died in 1990, achieved some degree of vindication when, in the late 1970s, some directors, most notably Martin Scorsese, publicly hailed *Peeping Tom* as a classic of the genre.

Around the same time that *Psycho* and *Peeping Tom* were introducing audiences to a new type of visceral horror, Britain's Hammer Film Productions was thriving

Homicidal photographer Mark Lewis (Carl Boehm) prepares to turn his instrument of death on Helen (Anna Massey) in *Peeping Tom* (1960), a brilliant, misunderstood film which effectively ended director Michael Powell's career.

with their remakes of the classic Universal monster movies. Aside from their exceptional production values, films such as *The Curse of Frankenstein* (1957), *Horror of Dracula* (1958), *The Two Faces of Dr. Jekyll* (1960), *The Brides of Dracula* (1960), and *The Curse of the Werewolf* (1961) were brilliantly marketed, catering explicitly to the burgeoning teenage audience who had disposable income to burn. They were filmed in lush color, perfect for the bloodier spectacles which censors were allowing with greater frequency, and blatantly exploited the latent sexuality of the Victorian texts on which they were often based.

Interspersed between the vampires, werewolves and mummies were a handful of well-crafted psychological thrillers. The best of these tales of madness and murder, which include *Taste of Fear* (1961), *Maniac* (1963), *Paranoiac* (1963), *Nightmare* (1964), *Hysteria* (1964) and *Fanatic* (a.k.a. *Die! Die! My Darling!*, 1964), were penned by Hammer in-house scribe, Jimmy Sangster, and directed by Freddie Francis. Unfortunately, they never received the respect they deserved, and along with William Castle's equally entertaining "mini–Hitchcocks"—*Homicidal* (1961), *Strait-Jacket* (1964), *I Saw What You Did* (1965)—were often discounted as *Psycho* imitators.

Besides Great Britain, the strengthening pulse of the horror film was found, of all places, in Italy, where a generation of Neorealism had left the impression that the Italians were too preoccupied with post-war strife and documentary-style dramas to indulge in the fantastical pleasures of horror. However, the 1960s saw the birth of an Italian horror movement that for the next generation would only be surpassed by that of the United States.

The dominant form of Italian horror, at least until the early 80s when it was supplanted by a slew of zombie films, was the *giallo*. Its name refers to the yellow covers of a series of Italian crime paperbacks. The defining feature of these *gialli* is a faceless murderer, who often, but not always, wears a pair of black leather gloves and kills his usually female victims in a variety of gruesome, yet beautifully shot and composed, death sequences.

The pioneer of the *giallo* was Mario Bava, a former cinematographer whose father, Eugenio Bava, had been a cameraman in the days of the silent film industry. Because of his background, Bava's films usually distinguish themselves by their lavish color palates and striking, almost ethereal lighting, a stylistic tradition continued by his protégé, Dario Argento. Although Bava's *The Evil Eye* (1963) is usually considered the first *giallo*, his 1964 film, *Blood and Black Lace*, was the most important, and certainly the most popular of the early *gialli*. *Blood and Black Lace* is set in a Rome fashion salon, run by Christiana (Eva Bartok), where everyone seems to be involved in drugs or some other illicit business. When one of the models, Isabella (Francesca Ungaro), is murdered, everybody seems a bit too eager to get their hands on her diary. Ironically, the unlucky few who do manage to obtain it are all done in by a masked figure who murders them in especially horrible ways; one model is mutilated by an iron claw while another has her face burned off on a red-hot stove. The "twist" ending reveals Max (Cameron Mitchell)—who was being blackmailed by Isabella—to be the killer. Christiana had carried out a token murder to shift suspicion away from Max, who was also her lover. Evidently not too moved by Christiana's sacrifice, Max tries to kill her as well, but his plan backfires when she returns, injured, but very much alive, and shoots him to death.

Admired for its impressive visuals as much as it was attacked for both its confusing plot and extreme violence against women (two denouncements which would continue to plague the *giallo*), *Blood and*

Tao-Li (Claude Dantes), just another beautiful model slain in an early Mario Bava *giallo*, *Blood and Black Lace* (1964).

Black Lace set the Italian horror film on a course it would follow, with varying degrees of success, for the next 30 years. The films it influenced are too numerous to count, and although Dario Argento would soon inherit the mantle as Italy's supreme fearmaker, Bava, who died of a heart attack in 1980, will forever be remembered as the godfather of Italian horror.

The course of the slasher film was not determined as most assume in the shower of the Bates Motel, but in a small drive-in theater in, of all places, Peoria, Illinois. The theater was chosen not for its visibility, but for its isolation; if the picture it was showing flopped, as was expected, nobody would ever know. Little did the patrons at that small Midwestern theater realize they were about to make history. For the next 75 minutes, they were treated to a spectacle the likes of which had never

been seen before: amputation, scalping, flagellation, mutilation, tongue-ripping, eyeball-gouging and brain-stealing, all shown in full blood-red color.

The movie was *Blood Feast* (1963). The horror film would never be the same again.

Blood Feast was directed by the one and only Herschell Gordon Lewis, known by such colorful monikers as the Godfather of Gore, the Sultan of Sleaze, the Baron of Blood and the Mad Hatter of Splatter. Most find it difficult to believe that this mild-mannered, well-educated former advertising executive and college professor was responsible for some of the most vile, gruesome, over-the-top and genuinely sickening films ever made. Lewis single-handedly invented the "gore film." Ironically, it is the atrocious acting, laughably extreme violence, bargain-basement special effects and subtle touches of

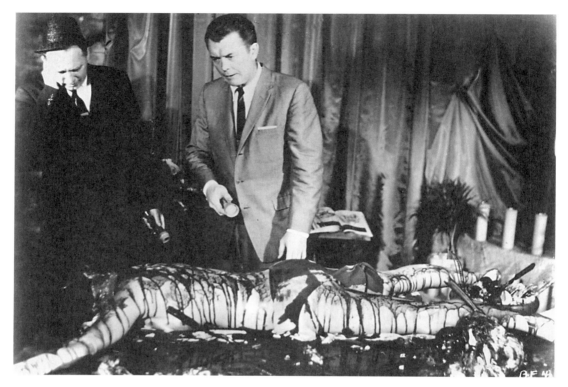

Frank (Scott Hall) and Pete (Bill Kerwin, billed as Thomas Wood), as inept a pair of investigators as you'll ever find, discover the flogged body of one of Fuad Ramses' victims in the first ever "gore film," Herschell Gordon Lewis' *Blood Feast* **(1963).**

black humor—all hallmarks of a Lewis film and the very aspects which prevented him from ever breaking into the mainstream—which have endeared him to fans for nearly 40 years.

As John McCarty writes in *The Sleaze Merchants*, "Lewis had the uncanny ability to spot a trend and exploit it before anybody else did." He began his feature filmmaking career with *The Prime Time* (1960), a fairly typical juvenile delinquency film probably best-known for being the screen debut of future horror actress Karen Black. Next came *Living Venus* (1960), a rather serious film based loosely on the then-controversial lifestyle of *Playboy* founder Hugh Hefner. This was followed by *The Adventures of Lucky Pierre* (1961), the first "nudie cutie" shot in 35mm color; a series of nudist colony films,

Daughter of the Sun (1962), *Nature's Playmates* (1962) and *Goldilocks and the Three Bears* (1963); and *Scum of the Earth* (1963), a darker version of *Living Venus* and the first "roughie," films which combined sex and violence with a purposely amateur style of filmmaking in order to achieve a realistic look.

While in Florida, shooting the nudie *Bell, Bare and Beautiful* (1963), Lewis and his partner David F. Friedman, a former carny and advertising-marketing-publicity genius, realized that if they were to stay ahead of the exploitation game they would need to change directions. The liberalization of censorship constraints meant that the nudity which Lewis and Friedman depended on to attract their core audience was beginning to creep into mainstream Hollywood films. As a result, the two came up with a list of subjects they could mine for exploitation value before finally settling on the one which would forever define both their careers—gore.

Lewis' first gore film was to be called *Something Weird*, a title which he loved and which would later be used for his 1967 psychedelic film about ESP and LSD. However, the Suez Motel in North Miami Beach where the cast and crew of *Bell, Bare and Beautiful* was staying had a six-foot-tall Sphinx in front of it. This odd, kitschy touch inspired Lewis to conceive what would become *Blood Feast*, the story of Fuad Ramses (Mal Arnold), an insane Egyptian caterer who cooks the limbs and organs of his pretty young victims in order to create a blood feast for the goddess Ishtar.

Lewis has been famously quoted as referring to *Blood Feast* as being like a Walt Whitman poem: "It's no good, but it's the first of its type and therefore deserves a certain position." The film, which had only cost $24,000 and was shot in 35mm color, was a smashing success. This was due in part to Friedman's shrewd publicity stunts, which included distributing to theater patrons vomit bags which read, "You May Need This When You See *Blood Feast*," and secretly obtaining an injunction against the film in Sarasota, Florida, which naturally only drummed up more interest.

Immediately after *Blood Feast*, Lewis and Friedman forged ahead with their next project, *Two Thousand Maniacs* (1964), a far more accomplished although no less gruesome film about a small southern town named Pleasant Valley, where the ghosts of massacred confederates have reappeared to seek revenge on a group of northern tourists who have stumbled into their midst. The film contains such memorable scenes as a quartering, where each of a victim's limbs are tied to different horses which run off in opposite direc-

tions; the barrel roll, where a man is placed in a wooden barrel with nails driven into it and then rolled down a hill; and "The Old Teetering Rock," a devilish variation on the dunking booth where an accurately thrown ball releases a gigantic rock onto a prostrate victim. Although not as successful as *Blood Feast*, *Two Thousand Maniacs* still made money, prompting Lewis and Friedman to make what would become the last entry in their "Blood Trilogy," *Color Me Blood Red* (1965). For Adam Sorg (Don Joseph), an obviously unstable painter, only one shade of red pigment will suffice. Guess what is the only substance which displays this color? And guess how he obtains it?

After *Color Me Blood Red*, Lewis had a falling out with Friedman over some financial dealings, left the gore film behind and went on to make a series of eclectic films, from the hillbilly flick *Moonshine Mountain* (1964) and the sci-fi fiasco *Monster A-Go-Go* (1965), to two lackluster children's films, *Jimmy the Boy Wonder* (1966) and *The Magic Land of Mother Goose* (1967). The lure of blood would prove too strong, however, and Lewis soon found himself back in the genre with *A Taste of Blood* (1967), a vampire tale sometimes referred to as "The *Gone With the Wind* of Gore." *A Taste of Blood* was so well-made for a Lewis film that it prompted Roger Corman to offer him a directing job which Lewis politely declined. *The Gruesome Twosome* (1967), a full-fledged gore film about a deranged mother and her son who scalp young girls to obtain wigs for their wig shop, came next, followed by the motorcycle-gore film, *She-Devils on Wheels* (1968).

After yet another series of nudie films, Lewis directed his penultimate gore film, the aptly titled *The Wizard of Gore* (1970). The film has a rather compelling premise. Montag the Magnificent is a magician who specializes in onstage Grand

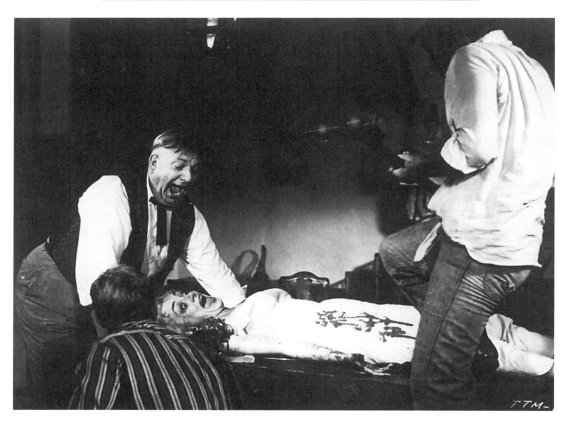

The residents of Pleasant Valley betray their town's name in Herschell Gordon Lewis' *Two Thousand Maniacs* **(1964). Here, Mayor Buckman (Jeffrey Allen), who moonlights as the town doctor, howls in glee as Bea (Shelby Livingston) has her arm hacked off.**

Guignol–type tricks. The snag is that his volunteers are found dead, soon after, from the exact same wounds they suffered during the show. *The Wizard of Gore* is a feast of Lewis depravity: a spike is driven into a woman's brain, an industrial press separates a willing beauty from her innards, and a sword-swallowing act culminates with the removal of the victim's intestines.

Lewis' last film was *The Gore Gore Girls* (1972), a film so ridiculously extreme, even *he* admits it was joke. As hard as it may be to believe, there were those who didn't find the humor in a woman having her nipples snipped off, only to have white milk flow from one breast, while the other spewed chocolate. Many were tiring of Lewis' antics, and he in turn was tiring of

the rigors, dishonesty and overall nonsense endemic in the business.

Herschell Gordon Lewis left behind a legacy far richer than he could have ever imagined. Without *Blood Feast* there never would have been a *Night of the Living Dead*, a *Texas Chainsaw Massacre* or a *Friday the 13th*. As important as Lewis' influence was to the slasher film, it cuts much deeper, to the very core of popular culture and underground entertainment. The alternative rock group 10,000 Maniacs chose their name as an homage to Lewis. John Waters, exploitation director par excellence, is a huge Lewis fan. He titled his 1970 feature *Multiple Maniacs* and referenced *Blood Feast* in his 1994 black comedy *Serial Mom*. Frank

Henenlotter, director of the dreary cult favorite *Basket Case* (1981), dedicated the film to Lewis.

Now living comfortably in Florida, Lewis never really gave up his gift for persuasion. He is one of the adverting industry's most respected direct response writers and has written over a dozen books on the subject. His days of gore are long over, but despite the fact that many critics feel that both he and his works should be forgotten, Herschell Gordon Lewis will always be remembered for what he was—an American original.

Night of the Living Dead (1968) was instrumental to the slasher film, not as a thematic or stylist antecedent, but as a template for how to make an effective and lucrative horror film on a minuscule budget. Before *Night of the Living Dead*, most successful horror films had been studio productions. The Universal classics had the full backing of that studio. Val Lewton's films—B-movies which sometimes used the discarded sets of high-profile projects—were still produced by RKO, a major studio. Even Corman, Castle and Hammer, independents in the traditional sense, were far more studio-oriented than the renegade company which put together *Night of the Living Dead*.

Credit for *Night of the Living Dead* is usually given to the film's director, George Romero, although its producers, Russell Streiner and Karl Hardman, both of whom have unforgettable roles in the film, were no doubt instrumental to its success. In 1967, Romero, a Bronx native who had made 8mm films as a teenager, was living in Pittsburgh and looking for a way to break into the film industry. His company, Latent Images, an industrial film and commercial production company, formed a partnership with another Pittsburgh advertising firm, Hardman Associates, in hopes of making a low-budget horror film. The company was called Image Ten,

named after the number of investors who had contributed to the production.

The plot of *Night of the Living Dead* is exceptionally simple. Zombies, revived by an excess of radiation accidentally released from a space probe, have begun feasting on the brains (or really any part they can get their hands on) of the living. They are, however, not indestructible. As the mainly ineffectual sheriff says, "Beat 'em or burn 'em. They go up pretty easy." Despite their plodding, practically crawling advance, the zombies have managed to corral a small group of people in a deserted farmhouse. Only the hero of the group, Ben, a strong-willed black man, does anything remotely effective in staving off the attack. Eventually, the hordes of living dead are vanquished by a posse of locals—most of whom are as equally mindless as the zombies—but not before each of the characters has met their grisly end.

Night of the Living Dead is subversive on many levels. It shrewdly mocks the futility of the military industrial complex which was carrying the United States deeper and deeper into Vietnam and thumbs its nose at the notion of technology as a panacea, or even as an effective weapon against the zombies. In fact, it was the failure or malfunction of modern technology which was directly responsible for the zombie resurrection. The film also had the audacity to designate a proactive and aggressive black man as its hero, who was not only resourceful but intelligent, at a time when the empowerment of blacks across the country was making the majority of Middle America slightly uneasy. Ben's death at the hand of an ignorant trigger-happy mob—which foreshadowed today's current epidemic of needless firearm deaths—was a parallel to that year's defining legacy, the death of two of the country's most rational and dynamic leaders, Robert F. Kennedy and Martin

The dead have come to life in George Romero's 1968 zombie classic *Night of the Living Dead*.

Luther King, Jr., both of whom were shot by assassins.

The offspring of *Night of the Living Dead* and Romero's two sequels, *Dawn of the Dead* (1979) and *Day of the Dead* (1985), are too plentiful to name. They run the gamut from the polished and the inventive (*Zombie* [1979], *Dead and Buried* [1981], *The Evil Dead* [1982]) to the tasteless and pointless (*Zombie Lake* [1980], *Night of the Creeps* [1986]).

Mario Bava's *Hatchet for the Honeymoon* (1969) follows John Harrington (Stephen Forsyth), a Paris fashion salon owner who, as he matter-of-factly announces less than five minutes into the film, is a completely mad paranoiac. He lives with his nagging wife who refuses to grant him a divorce, driving him to butcher young brides-to-be with the titular weapon. With each killing, Harrington recalls another clue to the murder of his mother which has haunted him since childhood. This prompts him to commit more and more murders until the final piece of the puzzle is in place. With a preposterous plot, even by the liberal standards of the *giallo*, *Hatchet for the Honeymoon* is forced to rely on Bava's hallucinatory images. Some of these are quite effective, especially the scenes in which Harrington's wife, whom he has murdered, returns as a ghost to drive him deeper and deeper into insanity. These scenes, however, are few and far between, and *Hatchet for the Honeymoon* ultimately fails to live up to its promise.

In 1970, Dario Argento burst onto

Stephen Forsyth stars as John Harrington, a self-professed paranoiac, in Mario Bava's darkly comic *Hatchet for the Honeymoon* (1969).

the Italian horror scene with *The Bird with the Crystal Plumage*, a stylish *giallo* in the tradition of those of his mentor, Mario Bava. The film's plot involves Sam Dalmas (Tony Musante), an American writer living in Rome, who witnesses a vicious knife attack on a woman while walking by an art galley late at night. Plagued by the notion that he saw some revealing detail he can't quite remember, Sam begins to investigate a series of related murders, bringing himself closer and closer to the killer.

Like most of Argento's films, *The Bird with the Crystal Plumage* is an extremely complicated (some would say convoluted) work. He eschews conventional narrative logic, choosing instead to create a world based on random chance and unlikely coincidence. Throughout his illus-

trious career, this has always been the knock on Argento; his films, while visually engaging, move ahead with little rhyme or reason. But even in his formative years, Argento was a master stylist. He opens the film with live-action shots which then revert to still photographs from the killer's camera. This freeze-frame disruption of linear causation recalls the final shot of Truffaut's *The 400 Blows* (1959). Argento, like Truffaut, began his career as a film critic, allowing him to study the styles of other directors before establishing his own distinctive voice. Although *The Bird with the Crystal Plumage* is nowhere near as striking as his later works, it hinted at greatness to come and began Argento's ascent to the pantheon of European horror directors.

Sam Dalmas (Tony Musante), an American writer living in Rome, is trapped behind a glass door, unable to stop a brutal murder in Dario Argento's first *giallo*, *The Bird with the Crystal Plumage* (1970).

With 1971's *Twitch of the Death Nerve*, Mario Bava made a film so bloody and outrageous some consider it a grim comedy. The plot involves a handful of hateful individuals who each lay claim— no matter how flimsy—to a piece of prime bayfront real estate. It is assumed legal ownership reverts to the one who can survive the ensuing massacre, since none of the characters are above slicing, dicing and hacking away at their rivals. The film's ending, in which the children of the two remaining murderers blow away their parents with a shotgun, is a bizarre and surreal twist from way out of left field. Today, *Twitch of the Death Nerve* is best-known, however mistakenly, as the film which

served as the inspiration for the *Friday the 13th* series, especially *Friday the 13th Part 2*.

That same year, Sean S. Cunningham, the man responsible for *Friday the 13th*, was contacted by a group of Boston theater owners. They had been impressed by the success of his pseudo-documentary sex flick *Together* (1971) and offered him $90,000 to make a horror film. What they could never have anticipated was that both Cunningham and Wes Craven, the man whom he hired to write and direct this film, would one day be responsible for two of most famous and influential slasher films ever made, *Friday the 13th* and *A Nightmare on Elm Street*, respectively. It

In Mario Bava's over-the-top blood bath *Twitch of the Death Nerve* (1971), the characters will do anything to get their hands on a piece of bayside real estate. In this scene, Albert (Luigi Pistilli) stakes both his claim and Simon (Claudio Volonte).

was, however, their first full collaborative venture which set their careers on a path from which neither has been able to stray.

The script for their horror film, which was originally called *Sex Crime of the Century*, was allegedly written by Craven in a single weekend. He had recently seen the Ingmar Bergman film *The Virgin Spring* (1960) and decided to update the story in a modern setting. Soon changed to *Night of Vengeance*, Craven's screenplay tells the story of two teenage girls who go looking for some dope on their way to a rock concert. They are kidnapped by four escaped criminals who rape, humiliate, torture and eventually murder them: Krug Stillo (David Hess); his heroin addict son Junior (Marc Sheffler); his girlfriend Sadie (Jeramie Rain); and Fred "Weasel" Padowski (Fred Lincoln). Soon after, the group stops off at the home of one of the girl's parents (it was a stretch in Bergman's film and it's a stretch here, but needless to say, plausibility is not the point of the film). After the parents come to the painful realization that they have been entertaining their daughter's murderers, they resort to their own even more brutal brand of vigilante justice.

The film was shot in October 1971 in Westport, Connecticut, in and around Cunningham's rented house. It was released in July 1972 under the title *Krug and Company*. For subsequent screenings in upstate New York, the title was changed back to *Sex Crime of the Century*. By the time August rolled around, the film had undergone another name change. It was now called *The Last House on the Left*, the least logical, but most effective of all the titles. Under it, the film would go on to make nearly $18 million.

Aided by its famous slogan *(To avoid fainting, keep repeating, it's only a movie … only a movie … only a movie…) The Last House on the Left* tore through theaters, alternately attracting and disgusting audiences. It was one of the earliest rape-revenge films and among the first to broach the question whether cinematic violence, no matter how debased, could have any socially redeeming value. Craven has always maintained that *Last House* was not exploitation for the sheer sake of exploitation, but a response to the highly stylized form of violence, *à la* Peckinpah, which had become commonplace in cinema. By refusing to cut away from scenes of realistic violence, Craven wanted to shock and horrify rather than titillate the audience. Others, however, were only out for a quick buck, and a succession of films with similar titles—*Last House on Dead End Street* (1977), *The New House on the Left* (1978), *The House on the Edge of the Park* (1980)—and vaguely similar plots, soon followed.

Throughout his distinguished career, Brian De Palma has been continuously overshadowed by both his legendary contemporaries—Francis Ford Coppola, Martin Scorsese, Steven Spielberg and George Lucas—and the man he has forever been accused of imitating, the Master of Suspense himself, Alfred Hitchcock. It is only fitting then that his greatest work was overshadowed at the time of its release by arguably the most popular and terrifying horror film in history. Released in 1973, and all but forgotten by the time *The Exorcist* hit theaters that Christmas, *Sisters* is

Mari Collingwood (Sandra Cassell) is attacked, raped, mutilated and murdered by Krug Stillo (David Hess) in Wes Craven's *The Last House on the Left* (1972), a graphic retelling of Ingmar Bergman's *The Virgin Spring* (1960).

the story of a Siamese twin (Margot Kidder) unhinged by the death of her other half. Like Norman Bates in *Psycho*, her homicidal impulses are activated by sexual arousal. The similarities end there, however, and *Sisters* is less a paean to *Psycho* than a complex psychological thriller in the tradition of the Italian *giallo* which Dario Argento had already begun to reinvent. Its violence, while brutal, is more stylized than graphic. After *Sisters*, De-Palma veered away from pure horror, choosing instead to embrace various aspects of the slasher film within the confines of psychological thrillers such as *Dressed to Kill* (1980), *Blow Out* (1981) and *Body Double* (1984).

Tobe Hooper's *The Texas Chainsaw Massacre* (1974) was less an actual massacre than a brilliant exercise in the power of suggestion, despite claims of its legendary bloodletting. It shrewdly hints at unspeakable brutality while actually showing very little. It is still, however, an exceptionally visceral film, one which proved that realistic violence was just as attractive to audiences as the cartoonish gore of H.G. Lewis and *Night of the Living Dead*.

The Texas-born and -bred Hooper is a bona fide cinephile who attributes his love of film to the fact that his father owned a movie theater in San Angelo where the young Hooper would spend

Emil (the always creepy William Finley) plans to give crazed Siamese twin Danielle/Dominique (Margot Kidder) a taste of her own medicine in Brian De Palma's *Psycho*-inspired *Sisters* (1973).

countless days and nights. After a theatrically distributed short, a bizarre feature and a documentary on the rock group Peter, Paul & Mary, Hooper went on to make the film which would live in infamy in the annals of horror cinema. The idea for *The Texas Chainsaw Massacre* was culled from a combination of Hooper's trip to a Montgomery Ward department store, where he was delayed in a row displaying chain saws, and the childhood story he used to hear from his relatives about Wisconsin mass murderer Ed Gein. Although closer in truth to the actual Gein case than *Psycho*, and despite a shrewd marketing ploy which convinced most people that the film was based on a true story, *The Texas Chainsaw Massacre* still takes tremendous liberty with the facts.[1]

The Texas Chainsaw Massacre was an extremely difficult and demanding production for all involved. Despite his previous efforts, Hooper had little experience dealing with investors. He and co-writer Kim Henkel were forced to hammer out a script and art director Bob Burns designed some "bone furniture" before any money was raised. The on-set exploits were no less taxing. The decomposing animal remains strewn about the farmhouse reeked of formaldehyde and the film's two stars, Marilyn Burns and Gunnar Hansen, both received minor injuries during shooting.

The film begins with a jolt: Blinding flashes from a flashbulb reveal the carnage while a voice-over by a then-unknown John Larroquette gives a news report about the crimes. Before long, a van of teenage hippies, among the last of a disappearing generation, comes barreling down the Texas highway. Naturally, they run out of gas near a seemingly abandoned farmhouse. What happens next is nowhere near as important as the palpable feeling of unmitigated random terror which Hooper expertly builds. One by one the group is captured, murdered and presumably skinned by Leatherface, a chain saw–wielding maniac who wears a mask fashioned from the flesh of his victims.

While conflicting reports place *The Texas Chainsaw Massacre*'s final budget anywhere from $93,000 to just under $250,000, with a gross of more than $20 million the film was a staggering success. With its lurid title and infamous tagline (*Who Will Remain and What Will Be Left of Them?*), it played especially well on the southern drive-in circuit which historically has always been more receptive to exploitation films. It would be wrong, however, to discount *The Texas Chainsaw Massacre* as a mere novelty. It is a powerful disturbing film in which Hooper combines the desolation of the barren Texas locale with a renegade filmmaking style to produce a dynamic study of rampant madness. In fact, New York City's Museum of Modern Art added the film to its permanent collection, validating its claim as legitimate, albeit unconventional art. There, for all eternity, among the Dalis and Pollocks, resides a print of *The Texas Chainsaw Massacre*.

Over the past decade, *Black Christmas* (1974), a Canadian slasher which was a hit in its own country but limped out of theaters in the United States after relatively little success, has become the darling of slasher enthusiasts due to its preempting of the stylistic techniques generally thought to have been pioneered by *Halloween*. It was directed by the chameleon-like Bob Clark, who made his horror debut with the low-budget cult hit *Children Shouldn't Play With Dead Things* and went on to helm the well-respected Sherlock Holmes mystery *Murder by Decree* (1979), before breaking into the mainstream with *Porky's* (1981), a hysterical nod to the 1950s which ushered in a new wave of risqué teenage comedies.

Black Christmas opens with a long shot of a sorority house, bedecked with all

In one of the most horrific scenes in Tobe Hooper's classic slasher *The Texas Chainsaw Massacre* (1974), Pam (Teri McMinn) falls into the clutches of Leatherface (Gunnar Hansen). The character of Leatherface was loosely based on Wisconsin mass murderer Ed Gein, who also served as the inspiration for Robert Bloch's *Psycho*.

the Christmas trimmings. A mournful rendition of "Silent Night" plays over the credits. Suddenly, in what is probably the slasher film's definitive point-of-view shot, the killer (camera) approaches the house, scales the trellis and enters through an attic window.

Inside, a party is winding down. Most of the students are leaving for the Christmas holiday, although a few girls, including Barb (Margot Kidder) and Jess (Olivia Hussey), along with their house mother, Mrs. Mac (Marian Waldman), have chosen to stay behind. Their holiday cheer is soon interrupted by a series of phone calls, far more obscene and nefarious than the typical prank. When one of their sisters suddenly disappears (suffocated by the killer who is hiding in the attic), and a young girl is murdered in a local park, the police, led by the always welcome John Saxon, are called in. In a terrifying twist which would be reused far more extensively in 1979's *When a Stranger Calls*, the phone calls are traced and found to be coming from inside the house. Suspicion falls on Jess' boyfriend Peter (Keir Dullea), an aspiring pianist who threatens her when she admits to wanting an abortion. When Peter arrives at the house to apologize, Jess, thinking he is the killer, stabs him to death with a poker. Traumatized, she is left alone to recover, as once again, the ringing of the telephone sounds throughout the house.

Unlike the slashers which would follow it, *Black Christmas*' killer is never exposed, nor is his motivation ever explained. The most we see of his him is a fleeting glimpse of his eyeball as he hides behind a door, waiting to attack Jess. There is never any attempt to rationalize or justify his madness. He is simply insane. A few books, including the usually accurate *Encyclopedia of Horror Movies*, mistakenly point out that the killer is Peter, when in fact it is fairly obvious that his identity remains a mystery. Allegedly, a year later, Clark penned a sequel to *Black Christmas* called *Halloween*. Ironically, it was rumored that at this very time he was working on another unrelated project with John Carpenter, the man whose name would soon become synonymous with Halloween.

Clare (Lynne Griffin) becomes the first victim of the mysterious slayer in Bob Clark's revered yuletide slasher *Black Christmas* (1974).

After his impressive freshman effort *The Bird With the Crystal Plumage*, Dario Argento struggled to find his niche with two inferior *gialli*, *The Cat O'Nine Tails* (1971) and *Four Flies on Grey Velvet* (1972), and one comedic Western, *Le Cinque Giornate* (1973). Then, in 1975, he hit his stride with *Deep Red*, the film which best illustrates both his strengths and weaknesses as a director. At times, the film is almost impossible to follow. It is a psychological mystery drenched in disturbing childhood imagery which is unduly unsettling by its sheer nature. It is also the film in which Argento first displays his propensity for beautifully orchestrated violence. The scene in which Giordani (Glauco Mauri) has his teeth bashed in on the corner of a fireplace is enough to send chills up the spine of any viewer. After *Deep Red*, Argento took a hiatus from the *giallo*, choosing instead to focus on his unfinished "Three Mothers Trilogy" which includes the critically acclaimed *Suspiria* (1977) and *Inferno* (1980).

The Redeemer (1976), better known as *Class Reunion Massacre*, has all the trappings of a standard slasher: an isolated empty high school, a diabolical madman, and a group of six former friends who don't find it the least bit odd that they're the only ones in attendance at their ten-year reunion. What follows is not only a far cry from a standard slasher, but far less satisfying and gruesome than the back of the oversized Continental Video box would

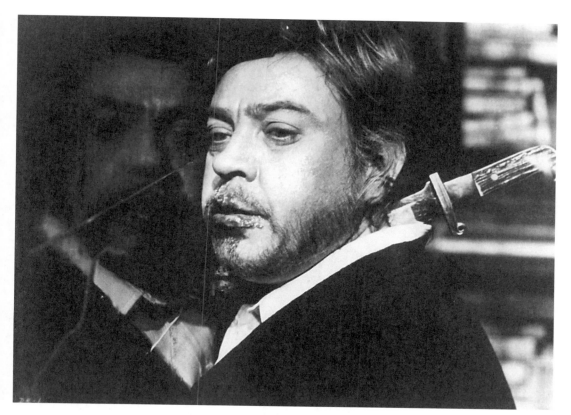

It's been a rough day for Prof. Giordani (Glauco Mauri) in Dario Argento's *Deep Red* (1975). After getting his teeth bashed in by a mysterious attacker, he's finished off with a dagger to the neck.

lead you to believe. Despite some truly nightmarish sequences, complete with Argentoesque imagery—a murderous mannequin who is a more effective killer than the actual "Redeemer"—and a weird, dreamlike quality, *The Redeemer* is hampered by both an impenetrable prologue and epilogue and a dubious sense of morality. The Redeemer of the title, you see, has invited the six guests back to their high school to punish them for their "sins," which include such blasphemous acts as lesbianism, a healthy appetite and, the best one yet, being a criminal defense attorney. Director Constantine S. Gochis spends an inordinate amount of time making sure the audience is aware that the Redeemer has two thumbs on his left hand. As to what this has to do with the logic of the film, your guess is as good as mine.

Since low-budget independent producer-director Charles B. Pierce was a former advertising executive, it is hardly surprising that the most compelling aspect of his benign and plodding slasher, *The Town That Dreaded Sundown* (1976), was its title and marketing campaign. In 1972, Pierce scored a modest hit with *The Legend of Boggy Creek*, a pseudo-documentary about a Bigfoot-like creature loose in Arkansas. The film became a favorite on the southern drive-in circuit because of its fairly realistic recreations of the alleged event. Four years later, Pierce again drew his inspiration from an actual event. *The Town That Dreaded Sundown* is based on a spate of murders which occurred in 1946 in Texarkana, a small town which straddles the Texas-Arkansas border. The hooded murderer was dubbed the "Phantom

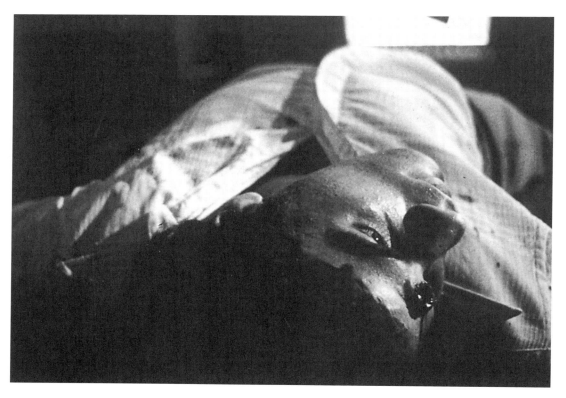

John (Damien Knight) is quickly dispatched by a single gunshot in a very un-slasher-like killing in Constantine S. Gochis' unbearably weird *The Redeemer* (1976).

Killer" for his ability to foil authorities and evade capture. Somehow Pierce was able to take this inherently cinematic story and give it all the excitement of a police report. *The Town That Dreaded Sundown* looks as if it was made, not set, in 1946, and despite some creative touches like death by trombone, the film never establishes any momentum. The Phantom Killer was never caught and, although it was suspected that he committed suicide in a desperate effort to avoid being captured, the open nature of the case was a further detriment to an already boring film.

Equally boring was *The Toolbox Murders* (1977), about which the only thing noteworthy is its conspicuous lack of suspense. This drab and painfully dull film achieved a small cult following on the basis of its inclusion as a video nasty. The most clever aspect of the film, by far, is its title. And as it suggests, good-looking women—at least by the standards of this low-budget dreck—in a California apartment building are murdered by a tool-wielding madman. The murders—by nail gun, powerdrill and hammer—are so telegraphed and staged that director Dennis Donnelly seems to be crying out, "Please notice me!" It doesn't help that early on he employs an incoherent montage which looks more like an editing exercise directly out of Film Techniques 101.

Cameron Mitchell plays the toolbox murderer, whose teenage daughter was killed in a car accident. Predictably, he goes nuts, blaming her death not on

The "Phantom Killer," a hooded psychopath who terrorized the small town of Texarkana in 1946, tries to claim his next victim in Charles B. Pierce's dull, plodding slasher *The Town That Dreaded Sundown* (1976).

happenstance, but on all like-minded adolescents. After knocking off various tenants in the building, he kidnaps a young girl who he views as some incarnation of his daughter. Psychosis must run in the family, for when the abducted girl's brother gets too close to the truth, Mitchell's unstable nephew gleefully eliminates him. The film ends with the kidnapped girl's rescue. However, in an unnecessary and downbeat twist, a postscript informs us that not only was *The Toolbox Murders* based on an actual case, but the kidnapped heroine was subsequently confined to an asylum.

Five years after *The Last House on the*

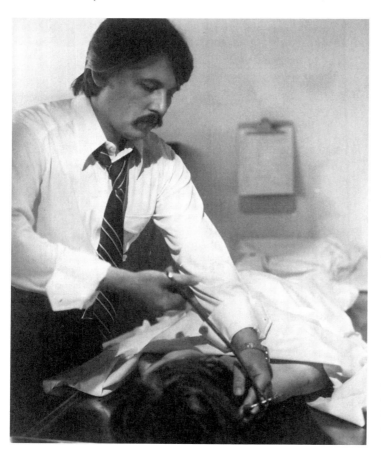

A nail is removed from the head of a female victim in the grim, misogynistic and utterly suspenseless *The Toolbox Murders* (1977).

Left, Wes Craven again pushed the envelope of good taste with *The Hills Have Eyes* (1977), in which a murderous pack of desert nomads attack a retired cop and his family as they travel across the desert. The film is loosely based on the exploits of Alexander "Sawney" Bean, an infamous Scottish cannibal, and his inbred family. Bean was a degenerate highwayman who lived in a seaside cave with his common law wife for over 25 years. During that time he spawned eight sons, six daughters, 18 grandsons and 14 granddaughters— all through incest. The Beans preyed upon travelers who ventured too close to their lair, murdering with impunity and disposing of the bodies in the most disgusting fashion—the mangled body parts which they couldn't eat right away were pickled for a later meal. Finally, after more than 1,000 unexplained disappearances, for which a few local innkeepers were unjustly and mistakenly executed, a hunting party of over 400 men and bloodhounds—led by the king himself—discovered the ghastly clan. Justice was quick and brutal; the Bean men were dismembered and slowly bled to death while the women and children were burned alive.

Like *The Last House on the Left*, *The Hills Have Eyes* embraces a sleazy realism while seriously exploring complex philosophical questions. It is similar to *The Texas Chainsaw Massacre* in that both films draw their terror from the frenetic primal violence of the "uncivilized." The film was shot on 16mm, a financial rather than artistic decision which nonetheless accentuates its grit. Always probing the darkest region of the human condition, Craven, the former professor, wanted to show what happens when you strip away the defining essence of the civilized man (i.e. his home, his amenities, his nuclear family). Does he crumble in the face of mortal danger? Or are his dormant animalistic tendencies triggered by the survival impulse? As in the Sawney Bean case, the civilized folk in *The Hills Have Eyes* enact a revenge which is just as brutal and depraved as the crime against them. The film's dark ending further reinforces the main theme of *The Last House on the Left*, that we are all capable of the most unspeakable atrocities when our normalcy is threatened.

Jupiter (James Whitworth), the "papa" of the cannibal clan in Wes Craven's *The Hills Have Eyes* (1977), gets a hold of Brenda (Susan Lanier), an unlucky traveler whose camper breaks down in the middle of the desert.

It would be convenient to assume that the slasher film grew out of a natural progression, that every new release pushed it closer and closer to some universal definition. This wasn't the case, however. Contrary to what many film historians think, the emergence of the slasher film wasn't the result of a gradual evolution, but a big bang. And that big bang was *Halloween*.

CHAPTER 3

Halloween: The Night *He* Came Home

On October 25, 1978, the boogeyman was born.

John Carpenter's *Halloween* would go on to become not only the most important slasher film, but one of the most successful independent movies ever made. Produced for a paltry $300,000, the film grossed over $50 million—well over 150 times its production cost. *Halloween* is an example of low-budget filmmaking at its finest, but more importantly, it is an almost perfect exercise in terror.

Over the years, as its reputation has grown, *Halloween* has forged its own mythology, which, as is often the case, has less to do with fact than with the romantic notion that the film stumbled upon its success by accident. *Halloween* was not some cinematic dark horse, destined to fail but somehow plucked from obscurity and given blockbuster status. It was a carefully calculated, albeit risky, business decision.

Halloween was the brainchild of independent distributor-producer Irwin Yablans. Yablans, who had acquired Carpenter's previous film *Assault on Precinct 13* (1976), which he planned to release through his distribution company, Turtle

Releasing, was developing a concept he called "The Babysitter Murders." The basic premise involved a group of babysitters being stalked by a psychopath. Yablans describes the sequence of events leading up to the production of *Halloween*:

I had started up this distribution company called Compass International. Well, actually, it was called Turtle then I changed it to Compass, but I quickly found out that it was going to be difficult to find pictures of any quality for distribution through pickup and paying for them at the various sales or film conventions. So I started making pictures, but we had no money to make pictures really. Then I got a call from Phil Gersh. Phil Gersh was John Carpenter's agent. At the time, John was a graduate student who had made a picture called *Siege* for about $180,000 and could not get distribution for it. Well, I was the last stop, I suppose. I looked at the film and I thought it showed a lot of talent and a lot of promise and I agreed to distribute it, but I wanted to change the title, which we did, to *Assault on Precinct 13*. I opened it in a few theaters in America and it didn't do very well. You know, it was just a small little picture. So I took it to Milan, because we had foreign rights as well, to see if I could get some foreign sales, but I wasn't very successful there either.

On the way home, I stopped in London and as I was waiting to fly out the next day, I got a call at the Hilton Hotel from a fellow named Michael Myers who owned a company called Miracle Films. He wanted to talk to me about the picture. I really didn't want to bother. I was kind of discouraged and I really didn't want to listen to one more pitch, so I told him no but he persisted and he came to my hotel. He came up and told me that he thought the picture was brilliant and I kind of liked him because he saw the same things in it that I did, and you know, you always like someone to confirm your own brilliance. And he said he wanted to enter the film into the London Film Festival, which surprised me to no end. But it wasn't the first time a picture bombs out in one country and for some reason attracts the attention of film buffs in another—Jerry Lewis in France. So we made a deal. He gave us a small guarantee of some sort. And lo and behold it [*Assault on Precinct 13*] wins a prize and becomes the darling of the festival and Carpenter becomes this great young director.

That was all I needed. I thought to myself, you know what, I think I'll make my first picture with this guy because he's talented and no one wants him because they don't know him.... So on the way back, I said to myself, you know, I loved *The Exorcist*, I loved *Psycho*, and I've always been a fan of horror movies, so I think to myself, I can make a horror movie with this guy. Then I thought, I won't be able to spend much money—all this thought process was on the airplane coming back from Milan to New York—and I thought, why not a babysitter movie? A babysitter in jeopardy, because everyone's either had a babysitter, been a babysitter, had children, you know, everybody can relate to it.... Then I thought to myself, well, if we can do it all in one night, we can probably do it for a price because we can keep it tight. Then Halloween just popped into my mind because, I guess,

well, that's the scariest night of the year. Then I said to myself, well, I'm sure it's been used, I'm sure the title is gone, I'm sure the premise has been used. I got back and I called Carpenter the very next morning, and I said, "John, how would you feel about making a movie about babysitters in jeopardy, and, wait a minute, doing it on one night, on Halloween...."

The plan was risky, but Yablans, while an inexperienced producer, was a shrewd businessman. He had seen what both *Night of the Living Dead* and *The Texas Chainsaw Massacre* had accomplished with a minuscule budget, a largely unprofessional cast and crew, and no guaranteed distribution. He also sensed, instinctively, that he had hit upon a extraordinary idea. But more importantly, he had enormous faith in Carpenter.

The son of a music teacher, Carpenter initially thought of following in his father's footsteps. In fact, he still composes the scores for many of his own films. But instead of pursuing a career in music, he attended film school at the University of Southern California. As part of the "movie brat" generation—those directors who came of age in the early '70s and revolutionized the Hollywood studio system—Carpenter scored his first legitimate success while still in film school. *The Resurrection of Bronco Billy*, a short film which he co-wrote, scored and edited, won an Academy Award. Although he had directed *Dark Star* (1974), an extended student film he made with future *Return of the Living Dead* (1985) director Dan O'Bannon, and had written the script for what would eventually become *The Eyes of Laura Mars* (1978), Carpenter was itching to break out on his own as a director of substance. He describes his reaction when Yablans approached him with the concept for the "The Babysitter Murders":

"The Most Frightening Flick in Years" announces the marquee of the Rivoli theater in New York about *Halloween* (1978). Notice the advertisement for the upcoming film, *1941* directed by a little-known director named Steven Spielberg.

My first reaction was joy because I needed a job. At that point in my career, I had been writing screenplays for several years and hustling around and trying to get movies going. And this was an opportunity to direct, and it became even more appealing when I made a deal with Irwin that I would not only do it for the money, but I would also have final cut. Then I felt I had a chance at making my own film, which I was not able to do when I would direct TV movies. It was a different situation…. On *Assault on Precinct 13* I had had final cut and I wanted it back.

Carpenter assured Yablans he could bring the film in for under $300,000, a ridiculously low sum, even in those days. Yablans immediately contacted Moustapha Akkad, an Arab financier whose highly

controversial film *Mohammad, Messenger of God* (released in 1977 as *The Message*), was distributed by Yablans. Akkad would eventually enjoy the dubious distinction of being the only individual associated with each of *Halloween*'s sequels in some capacity.

Initially, Akkad didn't believe that the film could be completed for only $300,000. Realizing that the fate of his production hinged on Akkad's investment, Yablans arranged a meeting in Los Angeles between himself, Carpenter and Akkad, at which he reiterated his belief that the film could be done for $300,000. Carpenter assured both men that not only *could* it be done, but that he *would* do it. He agreed to write, direct, compose and perform the music, all for only $10,000 plus a percentage of the profits, which, at that point, nobody imagined would be very much. Akkad still seemed unconvinced, so Yablans attempted a bit of reverse psychology. "I said, 'John, look, $300,000 is a lot of money,'" Yablans recalls. "'It's a big risk and I'm not sure that Moustapha wants to take the chance.'" Luckily, Akkad took the bait and production on *Halloween* was underway.

In retrospect, the element most integral to *Halloween*'s success may have been its title. The singularity of the name "Halloween" seemed to strike a collective cord within the consciousness of American moviegoers, conjuring up haunting images of ghouls, mystery, death and, most importantly, evil. It's hard to imagine "The Babysitter Murders" or some derivation of, eliciting the same response. As the originator of the concept and title, Yablans wanted to impress upon Carpenter his creative vision:

I grew up with radio, *Inner Sanctum, Lights Out*, radio horror shows. I think that's why great writers came from that time, because you had to be descriptive ... and I said I want it to be like a radio show. I want it to be spooky, scary, but leave much of it to the audience. And John, he got it. I mean, he understood that immediately. I think that one of the great successes of *Psycho* and *The Exorcist* was the anticipation. Hitchcock did that very well.

Halloween was shot over the course of 20 days in the spring of 1978, mostly in Pasadena, California. Its slick feel and crisp cinematography are deceiving in that they mask just how little money the production really had. The saga of its low-budget exploits have been well-documented, and some of the more colorful behind-the-scenes stories have become legendary.

The town of Haddonfield was named for the hometown of *Halloween*'s producer, co-writer and then-girlfriend of Carpenter, Debra Hill, who grew up in Haddonfield, New Jersey. It was Hill whose hands doubled for the young Michael Myers in the film's infamous opening. "We couldn't afford another kid to hold the knife later that night, so that's my hand holding the knife that stabs Michael Myers' sister. I had the littlest hands," said Hill. Many of Haddonfield's street names were taken from Carpenter's hometown of Bowling Green, Kentucky. Jamie Lee Curtis, the film's heroine, was cast partly because of her horror pedigree. Her mother, Janet Leigh, had starred in Hitchcock's *Psycho*, a film which *Halloween* constantly references. Carpenter initially wanted Anne Lockhart, daughter of *Lassie* star June Lockhart, for the role of Laurie Strode, who incidentally, was named after one of Carpenter's old girlfriends. However, the buzz generated by casting Curtis was far too great to pass up, and on a budget such as *Halloween*'s, Carpenter couldn't afford to squander any opportunity to drum up publicity.

The task of creating an Illinois October in the heart of sunny California with its endless sunshine and leafy palms fell to production designer, art director and location scout, Tommy Lee Wallace, an old friend of Carpenter's and boyfriend of Nancy Loomis, one of *Halloween*'s co-stars. Fake leaves were strewn along the streets and economically reused in later scenes to give the illusion of autumn. Except for the now notorious flub where cars bearing California license plates can be seen driving on the streets of Haddonfield, Illinois, the production design perfectly captures the familiarity and subtle nuances of small-town U.S.A. Wallace was also responsible for creating the look of a villain whose visage is now almost as recognizable as the Phantom of the Opera, the

Wolf Man and the Mummy. But the face of one of horror's most terrifying psychopaths was nothing more than an innocuous Captain Kirk mask which Wallace bought for a few bucks on Hollywood Boulevard. The eye holes were widened and the mask was spray-painted a bluish-white. "The idea was to make him almost humorless, faceless, this sort of pale visage that could resemble a human or not," said Hill. Carpenter describes the reason behind his decision to use this particular mask:

> There's a very famous book I read years ago called *The Mask of Sanity*. It's about psychopaths. It describes in really incredible detail that they wear this mask, that to us they appear human, but underneath they're just machines. They don't have any regard for us. I was always chilled by that. So it was kind of a literal interpretation. And that went along with Halloween of course. Everybody is dressed up in costumes. I had a choice between a clown mask, which would be obvious, and this one, which was really creepy.

Despite the incredible pressure that the entire production team was under, Yablans knew he made the right choice in entrusting Carpenter with his project:

> Right from the beginning, John was always the kind of guy, even then, who had this *auteur* mentality. Now, even though he was going to work for $10,000, we gave him 10 percent of the picture as well, which he probably thought he'd never get a nickel on. But even then he insisted that it be "A John Carpenter film." Even then, his ego always stressed that. That impressed me as well because it showed me that this guy really believes in himself. Anyway, he goes off and makes the picture and I spent a lot of time going down there and talking to him but I really had nothing to do with the physical making of the movie because he was in total control. He was staying right on budget and

even then—I was a fledgling filmmaker in those days, I really hadn't made a lot of pictures—but I could tell it was all under control. It was smooth, there was a wonderful camaraderie as they made that picture, it was really a joy to behold. As a result, I learned about making an independent film myself. They were accomplishing a lot of stuff and I could tell from the dailies that we were okay.

Halloween begins, appropriately, on Halloween night, 1963. In arguably the greatest opening scene of a horror film, a marvelous, languid point-of-view shot which was inspired by the opening sequence of Orson Welles' *Touch of Evil* (1958), six-year-old Michael Myers stabs his sister to death. For 15 years he has remained incarcerated in a sanitarium in Smith's Grove under the watchful eye of his psychiatrist, Dr. Sam Loomis (Donald Pleasence). On October 30, 1978, he escapes, certain to return to Haddonfield to relive the bloody anniversary.

Laurie Strode (Jamie Lee Curtis), a virginal teenager who always seems to be one step ahead of her dimwitted friends, plans to spend her Halloween night babysitting some local kids. She gets caught up in a terrifying game of cat-and-mouse with Michael, who has indeed returned to finish the job. The town's teenagers, surprisingly likable for a slasher film, are knocked off one by one, while Loomis futilely tries to convince the local sheriff that his idyllic town has become a slaughterhouse.

Laurie manages to outwit Michael long enough for Loomis to arrive. The obsessed doctor pumps six rounds into his former patient, who then plummets to his death from a second story window. Or so it seems. When Loomis looks out into the yard, Michael has disappeared. For as Tommy Doyle, one of the kids whom Laurie is babysitting, prophetically states, "You can't kill the boogeyman."

Shots such as this in *Halloween* (1978), in which Michael (Nick Castle) hovers in the corner of the frame, are indicative of Carpenter's visual style.

It is difficult to overestimate the importance of *Halloween*. Many of the conventions which have become staples of the slasher—the subjective camera, the Final Girl, the significant date setting—were either pioneered or perfected in the film. It is the blueprint for all slashers and the model against which all subsequent films are judged. Of course, *Halloween* didn't invent these cinematic devices—*The Texas Chainsaw Massacre* leaves Marilyn Burns as the lone survivor while *Black Christmas* employs a subjective camera—but it was the first to create a slasher paradigm by bringing them together in a single film.

Halloween has aged well, and while its reputation as a brilliant film is well-de-

served, it is not, as some critics have proposed, a cerebral one. In fact, *Halloween* is a prime example of an anti-cerebral horror film. While well-made and technically proficient, it is certainly not psychologically complex. Yet numerous critics have undertaken a psychoanalytic reading of the film and have concluded that Michael Myers is symbolic of sexual repression. In his article, "An Introduction to the American Horror Film," Robin Wood discusses *Halloween*'s opening murder: "The girl is killed because she arouses in the voyeur-murderer feelings he has simultaneously to deny and enact in the form of violent assault." It is surprising that many other critics are of a similar opinion, considering

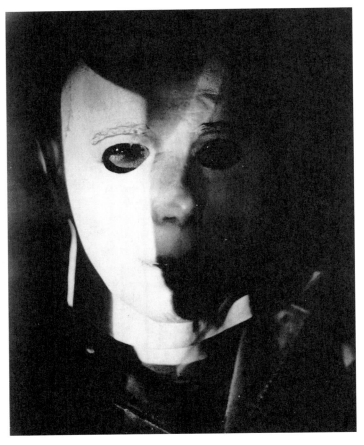

The face which began it all. In John Carpenter's *Halloween* (1978), the first true slasher film, Michael Myers, an irredeemably evil "boogeyman," turns an idyllic suburban town into a bloody nightmare.

that it is extremely difficult to try and force the film into any psychosexual context.

Michael Myers does not repress his sexuality, nor does he represent the repressed sexuality of any of the characters. This is never even remotely implied anywhere in the film. For as Dr. Loomis, Michael's psychiatrist for 15 years and the man most qualified to analyze him, says, he "is purely and simply evil." Why does Michael kill? Because like the shark in *Jaws* (1975), that's simply what he does. John McCarty summed it up best in *Movie Psychos and Madmen* when he wrote, "People, especially critics, tend to see what they want in films ... and the more meaningless a film, the more it is open to interpretation." Although his contention that *Halloween* is a meaningless film is a bit narrow-minded, his opinion about the overanalysis of film is dead-on.

A fascinating conceit which initially seemed as if it would become a constant of the slasher film, but which later films generally chose to eschew in favor of a more conventional killer, is the concept of an omnipotent, if not vaguely supernatural, boogeyman. There is no question that Michael Myers is human. He is not a zombie, vampire, ghoul or any other fantastic creature. Yet he routinely survives fatal wounds—including a sewing needle to the neck and numerous gunshot wounds to the chest—which would normally kill a mere mortal. Until *Halloween*, almost all films involving a stalking killer—including *The Texas Chainsaw Massacre* in which Leatherface, while deranged and psychotic, is clearly human—made a point to assure the audience that the villain could be destroyed. *Halloween* allows no safe harbor. Some series—most notably *Friday the 13th* and *A Nightmare on Elm Street*—took this omnipotence to even more ridiculous extremes. However, most found it more satisfying to create a villain who could be defeated by traditional means.

Many critics have accused Carpenter of forsaking plausibility in regards to Michael's mortality so that he could have some justification for bringing his boogeyman back in the event of a sequel. Carpenter insists, however, that this possibility never crossed anyone's mind. In 1978, nobody was making sequels, especially not for a horror film which wasn't expected to attract much interest anyway. It was solely a thematic reason—to show the indestructibility and pervasiveness of evil—that Michael isn't destroyed like a traditional monster at the end of the film. Says Carpenter:

It was all to make a new legend. There's something really creepy about the fact that evil never dies. It can't be killed. If as in the movie he really is just a force of evil, he's like nature. Well, in the end, he's back up again.

When detractors of the slasher film bemoan the senseless killing and rampant bloodshed in these movies, they invariably use *Halloween* as a prime example. Such ridiculous accusations only highlight their ignorance. In actuality, *Halloween* is one of the most restrained horror films. While there are stabbings, shootings and the occasional strangulation, not a single drop of blood in shed onscreen. When taking into consideration the graphic violence in the killing sprees of Stallone and Schwarzenegger, *Halloween* is benign in comparison. Yet it consistently raises the ire of such critics who find nothing reprehensible in dispensing vigilante justice against, say, an entire village of Viet Cong, but have a real problem with teenagers being dispatched in a creative manner. The irony here is the fact that it was exactly the relative innocuous nature of *Halloween* which endeared it to adoring fans. As Kim Newman states in *Nightmare Movies*, "Few films are as well made or inoffensive." As silly as it seems, the film which gave rise to some of the most abhorrent films ever made is really quite tame.

It was a conscious choice on the part of Carpenter to pare the graphic violence down to a bare minimum. Unlike *Psycho*, which at the time pushed the envelope in terms of what could be shown in a mainstream film, *Halloween* takes its cue from *The Texas Chainsaw Massacre*. Viewers are often astounded, even after immediately viewing Hooper's film, when told that never once does a chain saw make contact with human flesh.[1] Instead, the viewer must rely on a series of visual and audio cues—the humming of the saw, the ominously swinging meathooks, the scattered human remains—to imagine the horrors which will inevitably follow. *Halloween* is more graphic. We actually do see Michael murder his victims. But it is never—and this is where Carpenter *does* recall Hitchcock—at the expense of meticulously constructed tension. The murders punctuate the suspense, they do not overshadow it.

To their credit, some critics immediately recognized the merit of *Halloween*. It found a most unlikely supporter in Roger Ebert, who called the film "a genre classic." Ebert was undoubtedly as impressed with the director's technique as with the film itself, for Carpenter is a master craftsman. While he is not known for his signature style, in *Halloween* he successfully marries dramatic subtlety with kinetic, yet unobtrusive, camerawork.

Carpenter's Panaglide camera floats effortlessly through scenes, realizing Michael's point of view while sustaining an everpresent feeling of uneasiness. Studying the camerawork in later slashers, it is almost impossible to pretend the killer's gaze is anything more than a bumbling cameraman staggering around the set searching for the action. And while it was atypical for a director on a low-budget film like *Halloween* to be concerned enough with style to investigate the tools of his trade, Carpenter was always cognizant of the fact that both the "look" and theme of *Halloween* were inseparable from each other:

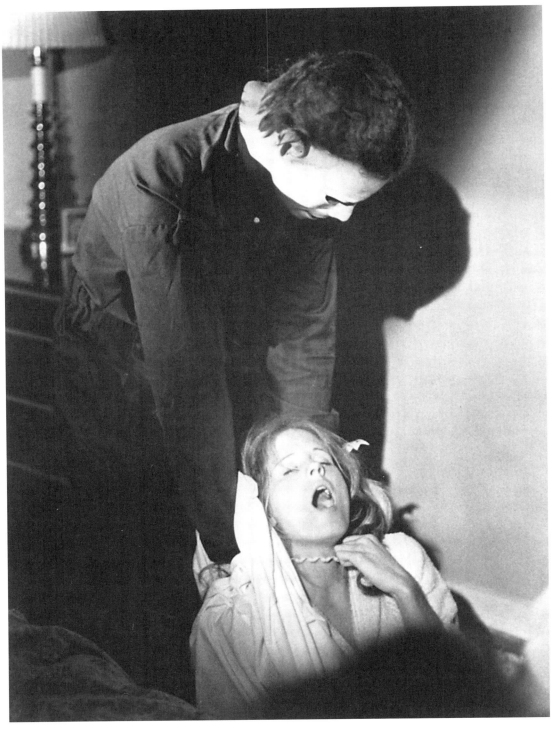

In *Halloween*'s (1978) most suspenseful and Hitchcockian scene, Michael (Nick Castle) chokes Lynda (P. J. Soles) with a phone cord as Laurie listens on the other end.

I had seen some examples of this Steadi-cam, the Panavision version is called Panaglide, it's a gyroscopic camera that you wear and I was very impressed with how it feels. This was the real secret to *Halloween*, because there's a float quality to it. And I've always thought that in some way the hand-held shot or the dolly shot doesn't really indicate point of view. And the whole movie is a point-of-view film. It's all seen through various eyes. So I just think that's responsible for a lot of it.

Carpenter also takes full advantage of the Panavision widescreen format in which the film was shot. He stretches the screen to its fullest, using every portion of the frame as a potential place for Michael to lurk. Some of the film's creepiest moments—Michael silently watching Laurie—were inspired by similar shots in *The Innocents* (1961), Jack Clayton's quietly terrifying version of Henry James' *The Turn of the Screw*.

Once *Halloween* was finished, Yablans knew he had something special, but it wasn't until he heard the score, which Carpenter composed himself, that he recognized the extent of the film's power. According to Carpenter, the music, which added an entirely new dimension to the film, was inspired by the score for *Suspiria,* which in turn took its cue from *The Exorcist.*

Yablans was now ready to use his experience and connections to try and set up distribution for *Halloween*, but first, he screened it for Akkad, who was busy making *Lion of the Desert* (1980). Until now, Akkad's interest in the picture had been purely financial. That all changed when he viewed it for the first time. Unduly impressed, Akkad demanded a credit, even though every credit had already been given away. In the end, Akkad won out. The first title card of *Halloween* reads: Moustapha Akkad Presents.

In the summer of 1978, before taking *Halloween* to Milan to try and sell the foreign rights, Yablans scheduled a sneak preview of the film in Westwood, California. He invited all the major studios to send representatives. No one showed up. Dejected, Yablans took his seat as *Halloween* began to play. Then, towards the end of the film, a curious thing happened. Yablans describes the experience:

> About 80 percent into the film, towards the end, the people started laughing and talking to the screen. I kept thinking that they were being derisive. But they were so into it that they were just relieving tension. They were getting involved and it was a *good* thing, which I learned as a result of watching it play many many times after that in theaters. The reaction was always the same way. It was this connection with the audience that makes the picture so unique.

Yablans took *Halloween* to Milan in October, just weeks before its domestic opening. This time, the reaction was immediate. By the time Yablans returned to the States, he had already made over $800,000 in foreign sales. *Halloween* had already earned a profit and it hadn't even opened yet. Instead of premiering *Halloween* in either New York or Los Angeles, Yablans decided to open it in Kansas City, a relatively small market, in order to get a feel for the film. By the time the picture was in its second week, it was already doing record business.

Next, *Halloween* opened in Chicago, where all the main theaters were owned by a man who offered to run the film at his four biggest drive-ins during Thanksgiving. Realizing that a drive-in, outside, in Chicago, in late November was a virtual death sentence for a film, Yablans told the theater owner he would give him the four drive-ins in return for his four best "hard tops." Much to the surprise of the theater owner, *Halloween* began shattering records in Chicago as well. By the end of the film's run, Yablans was owed hundreds of thousands of dollars. When the theater owner realized his potential profit, he called Yablans to discuss their arrangement. In those days, independent distributors were often swindled out of their percentage, a fact of which Yablans was all too aware. He went to see the theater owner, determined not to let this happen to him. Yablans remembers, verbatim, what he told the man:

> I said to him, "A man dreams a dream. He comes up with an idea. He finds someone who will work with him for very little money. He goes out and scrapes, he borrows, he begs, and finds someone to finance the picture. He finishes the movie. He can't get anyone to distribute the film so he does it himself. He pays all the advertising. He pays your house expense. He takes every risk imaginable; you do nothing. The picture then becomes a big success and you won't pay. See this [Yablans holds up the contract]. There will be a double-truck ad in *Variety* if you don't pay. On one side will be this contract printed just the way you see it. On the other side will be an open letter to Jack Valenti and [Yablans mentioned some federal bureau]. If you don't think I'll do it, you fat son of a bitch, then you don't pay me." Well, he paid every penny.

All across the country, *Halloween* found similar success. The reaction to it was the same everywhere; audiences immediately felt a connection to it—as if they were personally involved in the action—and made no effort to hide their emotions. Carpenter describes one particularly memorable screening:

> There was one audience I saw it with, it was a pure outside-of-Hollywood audience. That's when I realized, my God, listen to them. You know they were just going insane…. The whole participatory situation was going on. I remember the screening was in New York, I think it was for college kids. And I stood outside the door and couldn't believe it. It was a very emotional experience for them. They were really wrapped up in the images.

The film's one-sheet—a sinister looking pumpkin which subtly melds into a powerful hand clenching a glistening knife—decorated theater lobbies from New York to Los Angeles.[2] During this time, *Halloween* was being distributed through various subdistributors. Although Yablans admits that the film may have grossed even more had he opted to go with a major distributor, he doubts that the principals would have made anywhere close to what they came away with. Inevitably, in the face of this mind-numbing success, everyone's relationship began to deteriorate. "It was the same old story," said Yablans. "Everyone is a sore winner."

Explains Carpenter:

> You can't imagine what it's like until it happens. You just can't. It never happens like you think it will. When you're younger and you imagine this success, you think, oh, it will be like this. It never is.

Carpenter never recaptured the raw brilliance of *Halloween* in any of his later films. His sophomore horror effort, *The Fog* (1980), made two years after *Halloween*, is a reasonably effective ghost story which makes good use of the sleepy seaside setting, but never duplicates the eerie familiarity of Haddonfield. Today, in the wake of *Halloween*'s popularity, *The Fog* has been hailed by some as the more accomplished of the two films. It's not, and this seems to be a case of cinematic alchemy—a futile effort to make good films into classics. *The Thing* (1982), a poorly received but slick remake of the 1951 science fiction thriller, was the first in a string of remakes which Carpenter later continued with *Village of the Damned* (1995) and *Escape from L.A.* (1996).[3] *Christine* (1983), based on the Stephen King best-seller, suffered from the flaws of King's novel.

In the late 1980s, Carpenter enjoyed a mini-resurgence with *Prince of Darkness* (1987) and *They Live* (1988), but the films eventually proved too esoteric for the mainstream. The closest Carpenter has come to approaching his prior form is with *In the Mouth of Madness* (1995), a disturbing blend of fantasy and reality involving the disappearance of a King-like author. Unfortunately, he followed up with *Vampires* (1998), an eagerly anticipated but somewhat disappointing tale of a vampire hunter hired by the Vatican.

Just as teenagers would whisper the name of Michael Myers whenever they needed to conjure up a universal terror, Hollywood producers would invoke the name of *Halloween* whenever they needed reassurance that such an unlikely success was still possible. The belief that a film like *Halloween* could not only compete with the majors, but best them at their own game, played no small role in the rise of independent production companies such as Miramax and New Line Cinema. It was a new dawn for horror, and for cinema in general, when the classic movie stars of yesterday were facing stiff competition from a boogeyman.

CHAPTER 4

Deadly Prank Calls, Driller Killers and an Angry Young Woman

In late 1978, producers were still feeling their way around the slasher film. *Halloween* had whet their appetites for a similar hit. As good as *Halloween* was, it was not *The Godfather* (1972) and very few producers doubted that its success could not be duplicated. Almost every company, from the majors to the unheard-of, flirted with the notion of producing a cheap slasher, crossing their fingers and hoping for gold. It was with this goal in mind that they set out on their quest, a quest which resulted in a body of work far more diverse, controversial and complex than anything they could have imagined.

The year 1979 was a transitional one for the horror film—with different subgenres duking it out to see which would reign supreme—and initially, it did not appear that the slasher film would reap what *Halloween* had sowed.

Supernatural horror, unwilling to admit that its draw had been waning since 1976's, *The Omen*, offered *Alison's Birthday* (1979), a hodgepodge work borrowing heavily from superior films such as *Carrie*

(1976) and *Rosemary's Baby* (1968). While Peter Medak's *The Changeling* (1979) was all but overlooked, the haunted house film scored a coup with Stuart Rosenberg's *The Amityville Horror* (1979), an adaptation of Jay Anson's best-selling novel whose popularity can be attributed to the fact that it was based on the supposedly true account of a haunted Long Island home. *The Changeling*, a fabulously eerie and sophisticated story which deals with the idea of a spectral birthright, stars George C. Scott as a guilt-ridden composer whose wife and daughter are burned to death in a grisly car accident. In an effort to escape his painful memories, Scott moves into a lonely Gothic mansion, the former residence of an evil politician (Melvyn Douglas). Possibly too highbrow for its target audience, *The Changeling* has been relegated to a mere footnote in horror history despite its obvious attributes.

An eclectic and interesting assortment of monster movies—with both classic and modern sensibilities—also hit theaters. The most well-known of the bunch,

John Badham's *Dracula*, stars Frank Langella as the bloodthirsty count. Accompanied by a distinguished cast which includes Laurence Olivier and Donald Pleasence, *Dracula* was a critical and commercial disappointment. Two more vampire films, which couldn't be more dissimilar, were *Love at First Bite* (1979), a light but clever *Dracula* spoof, and *Nosferatu* (1979), the now classic Werner Herzog remake of F.W. Murnau's film of the same name, which stars Klaus Kinski as the pigmentless, rodent-like bloodsucker. In *Nightwing* (1979), directed by a slumming Arthur Hiller, swarms of vampire bats descend upon an Indian reservation; *Wolfman* (1979) was a low-budget werewolf film starring and produced by the little-known but prolific Earl Owensby; and *The Great Alligator* (1979) was an ill-conceived killer crocodile film, hearkening back to the nature-run-amok films of the decade.

Even zombies, true to their reputation, returned from the dead. The most successful and popular among them was *Zombie* (1979), a typically gory Lucio Fulci film which, although billed a sequel to George Romero's *Dawn of the Dead*, was really not a sequel at all.[1] *Bloodeaters*, just like *Night of the Living Dead*, the film which it blatantly rips off, was filmed in Pittsburgh. Its plot focuses on an experimental herbicide which turns people into zombies.

The biggest news of the year was Ridley Scott's *Alien* (1979), a terrifying film which nonetheless owes more to science fiction than true horror. Sigourney Weaver stars as Ripley, the unspoken leader of the *Nostromo*, an intergalactic vessel which has been overrun by the titular creatures, themselves a nightmarish combination of H. R. Giger and H. P. Lovecraft. The now famous scene in which an alien spawn bursts from the chest of crew member William Hurt was groundbreaking for its time. *Alien* took home the Oscar for Best

Visual Effects, as well as receiving a nomination for its art direction. Three sequels followed: *Aliens* (1986), which many think surpasses the original; *Alien 3* (1992), a gloomy although beautifully shot failure directed by David Fincher (*Seven* [1995], *Fight Club* [1999]); and *Alien Resurrection* (1997), an unnecessary follow-up which finds a clone of Ripley now battling the creatures.

At first glance, these films have very little in common with the slasher film. The impact of *Halloween*, however powerful, could not be immediate, and other forms of horror were attempting to carve a niche of their own. But as dissimilar from the slasher as a film like *Alien* seems to be, it is impossible not to notice the similarities. While the film's setting (outer space) is pure science fiction, the remote interior of the *Nostromo*, with its dark corridors and endless hiding spaces, is a far cry from the antiseptic, almost painfully white vision of most futuristic spacecrafts. Instead, it is linked to the slasher's milieu, those lonely camp sites, college dormitories and abandoned houses which have become the domain of knife-wielding maniacs. And what shall we make of Ripley, at the time a completely new breed of feminine heroine? Is she not infinitely closer to a Final Girl than to any of a handful of female leads from the science fiction films of the 1950s, most of whose only purpose was to validate the heroism of their male counterparts? Even the aliens of *Alien* do not really conform to the typical science fiction entity. These beasts, less protoplasm than insect, do not attack with phasers or deadly particle beams. They do not crouch silently in the void of some black hole. They stalk, just like any good killer in the slasher film.

All of this is not to say that *Alien* directly borrows from *Halloween*—the former was undoubtedly well into production before the release of the latter—but only to suggest that because of *Halloween*, the conventions of the slasher film were already firmly in place. Producers, however, were just getting their feet wet, and it would take the success of a few more slashers before they mustered the courage to dive in head first. But one thing was clear—the slasher film was more than a passing fancy. It was a serious trend in horror cinema which was building steam. And it was building steam quickly.

On October 23, 1980, on the PBS show *Sneak Previews*, an "inhumane and sexist" film was lambasted by Gene Siskel. In the March 1981 issue of *American Film*, his partner Roger Ebert mercilessly attacked the film in an article entitled "Why Movie Audiences Aren't Safe Anymore." In Britain, where freedom of artistic expression has historically been crushed by the boot of government censorship, it was at the core of the "video nasties" debate.

Ironically, the ignominious 1978 debut of *I Spit on Your Grave* created little interest, much less controversy. In the conventional sense, *I Spit on Your Grave* isn't really a slasher film. In fact, it isn't even a film as much as a series of highly disturbing skits designed to repulse. And if that was its mission, Meir Zarchi's low-budget rape-revenge opus more than succeeded.

Jennifer (Camille Keaton, reputedly the grandniece of Buster Keaton, the beloved pasty-faced comedian), the consummate New Yorker and writer for women's magazines, heads off to the country to begin work on her first novel. Upon arriving, she is harassed by four local hoodlums, one of whom is slightly retarded (or as his cohorts so delicately put it, "a half-idiot"). It isn't long before their immature taunts turn violent. Over the next 45 excruciatingly long minutes, she is "raped, beaten, and humiliated" (so goes the film's tagline) by each member of the group. Eventually, they tire and leave her for dead.

Over the next few days, Jennifer nurses herself back to health. She showers, repairs her tattered manuscript and attends church (although it is unclear whether her visit is to atone for past transgressions or for crimes to come). In the last half of the film, Jennifer gets her revenge. She pretends to have enjoyed the brutal rape in a seductive ruse which would make even the most hardened viewer uncomfortable. The four ensuing deaths are fittingly gruesome: she strangles one, castrates another, hacks one to death with an ax and feeds the last to the outboard engine of a motorboat. Her mission accomplished, the film abruptly ends.

The critics' initial response to *I Spit on Your Grave* was consistent and harsh, although the most passionate attacks didn't come until the early 1980s, when various activists used the film to drum up support for their cause. "This is, beyond a doubt, one of the most tasteless, irresponsible, and disturbing movies ever made," says the *Video Movie Guide*. "Regardless of how much you may enjoy 'bad' films, you will hate yourself for watching this one." Although there is something to be said for making it through the film's first hour without becoming violently ill, the *Guide* is not incorrect. *I Spit on Your Grave* is truly a vile film.

I Spit on Your Grave is the logical extension of films like *Ilsa: She Wolf of the SS* and its ilk, exercises in sleaze justified by the pretext of some greater social statement. In the case of *Ilsa*, it is the unimaginable horrors of the Nazi concentration camps. In the case of *I Spit on Your Grave*, it is rape. Of course, the argument can and has been made that by its sheer nature, the film is a severe indictment of rape and the objectification of women. But if this is truly the case, what is the point of spending so much time lingering on the graphic details of the assault?

After the backlash against the film,

some critics, apparently not knowing what to make of it, chose to intellectualize the film as some feminist experiment, notwithstanding the fact that it wallows in the degradation and humiliation of women far more than any slasher. However, even the most radical critics would be remiss to categorize *I Spit on Your Grave* as a feminist film. Still, it eventually began to attract its own supporters, among them Marco Starr, who, in "J. Hills Is Alive: A Defense of *I Spit on Your Grave*," calls the film "well made, interestingly written, beautifully photographed and intelligently directed."

While *I Spit on Your Grave* had a profound effect on the subsequent slashers which flourished in its wake, it did not, as has been proposed, spawn a series of imitation rape/revenge films. What it did was teach the slasher film a lesson it learned well. In the films which followed, volatile topics such as rape were shunned in favor of a more universal form of violence. There is a clear delineation of good and evil in every one of these slasher films, and although the "heroes" are often as dislikable as the killer, this is usually a result of poor acting or a sophomoric script rather than an attempt to form a complex and ambiguous hero-villain relationship. The violence in these films is so extreme, it becomes cartoonish. Graphic gore was acceptable as long as it was done in a grandiose and absurd manner. The moment it became too realistic, the censors squawked. Prolonged rape scenes made viewers uncomfortable and angry, while mutilations and decapitations left them cheering for more. *I Spit on Your Grave* is the best argument to be made for the slasher film as escapism, for the only way these films are truly unnerving is when they hit too close to home.

While *I Spit on Your Grave* had made producers wary of realistic violence, it didn't deter everyone from mining the humiliation-rape-revenge subgenre. Later films such as *Cannibal Holocaust* (1979) and *Cannibal Ferox* (1981) wallowed in this brutality, but even as these Italian bloodbaths were being shot, their backers knew that at best they could only appeal to a very provincial (and some would say disturbed) segment of the slasher audience. Since their budgets were nonexistent, the meager profits earned were of little consequence.

Utter the phrase, "Have you checked the children?" to anyone weaned on the slasher film and you'll no doubt get more than a few terrified looks. While Hitchcock made baths en vogue with *Psycho*, and Spielberg changed the vacation industry for a summer by transforming avid swimmers into beachcombers with *Jaws*, Fred Walton undoubtedly left a lot of parents sitterless because of his 1979 thriller *When a Stranger Calls*.

The source of *When a Stranger Calls*—and for Walton's short *The Sitter*, on which his feature film was based—is a staple of urban legend lore: A timid babysitter is harassed by threatening phone calls which are finally revealed to be coming from inside the house.

Contrary to popular belief, this did not really happen to a friend of a friend. Nor did it happened to a woman's daughter from your mother's hometown. And no, you didn't read about it in the paper. It is—much to dismay of the gullible—as its name suggests, simply a legend. Variations of the tale have been around since at least the early '70s and have been catalogued by urban legend guru Jan Harold Brunvand, author of numerous books on the subject.

However, it is one of those stories which is so firmly embedded in the fabric of popular culture that it is almost impossible to find a person who *doesn't* believe that it actually happened. Even Walton—the man most responsible for the tale's proliferation—is not immune to its legend:

> Every now and then I would run into somebody who would say, "Oh, yeah, I heard that story around the campfire when I was a kid," or "My aunt told us that story when we were kids".... When we finally starting shooting the feature [*When a Stranger Calls*], about the third or fourth day some stand-in pulls me aside and said, "I just realized the story that you're telling here, I want you to know that it happened in my hometown." She had grown up in Long Island somewhere. And she tells me this story about a babysitter and the phone calls, and as it turned out, it was the estranged husband and father of the children themselves.

In early 1977, Fred Walton was just another jobless college graduate. He had majored in English at Denison University, a small liberal arts school in Ohio, but had been unable to parlay that degree into a job in the entertainment industry. Steve Feke, his friend from college and his eventual co-writer and producer on *When a Stranger Calls*, had moved to Hollywood a few years earlier. Feke had a connection to the story editor of *Quinn Martin's Tales of the Unexpected* (1977), a short-lived television show vaguely reminiscent of *The Twilight Zone* (1959–65), who offered to help them get a writing job on the series.

One Saturday, while throwing around ideas, Feke told the now legendary story which had supposedly taken place in either Pacific Palisades or Brentwood. Walton had never heard the story before and immediately recognized its potential. Since neither of them thought it would be a story in which Quinn Martin would be interested, they decided to make it as a short film. The market for shorts at that time was much greater than it is today, and it was not unusual for them to be shown before features. It was also a practical way to break into the business just as George

Lucas, Randal Kleiser and other famous directors had done.

The production of the short *The Sitter* is a classic example of low-budget filmmaking. Feke, who had been working steadily, kicked in around $6,000. Friends of the pair contributed $1,000 here and there. But the most creative avenue of financing belonged to Walton. Since he had been willed his grandmother's Tiffany engagement ring, he gave his parents an option—either buy the ring from him, thereby keeping it in the family, or he would sell it to raise money for his short. Predictably, his parents immediately sent him the money.

The Sitter was shot over the course of three days on 35mm Kodak stock. Both Walton and Feke were adamant that it not look or feel like a student film. As Walton says, "It was a very slick idea, not some student film idea, some abstract arty thing." It was shot by Willy Kurant, Godard's cameraman on *Masculin, Féminin* (1966), who had just arrived in Hollywood and was desperate for work. The film was processed at MGM's lab, which, probably because it was the one which Stanley Kubrick used, had the reputation of being the best in the world.

The Sitter, which has a running time of 22 minutes, is basically a carbon copy of the first act of *When a Stranger Calls*, right down to specific shots and set decoration. But as professional as *The Sitter* was, the market for shorts was nowhere near as good as Walton and Feke had anticipated. Even worse, the industry professionals who did view it were not terribly impressed. At this point, the pair was close to $12,000 in debt. Still, they were certain that if they could somehow get nominated for an Oscar for Best Live-Action Short they would be guaranteed jobs. Unfortunately, to qualify for an Oscar a film had to have played in either a New York or Los Angeles theater for at least a week. Luckily, Feke had a connection who got *The Sitter* to screen before *Looking for Mr. Goodbar* (1977) for a week at Mann's Village Theater in Westwood. Walton remembers the screening vividly:

> We had never seen it on a huge screen, live, with an audience of people who didn't know us at all, so we were terribly excited. We sit down, the short begins, and all through the first ten minutes people are coming in and out of the theater, stumbling around the aisles, looking for seats, sort of glancing at the screen and saying, "Is that Diane Keaton?" Stuff like that. We were just dying, thinking, "oh, God, this is a disaster." Well, around the 15 minute mark, people got really quiet, and it really settled down. And when that big moment comes, when she opens the door and there's the cop. Everybody screamed.

As well as the screening went, *The Sitter* didn't get nominated for an Oscar. However, not long after, Feke was showering at the Y when he ran into a young industry lawyer named Bob Finkelstein. After hearing the story behind *The Sitter*, Finkelstein put Feke and Walton in contact with Barry Krost, a Hollywood manager, and Krost's partner, Doug Chapin. Krost had a relationship with Mel Simon, who at the time was new to Hollywood, having made a fortune building shopping malls in the Midwest. With Simon, Krost and Chapin now involved, the focus changed to making *The Sitter* into a feature film. Simon and Krost began shopping the project around to a variety of studios without much luck. Most of them were uninterested and did not find the script especially frightening or commercial. Although Columbia initially showed some interest, they were busy developing *Nightwing* at the time and ultimately decided not to make the film.

Frustrated at the studios' lack of foresight and commitment, Simon decided to finance the picture himself. Walton was slated to direct, with Feke and Chapin producing, and both Krost and Simon taking an executive producer credit. The shoot took a little over five weeks, with the first week being especially hard on the cast and crew. Unbeknownst to Walton, who had enough problems to worry about as a first-time director, his cameraman Donald Peterman was trying to quit. He was under a tremendous amount of strain and had gone to Feke and Chapin, who managed to convince him to stay on. Peterman, who Walton calls a "great and very talented guy," went on to shoot such films as *Flashdance* (1983), *Splash* (1984) and *Men in Black* (1997).

When a Stranger Calls was originally budgeted at $1.5 million, a substantial sum in those days, even for a financier like Simon. What nobody aside from the producers knew was that no distribution deal was in place. Walton just assumed that because of Columbia's prior interest in the film, they would be distributing it. It wasn't until Norman Levy, Columbia's president of distribution, announced in a screening with Columbia president Daniel Melnick that he could sell the picture, that Simon and Krost could breathe a sigh of relief. *When a Stranger Calls* eventually grossed over $20 million domestically, making it an extremely profitable independent film.

The first act of *When a Stranger Calls* remains faithful to the urban legend. Carol Kane is wonderful as Jill Johnson, the vulnerable high school teenager who has been hired by a neighborhood doctor and his wife to babysit their sleeping children. She begins receiving anonymous phone calls from a masculine stranger, asking her the ominous question, "Have you checked the children?" After the caller phones to ask Jill why she hasn't checked her charges, she contacts the police, convinced the perpetrator must be watching her. The

Jill Johnson (Carol Kane), an innocent high school babysitter, is terrorized by obscene phone calls in Fred Walton's nailbiter *When a Stranger Calls* (1979).

sergeant informs Jill that there isn't much the police can do at this point, but when the caller's messages begin to turn more obscene ("I want your blood ... all over me"), he agrees to tap the phone. Shortly after, the sergeant calls back. Frantic, he orders Jill to leave the house immediately. The perpetrator is calling from within. She escapes, shaken but unscathed. However, when Detective Clifford (Charles Durning) arrives, he finds both children have been brutally murdered in their beds.

Seven years later, the murderer, Curt Duncan (Tony Beckley), has escaped from the sanitarium in which he has been confined since the murders. The father of the slain children contacts Clifford, who is now a private investigator, and hires him

to track down Duncan. Clifford's first stop is the sanitarium, where he finds out that Duncan was an extremely violent patient, constantly on tranquilizers and depressants, and subjected to electric shock therapy.

Meanwhile, Duncan has become more of a pathetic wretch than a true villain (a subtle distinction not lost on the film's detractors). He wanders aimlessly around the local bars, searching futilely for companionship. An awkward and romantic failure, Duncan only accomplishes getting beat up by a local tough. In a last ditch attempt, he arrives at the home of Tracy (Colleen Dewhurst), an aging barfly who threatens to call the police when she realizes she has been followed home.

Detective Clifford, whose slowly growing obsession with killing Duncan is beginning to consume him, is not above using Tracy as bait. She halfheartedly agrees to assist him after hearing the lurid details of how Duncan mutilated the children with his bare hands.

The plan works perfectly. Duncan manages to get into Tracy's apartment, but when Detective Clifford breaks down the door his quarry is long gone. Alone and frightened, Duncan takes to the streets, a lifestyle for which he is ill-suited. While asleep in a homeless shelter, he is almost captured by Detective Clifford, but once again he manages to outrun the overweight investigator.

The story now reverts back to Jill, happily married with two children of her own. While out to dinner with her husband, the maitre d' informs her that she has a phone call. She picks up the receiver and hears the haunting refrain from her past, "Have you checked the children?" Hysterical, she rushes home, accompanied by the police, only to find her children and babysitter perfectly fine.

During the night, she compulsively checks on her son only to find that he has fallen asleep holding a piece of candy which she had never purchased. Naturally, she finds this odd and goes to wake her husband. To her horror, Duncan is in his place. A brief scuffle ensues, but Detective Clifford arrives in the nick of time and pumps a few rounds into Duncan's chest. Jill's husband falls from the closet, unconscious but unharmed, as Jill collapses into the arms of the detective.

Although its influence was far-reaching, *When a Stranger Calls* is not really a slasher film. While Walton incorporates many of the conventions and techniques of the slasher, *When a Stranger Calls* ultimately, as Dika says, "fails to comply with the significant combination that characterizes the formula." However, it was Walton's deft direction, especially his manipulation of perspective and spatial relationships, which laid the groundwork for later slashers to flourish. His fragmentation of the film's visual field not only mimics the subjective "look" defined by *Halloween*, but subtly turns it on its head. During one of the tensest moments of her ordeal, when Jill realizes that the caller might actually be a salient threat, she is shown in long shot through the living room window. This is done to mirror the stalker's gaze, as it had been done in *Halloween* and as it would be done in countless films to follow. The audience naturally assumes, as does Jill, that the killer is outside the house. Walton is toying with our expectations. Unless we are familiar with the story, as not many people were upon the film's release, we accept this as the subjective view of the caller. But, as is revealed in the climax of the first act, the killer is really calling from inside the house. The framing and distance of the shot tricks the viewer into identifying with a nonexistent stalker.

Carol Kane was not Walton's first choice to play the role of Jill Johnson. In *The Sitter*, the titular role had been played by an unknown but very competent all–American looking actress. This was the look which Walton wanted, the girl next door, clearly something Kane was not. However, she had done *Hester Street* (1975) a few years before and was coming off a small but meaty part in 1977's Best Picture *Annie Hall*. At the time, she was also a Barry Krost client and therefore a convenient choice. The initial problem with Kane is that, not unlike Nicholson in *The Shining*, she immediately brings a set of expectations to a role. Upon Jill's arrival, before there is even a hint of anything sinister, she already appears slightly unhinged. In retrospect, her eccentricity turned out to be an asset. She is, as Walton states, a "terrifically talented actress," and her uniqueness actually accentuates her vulnerability. Walton was acutely aware of how powerful this vulnerability was as it relates not only to the audience, but to the filmmaking process in general:

After the picture came out, friends of mine would say to me, half-jokingly, "Oh, we didn't realize you were so sick." As if I was some kind of sadist, gleefully scaring the crap out of people behind the scenes, you know, hiding behind doors and jumping out at them and stuff like this. And when they said this to me, I realized that to be able to make a good scary movie you have to be able to put yourself in the place of the victim, not the killer. You have to understand the fear, not the psychology of whomever is making the threat.

However, unlike most slasher films which ignore any characterization of the villain whatsoever, Walton spends an inordinate amount of time exploring Duncan's psychological makeup, more than he spends on Jill, Tracy or even Detective Clifford. He does such a good job probing the depths of Duncan's madness that he risks turning the film's villain into a rather sympathetic character. Some critics, not used to being challenged by a horror film, lashed out at Walton, and accused him of skewing the clear-cut delineation of good and evil usually found in these films. This ambiguity was not lost on Charles Durning, whose role as Detective Clifford is somewhat reminiscent of Popeye Doyle in *The French Connection* (1971). At one point during filming, after rereading the script the previous night, he approached Walton and said, "I'm the bad guy, aren't I?"

Durning isn't the bad guy, contrary to some reviews which refer to him as a fascist. He is an honest detective torn between protocol and vigilante justice. The way in which he plans to dispense this justice *is* particularly gruesome (he plans to stab Duncan with a lock picking tool), but considering that he was the one to discover the mutilated children's bodies, his hatred hardly seems excessive.

The character of Curt Duncan—played to perfection by Tony Beckley—was based on a college acquaintance of Walton's who had the uncanny ability to walk into a room and instantaneously make everybody else uncomfortable. Yet Walton felt tremendous sympathy for this man, evidenced by his somewhat compassionate portrayal of Duncan. While the film never holds back the details of Duncan's hideous crimes, it also acknowledges—some would say irresponsibly—that society has dealt Curt Duncan a poor hand which the harsh reality of city dwelling has done little to relieve. He is shunned by passersby as he attempts to beg for small change, thwarted and beat up in his efforts at love, and even abused in the sanitarium. The exorbitant amount of electric shocks he receives even raise the

eyebrows of the hard-nosed detective. Duncan is definitely a sick man, rendered deadly by the cruelties of society. Whether or not he is evil, Walton leaves that up to the audience.

Under Walton's manipulation, benign, inanimate objects take on a malevolent life of their own. As Danilo Bach, who scripted his 1986 film *April Fool's Day* (see Chapter 9), says, "Walton is a director of silence." As Jill becomes more and more frightened, so on edge than it seems she might crack at any moment, common households items—umbrellas, ice cream bars, shoes and especially canes—appear strangely sinister. As anybody whose childhood toys became Lovecraftian creatures the moment the bedroom lights were turned down knows, the mundane holds a special kind of terror. It is the whisper of shadows, not the madman's ax, which is most terrifying.

It is a shame that the promise Walton displayed with *When a Stranger Calls* never translated to future success, for he is an immensely talented director. In 1985, he directed an episode of *Alfred Hitchcock Presents*, "An Unlocked Window." While it would be heresy to compare it to the original, which Walton himself revered, it is not without its own creepy touch. In 1993, he was reunited with both Carol Kane and Charles Durning for the seemingly inevitable sequel to *When a Stranger Calls*, television's *When a Stranger Calls Back*. All things considered, *When a Stranger Calls Back* is a tense and satisfying thriller, heads and tails above the usual movie-of-the-week whodunit. It is unlikely that Walton will ever again make a film as influential as *When a Stranger Calls*, and although his name may slowly slip into obscurity, the phrase which he ushered into the lexicon of popular culture springs to the forefront of every babysitter's mind whenever a phone rings in an empty house.

While *When a Stranger Calls* eschews graphic violence in favor of quiet unspoken terror, *The Driller Killer* (1979)—while hardly as deliriously gory as its name suggests—revels in its milieu of gloom and sleaze. *The Driller Killer* was the first feature from New York City's prodigal son Abel Ferrara, who also stars (under the pseudonym Jimmy Laine) as Reno, the film's deranged protagonist. The film is a postcard to the city's seediest areas, from Alphabet City to the slums of Brooklyn. Ferrara's streets are not just mean, they're deadly. His city is as sick as the people who inhabit it, but like a son who loves his flawed father all the more for his faults, he accepts it with a sort of rueful indifference.

Given the time of its release, it is certainly no surprise that *The Driller Killer* found itself smack dab in the middle of the video nasties debate. But the decrees of British lawmakers meant little on the dirty streets of the East Village. It is rather comical to imagine Ferrara, the inveterate New Yorker, worrying about the judgments of a group of effete English judges halfway across the world.

It would seem easy to lump *The Driller Killer* together with such awful contemporaries like *The Toolbox Murders*, given both protagonists proclivity for power tools, were Ferrara not a skid row *auteur*. *The Driller Killer* is the first and last film which can be considered "gore-art." It has the trappings of the slasher film, the exploitation of the drive-in B-movie, but the formal and stylistic experimentation of the art film.

Already on edge because of a series of threatening phone calls, Jill Johnson (Carol Kane) inspects the empty house in *When a Stranger Calls* (1979).

The Driller Killer's hyperactive cinematography does not validate the killer's point of view but instead draws attention to the filmmaking process. It is the roving camera of a young Scorsese, whose watered-down version of Ferrara's city made his films more accessible to the mainstream. While Scorsese was hailed a young genius for his unflinching look at the dark underbelly of the city, Ferrara was largely ignored as a brooding however talented lunatic, a misconception not helped by his dead-on portrayal of the deeply disturbed Reno.

The narrative of most slasher films is fairly straightforward. There aren't many extraneous plot points to get in the way of the killings. *Driller Killer*'s narrative, however, is disjointed. It is a credit to Ferrara that it is never confusing, just chaotic. The entire film feels like a video from the Velvet Underground–like band whose music plays no small part in Reno's descent into madness. *Driller Killer* is a melange of volatile themes slowly reaching a boiling point. Reno is a prisoner of self-doubt, self-loathing and fear. Confronted by economic strife, sexual confusion and artistic failure, he finds relief the only way he knows how—murder.

Reno, a tortured artist, lives with his bisexual girlfriend Carol (Carolyn Marz) and her lover (Baybi Day) in a squalid apartment. Unable to finish his long-delayed masterpiece, Reno is spurned when he asks his art dealer Dalton (Harry Schultz) for an advance in order to finish the piece. To make matters worse, an awful punk rock band, which never stops rehearsing, moves into the above apartment. Wracked with anxiety, Reno lashes out at Carol. This is the one aspect of the film which strains its credibility. It is never clear why Carol, a compassionate, beautiful and ambitious woman, would ever stay, or get involved in the first place, with an abusive and downtrodden lout like Reno.

Pushed beyond the breaking point, the already unstable Reno takes to the city streets and begins murdering vagrants with a powerdrill. He finds, however, that he cannot squelch his insatiable appetite for blood. After Dalton mockingly critiques his artwork, he finds himself on the receiving end of Reno's drill. Reno then travels to the home of Carol's ex (Richard Howorth)—where she is now living—and murders him, abruptly ending the film as the screen fades to red.

The Driller Killer's ambiguous ending had many critics scratching their heads. If this was a slasher film, they wondered, how could the requisite bloody demise of the villain be neglected? And more importantly, *was* Reno the film's villain? He was the protagonist, certainly, but a true villain? Not really. He was too pathetically human to be completely evil. Ferrara thumbed his nose at these queries. *The Driller Killer* is unapologetic, angry nouveau art, a film which was far ahead of its time. Ferrara has never been a director of restraint. If the ending of *The Driller Killer* made some people uncomfortable, that's because it was supposed to. Reno isn't captured. There is no justice, no punishment. For all we know, he continues to kill. Not because he's some sort of brilliant psychopath. Not because Ferrara is trying to make a deeper sociopolitical statement. But because in the city there is strife, there is pain and, above all, there is death.

The Driller Killer can be accused of many things, but not of advancing the myth that the victims of slasher films are always vulnerable young women. Reno's victims fall into two distinct categories, the unknown derelicts he is so terrified of becoming, and those people who, as he perceives it, have wronged him. *The Driller Killer* is a film rife with sex, but it is far from a sexy movie. Ferrara is certainly not above a bit of exploitation—there is a gratuitous shower scene between Marz and her lesbian lover—but his murders are far more disturbing than titillating. The dominant relationship in *The Driller Killer* is not between sex and death, but between death and the city.

In his next film, the far more subversive and equally contentious *Ms. 45* (1981), Ferrara again explores the dark side of urban life, but this time holds the individual, not the city, accountable for the crimes. While not a slasher film, *Ms. 45* is extremely similar to *I Spit on Your Grave*, a film to which it is often compared. Thana (Zoe Tamerlis), a mute garment worker, avenges her two brutal rapes by dressing like a hooker and a nun and indiscriminately killing men. While the film drew some criticism for its parallels between sex, religion, death and rape, it found favor with some feminists who applauded the empowering, however violent, way in which Thana found her symbolic voice.

Ferrara never returned to the slasher film, which is a shame since his idiosyncratic style could have given it a much needed boost of intelligence and complexity. He did, however, remain on the streets of his beloved New York, continuing to explore the dark recesses and forgotten alleyways of the human condition. His later films—*Fear City* (1985), *The King of New York* (1990), *Bad Lieutenant* (1992)—tend to champion the deeply flawed antihero. There is no doubt that Ferrara's film are hard to take. He has an uncanny and mischievous knack for making audiences uncomfortable. As a result, his films have been unfairly written off and he has

never received the respect he deserves as a director.

Silent Scream (1980), a timid slasher with strong Gothic underpinnings, dispenses with the usual teenagers in peril motif in favor of a cadre of hardened horror vets: Cameron Mitchell (*Blood and Black Lace, The Toolbox Murders*), Yvonne De Carlo (*Satan's Cheerleaders* [1977]) and the legendary Barbara Steele (*Black Sunday* [1960], *The Horrible Dr. Hichcock* [1962]). Unfortunately, their involvement is all but wasted by director Denny Harris, who seems unaware how to effectively mine their considerable talents; Mitchell's role is brief and ineffectual, De Carlo is barely given any lines, and Steele, the darling of European horror, is not introduced until halfway through the film.

Mrs. Engels (left, Yvonne De Carlo) visits the asylum where her lobotomized daughter now resides in Denny Harris' *Silent Scream* **(1980).**

Four college students, unable to find on-campus housing, take up residence in De Carlo's hilltop mansion, where she lives with her Norman Bates—clone son (Brad Rearden) and homicidal daughter (Steele), a former teen beauty whose botched lobotomy has left her with a thirst for blood. Far more intriguing than the film itself is counting the ways it apes *Psycho*, from a similar but less accomplished version of Bernard Herrmann's score, to identical shots, framing and camera angles. While *Silent Scream* received some favorable attention, it was most likely because of fans' appreciation for the stars' prior work, than for anything which the film itself contributed to the genre.

All the slasher films which followed within a year of *Halloween*, no matter how accomplished, suffered from one fatal flaw—they weren't *Halloween*. In most cases, these films were well into production by the time of *Halloween*'s release, and even had they wanted to, it was far too late for them to change course and fully exploit this now fertile climate. Ironically, many of these, especially *When a Stranger Calls*, were at least as accomplished, if not more so, than *Halloween*. Artistic competence, however, has never been indicative of a film's popularity. Audiences didn't want something different from *Halloween*, they wanted *Halloween*, and they didn't have to wait long. Soon after, came a film which took the formula a little further. It was sexier, bloodier and a bit more graphic and flashy. Critics may scoff and say that because of *Halloween*'s success any slasher film could have played the box office slot machine and come up sevens, but not any film had a brilliant marketing strategy, a little bit of luck and a shrewd director who knew just how to play his cards.

CHAPTER 5

Friday the 13th, Prom Night and a Head in the Fish Tank

The summer of 1980 was supposed to belong to *The Empire Strikes Back*. The sequel to George Lucas' space opera *Star Wars* (1977) was one of the mostly hotly anticipated films in history. No one doubted that it would tear through theaters, setting box office records and devouring the competition. And if by chance it faltered, if it didn't quite live up to its predecessor, horror and science fiction fans had an alternative. *The Shining*, Stanley Kubrick's long-awaited adaptation of Stephen King's terrifying novel, was finally making its big-screen debut.

As expected, *The Empire Strikes Back* became the reigning box office king that summer. But the closest challenger to its throne wasn't *The Shining*, but a low-budget independent slasher film which took the entire country by storm.

Friday the 13th was not some well-packaged marketing juggernaut. It was not some high-concept idea which Hollywood producers pushed through the movie machine assured of box office gold. In fact, it was nothing more than a vaguely sinister title thought up by a man who was brainstorming alone in his office.

Sean S. Cunningham was born in New York in 1941. Although early on he harbored dreams of becoming a doctor, he quickly changed his focus to the arts, working as both a stage manager and director in the theater before turning his focus to film. He cut his teeth directing some innocuous soft-core nudie films such as the pseudo-documentary *The Art of Marriage* (1970) and *Together* (1971), which managed to play at the Rialto Theater on Broadway for an astonishing 31 weeks. His next project, which he developed with close friend Wes Craven, was the notorious *Last House on the Left* (see Chapter 2).

Desperate for money to pay for the fledgling post-production factory which he had opened on West 45th Street in New York City, Cunningham produced *The Case of the Smiling Stiffs* (1974) for a Florida investor. The problem-plagued production struck a nerve with Australian audiences who found it utterly hysterical, although it was a dismal failure everywhere else. After producing a Spanish film, *Planeta Ciega* (1976), because the idea of a tax shelter movie intrigued him, he directed two adolescent sports films, *Here Come the Tigers* (1978), a *Bad News Bears* clone, and *Manny's Orphans* (a.k.a. *Kick*, 1979), a feel-good movie about a soccer team from a Catholic orphanage.

After months of playing the studios' waiting game, *Manny's Orphans* was finally optioned by United Artists as the pilot for a television series. Cunningham was relieved to get some money, but was also convinced that the film would have benefited from a different title. It was while he was playing around with different titles that he came up with the one which would be his legacy:

> I'm sitting around thinking about titles and I think, if I had something called *Friday the 13th*, I could sell that … and it just sort of stuck in my mind. It was a few months later that I then decided to come up with an ad for a movie called *Friday the 13th*, without having any movie. So Steve Miner and I put together this ad. It was great big block letters and read: *Friday the 13th. The Most Terrifying Film Ever Made.* It was in these block letters which then came crashing through a piece of glass.

For the slasher film, Cunningham's epiphany was the equivalent of Edison's light bulb. It set the slasher film on a course which would change the face of horror and, to a lesser degree, the face of low-budget filmmaking. He didn't have a script, he didn't have a cast or crew, he didn't even have an idea. But he had a title. And with a name like *Friday the 13th*, a title was enough.

The first thing Cunningham did was hire a commercial artist to design an ad for the prospective film. The ad incorporated the glass-breaking image and read: *From the producer of **Last House on the Left** comes the most terrifying film ever made. **Friday the 13th**. Available in December.* Said Cunningham:

I ran the ad in the summer around the Fourth of July in weekly *Variety*, a big full-page ad, and the phones started ringing off the hook. Everybody wanted this film. And I said, "Shit, I better make this film." So we scampered around and tried to write a script and get a cast and do it all, and we started shooting around Labor Day.

After Cunningham ran the *Friday the 13th* ad, various companies from all around the world began asking to see the film, a film which wasn't even written, much less made. The buzz which the title generated, however, enabled him to drum up $500,000 to begin production. Cunningham was initially hesitant to revisit the horror genre. "Several years earlier, Wes and I had made *The Last House on the Left*, which was quite successful as a cult film but it sort of followed both of us around," said Cunningham. "So much of my efforts in the interim was to be doing other things not steeped in the horror genre." Luckily for slasher fans, the necessity of paying his rent, at least until the *Manny's Orphans* television series took off, forced him to make the film, which he admits, was nothing more than a "potboiler." Together with screenwriter Victor Miller, who had no horror experience but whom had written both *Here Come the Tigers* and *Manny's Orphans*, he came up with a script with the working title of *Long Night at Camp Blood*. It was Miller who was responsible for the now immortal name of Jason Voorhees; he had used the name Jason in *Hide the Children*, a previous novel of his, and knew a girl in high school with the last name Voorhees and had always loved the sound of it.

Friday the 13th was shot in the fall of 1979 at No-Be-Bo-Sco, an abandoned Boy Scout camp just outside of Blairstown, New Jersey. Allegedly, the original Camp Crystal Lake sign can still be seen hanging in the camp's trading post, no doubt

Fun-loving counselors Brenda (Laurie Bartram), Ned (Mark Nelson), Marcie (Jeannine Taylor) and Jack (Kevin Bacon) are reprimanded by a local police officer, unaware that they all will soon meet their grisly end in Sean S. Cunningham's *Friday the 13th* (1980).

causing nightmares for the few unsuspecting scouts who still occasionally visit the place. Although Cunningham chose this location primarily because the empty cabins provided cheap lodging for his mostly non-union and non-professional cast and crew, the isolated setting plays a large part in creating the film's mood. By day, No-Be-Bo-Sco is a quaint summer hideaway, but at night, the darkness of the North Jersey woods becomes oppressive, slowly closing in on the characters and making escape seen hopeless. While Cunningham and his crew didn't have to brave the threat of a vengeful maniac running around, they did have to endure a less dire threat. "We were shooting at a Boy Scout camp," recalls Cunningham, "we had no money and we were sleeping literally in cabins, cabins with no heat and outdoor plumbing, and it got cold at night."

When the film was finished, Cunningham began screening it for potential buyers. Suddenly, the same studios which usually turned their collective noses up at the mere mention a horror film, and who never would have financed a picture such as *Friday the 13th*, were virtually trampling each other to obtain the rights. A bidding war erupted between Paramount, Warner Brothers and United Artists. Eventually, Paramount won out, with Warner Brothers buying foreign rights. Cunningham received $1.5 million in advance and the studio promised to spend $3 million on prints and advertising to promote the film. Said Cunningham:

What Paramount decided to do—and this was Frank Mancuso, who was the head of distribution at the time—he decided to take a chance. He was going to take this film, which had no stars in it and wasn't a studio picture, and open nationally. A national campaign, that had never been done. When he did that, he could have been a bum, it could have been a huge mistake. As it turned out, he became a genius. As a result, that's how it [*Friday the 13th*] became a cash cow and ultimately that's how Frank got to become the head of Paramount.

On May 9, 1980, *Friday the 13th* exploded onto screens all across the country, taking in nearly $40 million before its run was over. *Halloween* has warmed up the crowd and audiences were begging for the headliner. The film which could capitalize on this zeitgeist was poised to become a cul-

tural phenomenon. *When a Stranger Calls* was too cerebral. *Driller Killer* was too esoteric and gloomy. *I Spit on Your Grave* and *The Toolbox Murders* were barely seen, and both lacked a certain levity to offset their dark natures. But *Friday the 13th* was perfect. It was raw, amateurish and, for the time, extremely gory, but it was also playful, and had a slickness about it which raised it above the level of other similar low-budget productions. What's more, it was made by a young but tremendously talented and underrated director who harbored no illusions as to what he was making. "This isn't high art, it was good craft," Cunningham says about the film, thwarting those who have said that *Friday the 13th* just got lucky:

What I was doing was this, I was trying to make something that people had to go

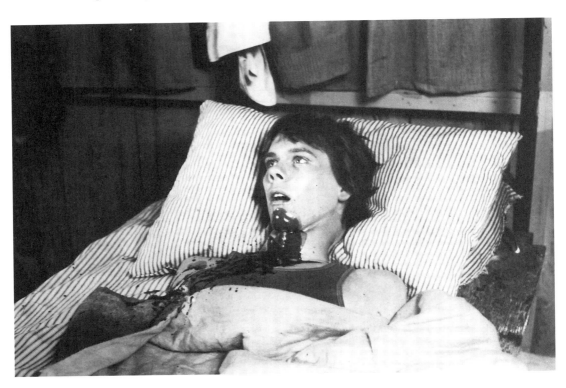

Jack (Kevin Bacon) is skewered after smoking a joint in *Friday the 13th* (1980). This shocking effect, courtesy of Tom Savini, was indicative of the graphic murders which had begun to populate the slasher film.

see. Because I was in the *movie* business, I wasn't doing high art or anything. I only had a certain amount of money and so anything that I decided to put on screen had to matter. Lots of the things that would be dedicated to telling the audience so much more about the people's lives and the characters and all that stuff became minimized, and the plot and the special effects became minimized too, to only include a kind of stripped-down version of a movie.

Friday the 13th opens in 1958 at Camp Crystal Lake. During a campfire singalong, two counselors sneak away to an empty cabin to indulge in nature's more carnal pleasures. They are interrupted by an unseen figure who proceeds to murder them both despite the girl's terrified pleas.

The film now jumps back to the present, 1980, and "Camp Blood," as it is affectionately known by the locals, has reopened under new ownership. But the bad luck which has marred its history continues. Despite warnings by a truck driver to stay away from the cursed place, Annie (Robbi Morgan), the new cook, is murdered after hitching a ride to camp.

At Camp Crystal Lake, Steve Christy (Peter Brouwer), the camp's owner, is busy preparing for the upcoming summer with the five counselors who have just arrived. Assisting him is headstrong artist Alice (Adrienne King), an old flame of his.

A thunderstorm hits the camp, forcing the counselors inside. They pass the time drinking beer, smoking a little pot and playing strip monopoly. But the fun is soon shattered when Camp Blood lives up to its name. Someone begins stalking the counselors and dispatching them in a myriad of ways: by spear, by ax and by knife. Before long, Alice is the only one left alive.

By this time, Mrs. Voorhees (Betsy Palmer), an old friend of Steve's, has arrived. She comforts a petrified Alice, although it is clear that she does not believe,

or is indifferent to, the alleged murders. From here it doesn't take long to figure out that Mrs. Voorhees is the killer. Years ago, her son Jason drowned at Camp Crystal Lake because the counselors who were supposed to watch him were busy making love. The unhinged woman has been waiting for revenge ever since. Various scuffles ensue before Mrs. Voorhees is finally decapitated by Alice in a gory finale.

The next day, a battered but victorious Alice is drifting aimlessly around the lake in a canoe, recovering from the previous night's events. Suddenly, in one of horror's great "jumps"—or as some would say, "cheats"—the morning stillness is shattered by Jason, the drowned child, who ascends from his watery grave to pull Alice to certain death.

Alice wakes up in the hospital, babbling incoherently about a boy in the lake, which the officers who rescued her naturally attribute to shock. Little did they know that this phantom boy would eventually become one of cinema's most notorious villains.

Cunningham never wanted to include this final scene, which is patently absurd by any stretch of the imagination, but eventually capitulated to his investors who wanted the film to end on a shocking note:

It was really an insistence from our investors. They wanted something really disgusting. And their idea of disgusting was the kid coming out of the lake.... I didn't want to do that, it just didn't seem to make any sense to me at all. But the question is, how could I accommodate that and then get something that actually worked in the movie. I had to figure out a way how to do that. So what I did was, I decided to make it a dream without telling the audience. So I put her in the lake and I did all the things which would say it was safe ... I figured if it really didn't work as well as I wanted it we could always just end with her in the lake. Have the sweet music. That's the kind of normal ending, you know the sun comes up, you crane back, and there you are bloody but unbowed. The world is back in balance.

But the ending did work, and even Cunningham admits that it was after watching the audience's reaction to this final scene that he realized he had something more than an ordinary horror film. Jason's makeup was designed by Tom Savini, who also handled all the other effects chores in the film. It was these effects—a spear through the neck, an ax to the face, one of the most realistic decapitations ever captured on celluloid—that incurred the wrath of censors. It wasn't only that the murders were so violent and bloody, but that they occurred in plain view of the unflinching camera, as if daring viewers to figure out the trick. Cunningham explains the essence of Savini's effects:

They weren't particularly graphic as we think of them today, given what's available, but what they really were, and this doesn't exist any more, is that they were part of a magic trick. Films have really changed in this regard. It used to be you would go to a movie and your eyes would get tricked. You'd see Lon Chaney turn into a wolf man before your very eyes. Now you know Lon Chaney didn't turn into a wolf. It just looked like he did when you're eight or nine years old. Or somebody got shot and blood came out of their chest. Now you know they didn't really get shot, but how the hell did they do that? And with Savini we were using a lot of misdirection, trying to get the audience to be looking one way and all of a sudden an arrow comes through somebody's neck, or so it seems. And you know the arrow couldn't have come through his neck, but man, it sure looked liked it. And since nobody expected it, it had a double or triple impact. I think without that graphic addition, I think the film would have been flatter. Would it have been as successful? No. I think it still

would have been successful because we still would have had that scene at the end. We could have done slightly more conventional special effects, but these seemed to work so well. And, like I said, people hadn't seen that stuff before. So it was all new.

Another aspect of the film which played no small role in its success was Harry Manfredini's haunting score, which includes the much analyzed vocal effect which, in later installments of the series, became used to signify Jason's presence in a scene. This effect, a combination of heavy breathing and unintelligible chanting, is actually the sounds "ki," for kill, and "ma," for mommy, spoken by Manfredini and then run through an echoplex.

In Dika's *Games of Terror*, she proposes that the slasher films which are most enjoyable to audiences are the ones which adhere most closely to the familiar structure. It is strange then that *Friday the 13th*, the archetypal slasher and easily one of the most popular of these films, actually deviates with some regularity from the conventions which have since become mainstays of the subgenre. The most obvious example is in the identity of its killer, surprisingly a woman. In 1980, the slasher film hadn't yet begun experimenting with the killer's gender in an effort to mislead audiences, as in later films such as *Happy Birthday to Me* and *Sleepaway Camp*. Yet Cunningham not only made his killer a woman, he cast Betsy Palmer in the pivotal role. Palmer was not cast, as rumor has it, because she could provide her own transportation to the set, but because audiences would never suspect that this wholesome actress might in fact be the killer. Explains Cunningham:

Betsy Palmer had been for many years the equivalent of Katie Couric. So not only was it a woman, but it was Betsy Palmer! Can you imagine Jane Pauley coming

Sean S. Cunningham took a calculated risk in making the killer of his infamous slasher *Friday the 13th* (1980) a woman. That she was played by Betsy Palmer, a wholesome television personality, added to the shock.

out? You might say, "Oh, she's doing a bit." But you wouldn't ever think she's the killer. So it was all meant as misdirection.

Still, Cunningham doesn't allow the audience an impartial perspective and implements unmistakable visual cues to convince the audience that the killer is a man. She drives a pickup truck, wears beaten work boots, possesses enough strength to fashion her slain victims in compromising positions, and is adept with both a hunting knife and spear. When her identity is finally revealed, it is not only a shock to our expectations within the context of this specific film, but to our previous expectations of the entire subgenre.

As in almost every slasher, in *Friday the 13th* sex and violence are inexorably tied together. As the prevailing theory goes, to satisfy the burgeoning sexuality

of the predominately adolescent male audience, numerous gratuitous scenes of nudity and sexual activity are inserted. To satisfy the hierarchical Puritanical ideology which still pervades our society, those same teenagers who engage in these illicit acts are punished in the most brutal manner possible. However, in *Friday the 13th*, Cunningham justifies this post-coital slaughter by validating it with thematic relevance. Mrs. Voorhees doesn't kill because of the sexual act *per se*, but in retribution for the death of her son, whose neglect was prompted by the overriding sexual urge of irresponsible camp counselors.

Despite the undying criticism that slasher films force viewers to identity with the killer's point of view, *Friday the 13th* rarely employs a true subjective camera. It is only in the film's opening scene, and only as it approaches the terrified girl, that the camera simulates the killer's gaze. After her amorous companion is murdered, the girl scurries aimlessly around the cabin, anxiously awaiting the inevitable, as the killer/camera closes in on her. The suspense is fleeting, for as anybody even vaguely familiar with the slasher film knows, the question is not *if* she will be killed, but *how* and *when*. At the moment before the death blow, the scene fades to white from a freeze-frame of her gaping mouth, forever frozen in a final scream.

For the rest of the film, the killer's point-of-view shots become less frequent and the camera becomes a disembodied entity. It lurks in the background, aimlessly stumbling around bushes and trees while keeping a threatening gaze directly on the counselors. These long-shots, presumably from the killer's location, are still subjective. As cheaply made as *Friday the 13th* was, the constant shaking of the camera is a clear stylistic choice, not the result of a broken tripod or nervous cinematographer. They do, however, remain ambiguous, never revealing the exact location of the killer. She could be anywhere within the film's visual space. Of course, the effectiveness of this technique depends a great deal upon how willing the audience is to play along with the conventions of the slasher. If we accept that the camera does not always reveal the exact location of the killer, but only alerts us to her presence, then both spatial and temporal relationships in the film are clearly defined. However, if we refuse to play along with *Friday the 13th*, and insist that the subjective camera must designate the killer's exact position within the frame, only two conclusions can be drawn. The first is that both space and time are malleable. For example, in the opening murder of the film proper, as Annie limps away from her pursuer, there is no logical way that the

woman could suddenly reappear in front of her. The second is that the killer is supernatural, not in the sense of being immortal, but in having the ability to disappear and suddenly materialize in a different place, thereby catching the characters by surprise.

After *Friday the 13th*, Cunningham washed his hands of the series until 1993, when he returned to produce *Jason Goes to Hell*, its ninth installment. He went on to direct the teen sex comedy *Spring Break* (1983); *The New Kids* (1985), a far more unsettling movie than *Friday the 13th* which he describes as "*Walking Tall* in high school"; and *DeepStar Six* (1989), an undersea thriller which ushered in a minor wave of like-minded films such as *Leviathan* (1989) and *The Abyss* (1989). While he stayed on the periphery of the horror game, producing films like *House* (1986) and *The Horror Show* (1989), the series he originated trudged forward, slowly but surely solidifying its rightful place as one of the greatest success stories in American cinema.

The July 24, 1980, release of Brian De Palma's *Dressed to Kill*, an eagerly anticipated *Psycho*-inspired pastiche of Hitchcockian themes and techniques, helped give the slasher film some much needed validation, especially in the wake of *Friday the 13th*. *Dressed to Kill* was no slasher film, at least in the eyes of the film community. It was a modestly budgeted thriller with A-list talent (Michael Caine, Angie Dickinson, Nancy Allen) and a young sought-after director who was just coming into his own as one of Hollywood's premier artists. It was also a complex film, intelligently tackling such thorny issues as rape fantasies and sexual deviance in ways which would have been impossible for the slasher film to address. However, *Dressed to Kill* unabashedly flaunts stylistic techniques which were being used with regularity by the slasher film. This did not prove that De Palma was derivative of both Hitchcock *and* the slasher film, but that the slasher film was closer to the mainstream than most cared to admit, and even more frightening, that its most controversial elements had begun to infiltrate the Hollywood product.

On the heels of *Friday the 13th* came *Prom Night*, one of the better early slashers in which Jamie Lee Curtis, in a role similar to the one she played so well in *Halloween*, joins with soon-to-be-funnyman Leslie Nielsen in a slasher *tour de force* of future box office stars. Although *Prom Night* was released nearly three months after *Friday the 13th*, the films were produced at the same time, so it is not surprising that *Prom Night* owes more to *Halloween*. According to Paul Lynch, the film's director, the inspiration for *Prom Night* goes back even further:

> I always did *Prom Night* based on Hitchcock more than anything else. Based on a little bit of Hitchcock and a little bit of De Palma. Not based on *Halloween* as much as I loved *Halloween*. For me, it was the kids and their situation that were interesting. The horror was second to that. It was the premise for me of *Psycho*, where you get involved with the people and out of the people you get some interesting horrific experiences. For me it was always the kids. I was interested in the characters and in what happened to them. The violence was secondary and there was no real reason to go beyond what we did.

Prom Night begins six years earlier in an abandoned building in which four children are playing a frightfully morbid version of hide-and-seek. The seeker chants "the killer is coming," while trying to terrify the "hiders" as much as find them.[1] When a fifth child stumbles into the game, the others descend upon her. In a freak accident, she falls to her death from the second story window. The four agree never to mention the incident again and the girl's death is eventually blamed on a convicted sex offender. But someone was watching. Someone who knows the truth and will never forget it.

Six years later, the children are all grown up. It's prom night, and as they ready themselves for that most unforgettable rite of adolescent passage each receives a threatening phone call from an ominous stranger. Like the doomed characters of any good slasher film, they ignore the warning, until a hooded maniac begins murdering them one by one. In a nicely choreographed final scene set to the pulsing beats of disco, Curtis reveals the killer. It's her own brother, and the brother of the little girl who was killed in the film's opening. For six long years, he has been waiting to take his revenge.

The final scene does have a sort of poignancy not typically found in slasher films. It's rather touching in a disturbing way, and a favorite of Lynch's, who calls the perfect synchronicity between the image and the soundtrack "pure unadulterated luck—the magic of film."

"The moment where Jamie looks at her brother, and her brother looks at her through the mask, and she knows that it's him. Well, the music hit the moment exactly, with such power it was staggering. And you were all whipped up in so much emotion by this piece of music. I mean, the scene was pretty good, but the music just took over with such emotion. It was just fabulous. And I've never had that happen since … it's a great movie moment for me."

Working primarily in episodic television, Lynch is one of the most energetic, upbeat and modest directors in the business, quick to deflect praise and even quicker to dispense it to his actors and crew. He is also a true student of film. He has a library filled with countless books on cinema and speaks in glowing terms of the often neglected films such as *House by*

Young Robin (Tammy Bourne) plummets to her death from the window of an abandoned building. This accident is the catalyst for the carnage to come in Paul Lynch's *Prom Night* (1980).

the Lake (a.k.a. *Death Weekend*), *Black Christmas* and *The Hills Have Eyes* which paved the way for *Prom Night*.

As a teenager growing up in Toronto in the mid–60s, Lynch became infatuated with Sue Lyon, the beautiful young blonde who had recently starred in Stanley Kubrick's *Lolita* (1962). Smitten with the teenage ingenue, Lynch began digging up anything he could find on the film and soon discovered that Kubrick had started out as a magazine photographer. A cartoonist by trade, Lynch bought a camera and starting taking his own pictures. With the help of William Gray, the future scribe of *The Changeling* who was an unemployed editor at time, he turned some of them into a 15-minute documentary. The film was sold to the Canadian Broadcasting Company and Lynch soon began working for them on a full-time basis, traveling all across North America shooting documentaries on stock car and horse races and directing some dramatic series. In 1973, Lynch made *The Hard Part Begins*, a well-received film about country music. A PA on the set suggested they shoot a documentary on Bob Guccione, publisher and editor in chief of *Penthouse* magazine, so in the summer of 1973 Lynch traveled to England to film the goings-on of Guccione's hedonistic empire. Guccione liked the completed film so much that he bought it, and for the next two years Lynch followed him and his entourage of beautiful women around the world before landing in Los Angeles.

In the spring of 1979, Lynch was ready to make a commercial film. He went to see Irwin Yablans, who after *Halloween* had become the first stop for slasher projects, with a pitch about a psychotic doctor called "Don't See the Doctor." Yablans didn't like the idea of mixing medicine and horror but instead suggested something about holidays. Lynch then offered an idea regarding cannibalism and Thanksgiving, a concept which Yablans found even more distasteful. On his way back from Yablans' office, Lynch passed a billboard which read: *For Your Prom Night. After Six Tuxedo Rentals.*

An idea for the film was born.

Early the next week, Lynch went to see Yablans with an outline for the film. Unfortunately, the producer was in New York and wasn't due back until the fol-

lowing week. At a party that Friday, Lynch ran into Peter Simpson, who had recently produced a successful family film, *The Sea Gypsies*. Simpson, who also owned a media-buying company, liked Lynch's idea and raised the film's budget through a public offering. Robert Guza, Jr., was called in to fill in the story which William Gray then scripted.

Initially, Lynch and Simpson wanted a well-known television actress for the lead female role. But when Curtis' manager got wind of the project and expressed his client's strong interest, the prospect of having of *Halloween*'s star in their film was too great to pass up. Lynch, in characteristically magnanimous fashion, admits, "Half of the success of the picture is Jamie Lee Curtis."

Curtis also received high praise from her co-star Leslie Nielsen, who found her to be an extremely intelligent actress. *Prom Night* was one of the last "straight" roles for Nielsen, known in the 1950s for such films as *Tammy and the Bachelor* (1957) and more recently *The Poseidon Adventure* (1972), before he reinvented himself as a comic genius with *Airplane!* (1980). Not above bringing a bit of lowbrow humor to the set, Nielsen carried around a small "fart machine," providing much needed comic relief. The rest of the cast was no less interesting. Towards the end of the film, there is a wonderfully effective scene in which David Mucci—the kid from the wrong side of the tracks who plans to spoil the prom—is decapitated. His head rolls across the stage in plain view of everyone in attendance. Mucci, who had a serious medical condition, was forced to be immobilized underneath the stage during the shoot. He was terrified something would happen while he was trapped there so Lynch held his hand during the entire scene to assure him everything would be all right. Robert Silverman, who plays the dimwitted school janitor Sykes and who, because of his suspicious leering, is fingered as a prime suspect from the beginning, was doing a bit more than acting—he was relearning. Years before in Toronto, Silverman had been struck by a car while crossing the street. The impact had thrown him against a wall. It took years of intense therapy for him to fully recover. His performance is authentic, and the fact that his injury left him obviously affected didn't faze Lynch, who wanted Sykes played a bit off-kilter anyway.

Prom Night was shot in Toronto over the course of four weeks in August and September 1979 on a budget of $1.6 million. Lynch remembers it as a high-energy shoot which was "terrific fun." Avco, a small company at the time, released 250 prints of the film in July 1980, a fair number for a slasher film but nowhere near the amount which Paramount put out for *Friday the 13th*. However, the film still took in nearly $15 million. *Prom Night* was successful enough to spawn three sequels: *Hello Mary Lou: Prom Night II* (1987), *Prom Night III: The Last Kiss* (1989) and *Prom Night IV: Deliver Us From Evil* (1991)—none of which have anything to do with the original nor do it any justice.

"When I was a kid, I just loved movies," said Armand Mastroianni, another director who was bitten by the filmmaking bug as a child. Growing up, he devoured all the Universal monster classics and made his own 8mm films with his friends. However, it was the Hammer films like *The Curse of Frankenstein* and *Horror of Dracula*, with their use of atmosphere and mood over cheap shock value, which had the greatest impact on the young Mastroianni. It was a style the young director learned well and emulated in his remarkably suspenseful slasher, *He Knows You're Alone*.

Mastroianni had no formal filmmaking education, although he started a film program while at the College of Staten Is-land, but received the kind of first-hand look into the industry which most aspiring directors only dream about. He cut school one day because he heard that *The Godfather* was being filmed on Staten Island and managed to sneak onto the closely guarded set. He even had the chutzpah to approach Francis Ford Coppola and ask the intimidating director if he could stay and watch. For the next three days, Mastroianni was invited back to the set. He witnessed the filming of some of *The Godfather*'s greatest scenes, including Connie and Carlo's wedding and the garden scene between Marlon Brando and Al Pacino.

While working on a comedy which he planned to shoot in Brooklyn, Mastroianni was introduced to producers Edgar Lansbury, the brother of Angela Lansbury, and Joseph Beruh. He pitched them the old urban legend about a couple who drive out to a deserted spot to make out, only to have an escaped mental patient kill the boy and hang him above the car. Midway through the pitch, Mastroianni noticed that neither producer seemed too interested or impressed. Suddenly, he was struck by the idea to use this scene as a self-conscious reference, as a film within his film. Now the producers were intrigued. Mastroianni's spontaneous brainstorm eventually formed the basis of *He Knows You're Alone*'s fabulous opening sequence, in which a girl is murdered in a movie theater while watching a slasher film.

Along with his friend Scott Parker, Mastroianni hammered out a script involving a psychopath who has been jilted on his wedding day. He takes revenge by murdering brides-to-be and anybody else who gets in his way. Rather than focus exclusively on the murders, Mastroianni chose to explore the heroine's slowly growing paranoia.

In an interview in the July 1999, issue of *Fangoria*, he says:

That was my intent in *He Knows You're Alone*. That was the time that *Friday the 13th* was about to come out, and there was a lot of very gory stuff being shown on screen. I thought it might be a good idea to head a little more in the opposite direction. Otherwise it would have just meant copying each other. I felt like de-emphasizing the violence somewhat and keeping it a little less graphic, hopefully making it more genuinely frightening by allowing audiences to use their heads.

He Knows You're Alone was only budgeted at about $300,000, but because it was shot on 35mm and went through a full mix it looks far more expensive. The 18-day Staten Island shoot, which wrapped just before Christmas of 1979,

was nerve-wracking for both the cast and crew. They were constantly moving from one location to the next, a necessary inconvenience which prepared Mastroianni for his later career in television. Despite the stress, Mastroianni managed to "keep it light on set." The consummate actor's director, Mastroianni is, by all accounts, wonderful to work for. His relaxed nature and collaborative philosophy puts the cast at ease and ultimately brings out better performances. "Directing is about listening," he says, "listening to people's ideas, listening to the actor's thoughts, making your choices and going with them."

Mastroianni can also be credited with giving one of Hollywood's biggest movie stars, two-time Best Actor winner Tom

Subtlety is hardly the strong suit of the killer in Armand Mastroianni's *He Knows You're Alone* **(1980).**

Hanks, his first big break. The director recalls that even in Hanks' early days, the soon-to-be comedic wunderkind was an extraordinary talent. He was also a sweet and charming gentleman, characteristics he has retained as a superstar. Hanks arrived early for his *He Knows You're Alone* audition and Mastroianni invited him into the office while he finished his lunch. The two began talking and by the end of the conversation the director was sold. He ran into the producers' office and convinced them to forgo the audition and immediately hire Hanks for a brief but memorable role.

On set, Hanks was more than an actor, he was the sounding board for the string of titles which the producers were trying to decide upon. "Everyday he would come to work and we'd go, 'Hey, Tom, can you come up with something new for this movie?'" Mastroianni remembers. Countless names were tossed around, including *Shriek* and *The Uninvited*, before they finally settled on *Blood Wedding*.

About two weeks before the Cannes Film Festival, the producers placed an ad in both *Daily Variety* and *The Hollywood Reporter* promoting *Blood Wedding*. This caught the eye of the studios, who offered to view the film in Los Angles immediately. 20th Century–Fox was first up, but for some reason they canceled the screening. Next, the producers brought the film over to MGM. When they arrived to pick it up, the screening had just started so they sat quietly in the back and watched alongside the studio brass. Michael Nathanson, vice-president of production, loved the film. He turned to the producers, who clearly were not supposed to be there, and told them to go back to their hotel and expect a call. The next day, Lansbury and Beruh found themselves having breakfast at the home of MGM president David Begelman.

Blood Wedding—whose name was promptly changed to *He Knows You're Alone*—was sold to MGM for about $2 million for both domestic and foreign rights. It was released in August 1980, and although it didn't do the business of *Friday the 13th*, it made close to $5 million and was a modest hit for the studio. Says Mastroianni about the horror climate:

That's the time when the studios would take a gamble on these low-budget independent slasher films and said, "Let's give them a few million bucks and see what we got. Take a shot." Not that they could make them for that, and later on when they tried to make the big-budget horror films they didn't work ... there's something about the grittiness of these independent films that the studios really couldn't duplicate because they would suddenly pump a lot of money in and give it a glossier look. It felt more pretentious, it didn't feel as documentary-style.

Still, MGM didn't plan to market *He Knows You're Alone* as a low-budget production. Although they had only paid $2 million for it—a drop in the bucket for a major studio—they were going to do everything in their power to insure that their investment paid off. Explains Mastroianni:

To justify the expenditure of picking up this film and putting it out, they actually shot an additional trailer that was never in the film. They decided to spend some money and build sets and then flew the actors out. I was there and everybody came out to Los Angeles. They built this set and we shot this sort of preview of a women sitting in front of a mirror, the lead actress [Caitlin O'Heaney], brushing her hair. It was never in the film. And you heard the narrator saying, "On the night before her wedding, every girl is frightened." And the camera is pushing in over her shoulder through the bedroom and she's brushing her hair. And you see her reflection in the mirror and then she stops

brushing her hair. She turns to the camera and suddenly a hand punches through the mirror.

After *He Knows You're Alone*, Mastroianni directed the vastly underrated *The Killing Hour* (a.k.a. *The Clairvoyant* [1982]), along with *The Supernaturals* (1985) and *Cameron's Closet* (1989), before turning his talents to television series and cable movies. One day while walking in Manhattan, Mastroianni spotted Martin Scorsese kneeling on the sidewalk. He walked up and introduced himself. Scorsese, who was in the middle of filming *The King of Comedy* (1983), stopped shooting, called over Robert DeNiro and introduced Mastroianni as "the guy who made *He Knows You're Alone*." The slasher film hadn't just reached the masses, it had touched one of the most well-respected artists in the film industry. By now, its impact was hard to ignore.

Bride-to-be Amy Jensen (Caitlin O'Heaney) **cowers in a corner, awaiting certain death in** *He Knows You're Alone* **(1980).**

CHAPTER 6

Trains of Terror, Funhouses, Horrible Holidays and a Maniac

The proverbial graveyard of horror is littered with the corpses of overlooked films which, for one reason or another, never found a niche with audiences and have been relegated to either video (now DVD) or obscurity. Sometimes, however, a film which has very little to offer will strike a cord with audiences and become an overnight sensation. Such is the case with Ulli Lommel's *The Boogey Man*, a supernatural slasher made for less than a half a million dollars which supposedly grossed more than $25 million worldwide.

Ulli Lommel was born in the American sector of West Berlin in the closing days of World War II. As a teenage star in Germany, he worked under famed German director Rainer Werner Fassbinder in such films as *The American Soldier* (1970) and *Chinese Roulette* (1976). Influenced by far more than just European art cinema, Lommel acted in exploitation pioneer Russ Meyer's 1965 film *Fanny Hill: Memoirs of a Woman of Pleasure*, and later went on to direct the king of American *avant garde*, Andy Warhol, in *Cocaine Cowboys* (1979).

It was his 1973 film *Tenderness of Wolves* which first brought him international attention. The story, which was also the inspiration for Fritz Lang's classic *M* (1931), details the gruesome crimes of Fritz Haarman, the famed Vampire of Hanover. From 1918–24 Haarman is thought to have killed over 50 boys—although he was only convicted of 27 murders—whom he lured into his apartment. After wining and dining his victims, Haarman went for the jugular. He would literally suck their blood and then cut the bodies into little pieces which he sold as steaks to the local townspeople.

The Boogey Man stars Suzanna Love (Lommel's wife at the time) as a young married woman who, as a child, witnessed her brother stab their mother's kinky lover to death. Twenty years later, she lives on her aunt and uncle's farm, along with her husband Jake (Ron James) and the mute brother (Nicholas Love) who has not spoken since the murder. Compelled to visit her childhood home, and the site of the tragedy, Love sees the ghost of the mother's

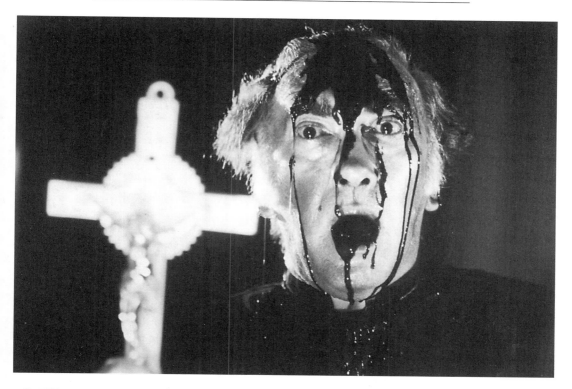

In Ulli Lommel's *The Boogey Man* (1980), even Father Reilly (Llewelyn Thomas) is powerless against the supernatural force unleashed by a broken mirror.

lover—who presumably is the "boogey man" of the title—in a bedroom mirror. She smashes the mirror to bits, which somehow releases his malevolent spirit.

For some reason, the spirit resides in one of the mirror's broken shards and brings death to either whoever touches it, or whoever it reflects light onto. A series of gratuitous deaths follow, including a fairly creative one in which an amorous girl is impaled on a skewer protruding from her boyfriend's mouth. Jake, seemingly struck by divine inspiration, suggests they throw the mirror in a well. For some inexplicable reason, this seems to destroy the boogey man.

The slasher film, which shows human acts so terrible they should be beyond our comprehension, hence the vicarious thrill of watching them, and the supernatural horror film, which deals with themes and events that actually are beyond our comprehension, have never really gone together. There have been few, if any, successful marriages, and *The Boogey Man* is no exception. Its muddled plot is not really complicated, just inane. None of it makes much sense, which makes it extremely tough for the film to generate any real suspense. While the murder scenes involving levitating farm tools are carried out with a certain flourish, instruments of death are far more frightening in the hands of some maniac then when controlled by an unseen force.

Despite its many flaws, *The Boogey Man* was an undisputed hit. Its success set the stage for *The Boogey Man II* (1982), an even more bizarre film which uses recycled footage from the original to create something which tries to be both a slasher film and a scathing indictment of Hollywood,

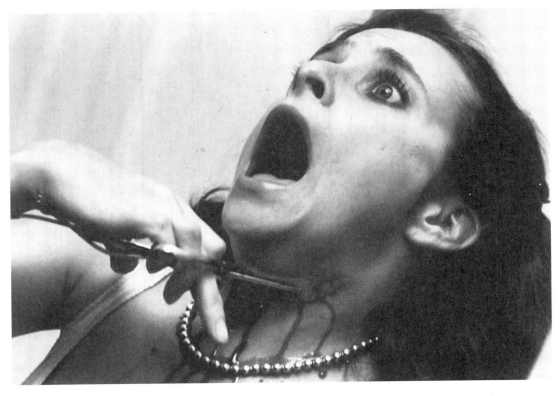

Unlucky teenager Jane (Jane Pratt) is overcome by the power of the Boogey Man.

an effort which fails miserably on both accounts.

Terror Train was Jamie Lee Curtis' slasher swan song.[1] She had gone from high school babysitter in *Halloween*, to prom queen in *Prom Night*, to graduating collegiate co-ed. It was the last time she would don a bad hairdo, lose a group of friends to a revenge-minded maniac, and scream for her paycheck in the genre she helped inaugurate.

Terror Train was released on October 3, 1980, at the height of the slasher film's popularity. Strangely enough, 20th Century–Fox, which had acquired the film as a negative pickup, moved up its release date from October 31 for fear that the market for such films was quickly drying up. In a *New York Times* article by Aljean Harmetz, "Quick End of Low-Budget Horror-Film Cycle Seen," which trum-

peted an end to the slasher film, Robert Cort, Vice-President of Advertising and Publicity for Fox, said, "The box office for these films has been dropping recently. By releasing *Terror Train* this Friday we hope we can give it some breathing room between the summer horror glut and the end-of-October glut." While this eulogy was horribly premature, and the film's gross of slightly more than $10 on a budget of less than $3 million was nothing to scoff at, it was far from the $45–50 million which Fox had optimistically anticipated.

Terror Train begins with a prologue involving one of the those collegiate pranks which you just know is going to end badly. The nebbish Kenny (Derek MacKinnon) is goaded by his friends into a tryst with the popular and beautiful Alana (Jamie Lee Curtis). It has always been somewhat of a mystery why the nerds in slasher films, supposedly the smartest of the lot, never question the intentions of the leading lady who suddenly takes an interest in them. But Kenny trusts his new paramour and allows Alana to lure him into her canopy enshrouded bed where a limbless cadaver, stolen from the mortuary, awaits him. Everyone has a good laugh at the cruel joke—that is, everyone except Kenny, who is so traumatized that he goes insane. And who said pre-med students don't know how to have fun?

Three years later, the graduating class has organized a New Year's Eve costume bash aboard an old steam locomotive. As one particularly inebriated guy toasts, "To my last big college party," you can bet that their unbalanced classmate whom they pushed over the edge a few years prior is the last thing on their minds. But somebody has a longer memory than the pranksters, somebody who has no qualms about killing the guilty one by one. When everyone except Alana, the film's Final Girl, has been punished, the killer reveals his identity. It is Kenny (no surprise there), who has been disguised the entire time as the beautiful assistant of a hired magician (a young David Copperfield).

The mission of director Roger Spottiswoode was simple: He was told to "try and write *Psycho* on a train with kids." No stranger to the film industry, Spottiswoode edited three of legendary director Sam Peckinpah's greatest films, *Straw Dogs* (1971), *The Getaway* (1972) and *Pat Garrett and Billy the Kid* (1973). He had also written a draft of *48 Hours* (1982), which hadn't yet been made. In September 1979, while Spottiswoode was recutting a few films for producer Sandy Howard, he was handed the script for *Terror Train*. Unbeknownst to him, until he spotted the film's poster in Howard's

Alana (Jamie Lee Curtis) realizes that there is no escaping the maniac in Roger Spottiswoode's *Terror Train* (1980).

office, he was listed as its writer. After some negotiating, Spottiswoode was hired to direct *Terror Train* on the condition that he would also edit it. As an unproven director, he was a gamble; as an editor, he was among the elite.

Spottiswoode was given six weeks prep for a 25-day shoot. Because there was no money in the budget for sets, he was faced with the nearly impossible task of having to shoot the entire film on an actual train. While the script, which he never thought was very good, was being rewritten, Spottiswoode had to find the train and transport it into Montreal, a nightmare in itself:

> There's a place called Traintown in Vermont which is wonderful. I think somebody had made a fortune in the stock market and his father was a train driver who was retiring and what he really wanted to do was to go on driving trains. So this guy had bought eight miles of train line and an old shedding and had turned it into a train museum. It was really great. It's still there. So we went there and we picked a lot of carriages. We then picked the engine, had them put together, and brought down an art department. We had no time left; we're four weeks before shooting. It would take a week to shuttle this thing up to Montreal, because it had to go so far, and then stop, and get permission to go to the next place. It's very complicated to move a train that is not a regular train and is being built on the move.

Luck smiled on Spottiswoode in one instance. He managed to secure the services of Stanley Kubrick's heralded cameraman John Alcott, who had shot *A Clockwork Orange* (1971) and had won an Oscar for *Barry Lyndon* (1975). Initially, Spottiswoode was a bit leery of Alcott's involvement, for he couldn't figure out why one of the world's most respected cinematographers would want to endure a shoot which looked to be highly problematic:

> This is a man who's done all these famous films. He had just done *The Shining* which hadn't come out but they had spent a year shooting it and they did one setup a day. I knew as an editor I wouldn't be able to shoot [*Terror Train*] without coverage, so I'd need lots of setups. I kept saying to Sandy, "This isn't going to work, he's going to be a prima donna." And he said, "No, no, you've got to meet him." So finally John shows up and of course he's this delightful man who took me aside and said, "Now look, I just spent the year with Stanley, and I've got to tell you I got bored out of my fucking mind. There's nothing better than having to shoot 20 or 30 setups every fucking day. Let me tell you. One a day was death."

The last thing that Alcott had to worry about on *Terror Train* was how to squelch his boredom. The logistical nightmare of having to transport wires and equipment, not to mention cast and crew, down the narrow corridors made the train nearly impossible to light. To make matters worse, the deal which the producers had negotiated didn't allow them to cut any holes in the train to position the lights. At one point, a representative from the film's completion bond company took Spottiswoode aside and told him that there was no way he was going to be able to complete the film without building sets. Thankfully, the one man who believed it could be done was John Alcott. "He's a real worker who takes pleasure in enormous challenges," said Spottiswoode.

Since there was no room for lights, and no money to build sets, Alcott was forced to devise an ingenious solution. He lit the train with hundreds of tiny bulbs whose wires were all connected to an enormous panel controlled by over 300 dimmers. Preferring to use the back of his hand rather than a light meter, Alcott would then radio his specifications to the electrician stationed on the panel. The impressive lighting schemes were produced by changing the bulbs and the voltage.

The efforts of Alcott, Spottiswoode and Curtis managed to raise *Terror Train* a notch above its contemporaries. While many of these films had a slightly larger budget, none managed to duplicate its style and oppressive atmosphere. The only aspect of the film which didn't translate well was Copperfield's magic tricks, which critics and audiences refused to attribute to the magician's own talent. In his review of *Terror Train* in *The Washington Post*, Gary Arnold says that Copperfield "seems to be getting rather too much critical assistance from the director and editor when it comes to dazzling the audience. The illusions suffer to some extent from the strong suspicion that they're largely the work of editing and optical tricks." Spottiswoode explains his theory why the on-screen magic tricks didn't work, despite the fact that all of them were a result of Copperfield's sleight of hand:

It seemed to me that magic wouldn't work very well in film and I was right about that. We did all of David's illusions in one take. I discovered when we previewed it and showed it to people that nobody knew or cared. The fact that you did it was just movie stunts, special effects. They just expected it. Even in the days before CGI, they expected things to happen and they gave no credit to David for doing it. It was strange. I think I've always known since then that magic doesn't work in films.

Terror Train was 20th Century–Fox's lone foray into the slasher film during the

Psychologically scarred from a cruel practical joke, the deranged Kenny (Derek MacKinnon) gets the last laugh in *Terror Train* (1980).

genre's most productive years. It didn't prompt the studio to follow Paramount's lead in acquiring similar films. For an industry spoiled by the success of *Halloween* and *Friday the 13th*, nothing short of a blockbuster was worth the aggravation. For Spottiswoode, however, it was well worth it. The young editor who had been weaned on European art films would go on to become one of Hollywood's most sought-after directors, alternating between intelligent fare like *Under Fire* (1983) and hugely successful action movies like *Tomorrow Never Dies* (1997) and *The 6th Day* (2000).

After *Halloween*, Irwin Yablans watched as others—most of them far less savvy and talented than he, Carpenter, Akkad and Hill—grew rich by mining the genre he had helped invent. He called such films as *Maniac*, *Prom Night* and *Terror Train* "obvious steals," and half-jokingly raised the possibility of suing them. It was, however, unthinkable for someone with his business acumen to rest on his laurels when there was still money to made in the genre. "I just sat down one day and thought about the ultimate film buff," said Yablans. "I thought about what he would do, and it just seemed natural that he would want to seek out revenge on people by using all his movie heroes."

With this seed of an idea, he hired Vernon Zimmerman to write and direct what would eventually become *Fade to Black*, the story of Eric Binford (Dennis Christopher, one year removed from his "break-out" movie, *Breaking Away* [1979]), an unbalanced young man who is so obsessed with Hollywood that he can't distinguish reality from moviedom. Fed up with his wheelchair-bound aunt's malicious harping, he pushes her down a flight of stairs, just as Richard Widmark did as Tommy Udo in *Kiss of Death* (1947). Having developed a taste for murder, and an equally strong one for fantasy, Eric dresses up as his cinematic heroes—Dracula, the Mummy, Hopalong Cassidy—and gets revenge on his enemies in ways which are consistent with whatever character he is impersonating at the moment. His spree comes to a fitting end on top of Mann's (formerly Grauman's) Chinese Theatre, which he naturally views as an homage to James Cagney's last stand as Cody Jarrett in *White Heat* (1949).

Fade to Black made $15 million on a $1.8 million budget. Still, for most everyone involved, the experience was disappointing. Zimmerman was in over his head, which forced Yablans, usually a hands-off producer, to be on set nearly every day. The director didn't appreciate this helping hand and consequently refused to be involved with the editing. As a businessman, Yablans should have been ecstatic with the return on his investment. His somewhat blasé attitude proved that slasher films, once considered lucky to break even, were now *expected* to generate enormous revenue. In the case of *Fade to Black*, however, it was more than the unspectacular box office count. Yablans always had the feeling that the finished film didn't do his idea justice:

> I wish I hadn't made that movie because I'd like to make it again. I thought the idea was so good. It comes from the concept that all of us, every one of us, our personalities and our whole persona are affected, whether we want to admit it or not, by movies. In countless ways we create ourselves as reflections of images we've either consciously or subconsciously absorbed through film.

What is ironic is that *Fade to Black*, a highly original, complex and probing concept, was practically nothing more than a slasher afterthought, while *Halloween*, which for all of its technical and stylistic gloss operates on the most primitive and instinctual level, ultimately altered the course of cinema. Perhaps Janet Maslin explained it best in her review when she said, "The trouble with *Fade to Black* is that it's supposed to be a thriller. It's much more amusing than scary...." Unfortunately, it was not amusing enough to sustain interest solely on premise alone. As a one-trick pony, *Fade to Black* soon grows tiresome, and as a slasher, it lacked the bite to keep audiences on the edge of their seats.

One director who can never be accused of lacking bite is Jeff Lieberman, the darling of cult movie enthusiasts because of his highly individual—some would say idiosyncratic—take on conventional genres. However, Lieberman is one of the few *auteurs* of the early slasher film whose talent never translated into mainstream success. His first two films were the nature-run-amuck, stomach-churner *Squirm* (1976) and *Blue Sunshine* (1977), a film which gives new meaning to the term "bad trip." For his next project, he was offered a film called *The Last Ritual* which he agreed to direct on the condition that he could amend the awful script. The producers had no qualms about Lieberman's request as long as the film didn't diverge from slasher formula. As a result, the giant snake ritual of the title was quickly shelved in favor of two inbred hillbilly twins (both played by John Hunsaker) inspired by *Deliverance* (1972).

Set in Silver Falls State Park in the gorgeous Oregon mountains, *Just Before Dawn*

follows five naive but experienced hikers who unwittingly invade the territory of a mountain family. While the obvious result is the civilized vs. uncivilized conflict of both *The Texas Chainsaw Massacre* and *The Hills Have Eyes*, Lieberman is less interested in the film's thematic message than in its ability to shock and upend viewers at every juncture.[2] His direction is nearly flawless, and almost every sequence in the film can stand alone as a shining example of his ability to generate suspense. Among the film's most unsettling scenes is a skinny-dipping episode in which Megan

Hopalong Cassidy is only one of the disguises worn by Eric Binford (Dennis Christopher) in Vernon Zimmerman's *Fade to Black* **(1980), the story of a crazed cinephile whose movie fantasies serve as the inspiration for his murders.**

(Jamie Rose) discovers that the person fondling her under the water is not her boyfriend, Jonathan (Chris Lemmon, son of Jack Lemmon), who has already swam back to shore. If *Just Before Dawn* is known for one thing, however, it is its final scene—the standoff between Constance (Deborah Benson), the lone surviving female, and the last hillbilly twin. In a fit of rage, a last ditch effort to survive, Constance rams her forearm down the hillbilly's throat, effectively suffocating him. It is brutal, outrageous and, most of all, unexpected, the typical hallmarks of a Lieberman work.

Another backwoods slasher, initially released around the same time as *Just Before Dawn*, was James Bryan's incomparably awful *Don't Go In the Woods … Alone* (1980). It was later retitled *Don't Go In the Woods*, for whatever silly reason, and is easily one of the worst films of the slasher cycle. Interspersed between a handful of almost impossibly suspenseless murders, the muddled plot involves a quartet of hikers who finally come to the realization that they are being stalked by some sort of primeval forest behemoth. More like a miniature half-baked *Deliverance* than *Friday the 13th*, the film it assumedly seeks to emulate, *Don't Go In the Woods … Alone* epitomizes every negative perception of slasher films: woefully inept actors, a script so absurd it dissolves into parody, nonexistent production values and bargain-basement (I'm being very generous here) special effects. On top of all this, it is burdened with one of the all-time irritating scores, egregiously overused at every juncture. In fact, it takes a fair amount of willpower just to refrain from watching the entire film on mute. The few striking shots of the Utah wilderness are without a doubt the film's high point.

New Year's Evil (1980) appears to have been made primarily to lay claim to one of the few holidays which hadn't already been gobbled up as the basis for a slasher film. Evidently, producers Menahem Golan and Yoram Globus thought that simply setting their film on New Year's Eve would insure success. Instead, director Emmett Alston manages to take an intriguing premise and inherently compelling plot and create a boring, bloodless slasher. Blaze (Roz Kelly), a celebrity rock deejay whose best days are clearly behind her, is hosting a televised New Year's Eve special in Los Angeles. Throughout the night, she receives a series of threatening phone calls from a man who identifies himself only as "Evil." Evil promises to kill someone each time midnight strikes in a different time zone across the country—first New York, then Chicago, Aspen and finally Los Angeles, where Blaze herself will be the final victim. In the film's lone twist, Evil is revealed to be Blaze's husband, thereby allowing him unfettered access to his final victim. Evil's psychosis is never sufficiently explained—more annoying than ambiguous—nor is his reason for the murder spree. Furthermore, it seems virtually impossible that Blaze could remain ignorant of someone as seriously disturbed as her husband. The low point of *New Year's Evil*, of which there are many, is the completely unsatisfying ending. Evil, realizing that escape from the police is impossible, jumps to his death from the roof of a building, easily the most uninteresting demise of any killer in the history of slasher films.

In *The Last House on the Left*, David Hess played a sadistic psychopath so convincingly that many were shocked to discover that he was actually a well-adjusted adult, much less the creative force behind one of the first mad Santa films, *To All a Goodnight* (1980). His lone directorial effort, while not a blatant rip-off of *Black Christmas*, owes quite a bit to Clark's film, right down to the muted lighting and Yuletide set dressings. At the Calvin Finishing School—which it seems is only finishing turning its students into sluts—Christmas break brings more than eggnog, presents and good tidings to all, it brings a plane-load of young men, eager to dispense their own brand of Christmas cheer to the willing ladies. Unfortunately for them, it also brings a lunatic Santa, whose sack of gifts includes an ax, crossbow and knife. As expected, one by one the cast is eliminated in a variety of unpleasant ways. What is not expected, is their ferocious sexual appetites, even once they discover that the killer is in their midst. One would have to ascertain that in *To All a Goodnight* murder is the ultimate aphrodisiac, for the characters barely have time to dodge the next errant crossbow arrow before hopping into bed with each other. The film attempts a "twist" ending with little effect; there are actually two killer Santas—a cook and the investigating officer—whose daughter was killed in a prank two years before when her classmates backed her over a balcony, from whose height it would seem that a sprained ankle, not a broken neck, would most likely result.

Derek Sullivan (Grant Cramer) might not be the killer in Emmett Alston's *New Year's Evil* (1980), but that doesn't mean he isn't seriously disturbed.

By late 1980, there weren't many holidays or pivotal rites of passage which hadn't already been used as the basis for a slasher film. Halloween (*Halloween*), Friday the 13th (*Friday the 13th*), New Year's (*New Year's Evil*), prom night (*Prom Night*), college graduation (*Terror Train*), weddings (*He Knows You're Alone*), even Christmas (*Black Christmas*) had been done; the slasher film had left its crimson stain on almost all of our national celebrations. Thanksgiving, however, the most American of holidays, remained untarnished. That is, until *Home Sweet Home* (1980), easily the worst of this bunch, left a permanent blemish on Turkey Day forever.

Home Sweet Home is a film so bad it defies even the lowest expectations. An eclectic and impossibly annoying group of people arrive at an isolated country home to celebrate Thanksgiving. In truth, the film could have been set on any day. The Thanksgiving holiday is only a hackneyed device used to bring them all together in a single location. After repeated viewings I'm still trying to figure out their relationship to each other. In addition to the wooden actors, all of whom seem to be transplanted from a cheesy porno film, is a teenage heavy metal guitarist all decked out in face paint who looks like some freakish Kiss parody. There is also an adolescent girl tastelessly thrown into the mix for no other reason than to show the maternal instincts of one of the nondescript characters. Luckily, before we can build up any real animosity towards them, an escaped mental patient, Jay Jones, begins the slaughter. Jones is played by fitness guru Jake Steinfeld, whose claim as "trainer to the stars" couldn't have been helped by his turn as the perpetually giggling, PCP-addled psychotic madman. The film ends when the aforementioned maternal character, the only remaining adult of the bunch, incapacitates Jones long enough—with a well-placed carving knife to his back—for the police to arrive and shoot him.

In the fall of 1980, two offbeat and highly individual horror films were released. While only tangentially related to the slasher film, both are sometimes categorized as such because of both the time of their release and the mode of their production and distribution. The two films, Kevin Connor's *Motel Hell*, which passes off excess as satire, and Charles Kaufman's *Mother's Day*, which does the same with cruelty, are similar only in their desire to parody (or as some critics who give them far too much credit would say, deconstruct) whatever genre they appear to be lampooning.

In order to solve the pressing global dilemma of "too many people, not enough food," Farmer Vincent (a sinewy Rory Calhoun, who gives it his all) has been producing a delicious line of smoked meats made from one part farm-raised hog

It's a bizarre harvest indeed for Farmer Vincent (Rory Calhoun) and his sister Ida (Nancy Parsons) in Kevin Connor's *Motel Hell* (1980).

and one part unlucky motorists who pass by his Motel Hello (the "o" in the sign is burnt out, giving some plot justification for the film's title). He and his sister Ida (Nancy Parsons), who both fully subscribe to the family saying "it takes all kind of critters to make farmer Vincent's fritters," "plant" their victims in a secret garden and then sever their vocal cords so the only sound the "stock" can make is a nauseating gurgle. Why they feel the need to bury their victims before butchering them is never explained, but it does make for some highly effective surreal imagery. Equally effective in a warped sort of way is the film's over-the-top climax, which *The Encyclopedia of Horror Movies* calls "one of the truly great moments in the Grand Guignol pantheon," in which Farmer Vincent, wearing a hog's head, engages in a chain saw battle with the town sheriff as a beautiful young victim tied to a conveyer belt inches closer and closer to a hacksaw blade. The *Encyclopedia* also refers to the farm as "the epitome of Reagan's America," in a reading of the film which goes far beyond what should be allowed considering the subject.

Like *Motel Hell*, *Mother's Day* supposedly satirizes the pervasive culture of consumerism, although I have a hard time seeing how an altogether unpleasant film about three outward bound women who are ravaged by a backwoods family is even remotely satirical. In his *New York Times* review of the film, Tom Buckley observes, "It is as though the persons responsible for it possess some fearsome power as yet unknown to science called antitalent." It is hardly surprising then that director Charles Kaufman is the brother of infamous Z-movie producer and Troma founder, Lloyd Kaufman. Like the deadly clan within the film, *Mother's Day* is a family affair for the Kaufmans: Lloyd received a producing credit, patriarch Stanley Kaufman had a brief acting role, and sister Susan Kaufman was responsible for the production design.

The film, which some people feel is one of Troma's best (as Lloyd Kaufman proudly states in his semi-autobiography *All I Need to Know About Filmmaking I Learned from the Toxic Avenger*) begins on a bizarre note. At some type of self-empowerment meeting, a grandmotherly woman (Rose Ross) agrees to give two vagabonds (a guy and a girl) a ride home. Just when it seems inevitable that the two are going to kill her—for what sordid reason we can only imagine—her two backwards sons spring from the nearby forest, behead the guy and pummel the girl to a bloody pulp before mother steps in to finish the job.

From here, it doesn't take too long to figure out that the three professional women and former college roommates who we soon meet are going to be the next victims. In the film's most sickening scene, two of the girls are captured and bound. The third is forced to play the lead role in a rape fantasy production which the two hillbillies put on for the pleasure of their approving mother. When the girl finally dies after being repeatedly raped and beaten, her two friends plot revenge. They manage to escape and dole out their gruesome justice with such items as an electric carving knife, Drano and a television set. But the kicker is saved for dear old mom, who the girls suffocate with an inflated plastic breast in what critics have seen as a fitting and symbolic revenge against a pathologically overbearing mother. Others have seen it for what it really is, typical exploitative nonsense from a company which has a permanent lease on bad taste.

Directly from *Friday the 13th*, Tom Savini went right to work on an even more controversial film, Bill Lustig's *Maniac* (1981), the story of a deeply disturbed loner, Frank Zito (the late Joe Spinell), who indiscriminately murders and scalps

Mother (Rose Ross) gleefully strangles a young woman in Charles Kaufman's supposedly satiric *Mother's Day* (1980). This violent and over-the-top film was produced by Troma, so even the specter of a grandmotherly sadist should come as no surprise.

young women. Savini brought with him the headless corpse (just a model, of course) of Betsy Palmer, which would be used in *Maniac*'s now infamous final scene. However, unlike *Friday the 13th*, which was beloved by slasher fans eager for the gorier murders which *Halloween* had failed to deliver, *Maniac* was universally loathed.

In his essay "Disturbo 13: The Most Disturbing Horror Films Ever Made," horror scribe Stanley Wiater states, "*Maniac*'s filmmakers' cold-blooded mentality is continually evident in its unrelenting misogynistic attitude that women are good for only two functions: fucking or killing (and not necessarily in that order)." In *Splatter Movies*, John McCarty writes that *Maniac* "gives new meaning to the word sleaze." Kim Newman describes Spinell as "slobbish, sweaty, ugly and

prone to horrible overacting." Even Vincent Canby, the legendary *New York Times* film critic who probably thought he was being far more clever than he was, compared Spinell's acting to "watching someone else throw up."[3]

It's hard to imagine that the man responsible for *Maniac* is one of the most affable, genuinely funny and generous directors in the business. Lustig, a native New Yorker who cut his teeth in the adult film industry, had always wanted to make a horror film. He especially admired the stylish European films of Mario Bava and Dario Argento.[4] Unfortunately for Lustig, before the success of *Halloween*, horror films were seen as more of a disreputable genre than a lucrative investment. Unfettered, Lustig, his childhood friend and co-producer Andrew Garroni and Spinell, whom Lustig had met on the set of *The Seven-Ups* (1973), pooled their money. Spinell, who contributed $6,000, signed over the checks he had just received for his role in *Cruising* (1980). Lustig kicked in $30,000 and Garroni added $6,000. Deals were cut with the labs, cast and crew. With deferments, the film's total cost was about $350,000.

Although *Maniac* didn't have much of a script, Spinell took his role extremely seriously. Along with improvising much of the dialogue, he did extensive research on serial killers, especially Henry Lee Lucas. The shoot, which began in the fall of 1979 and finally finished in April 1980, was both taxing and rewarding. According to Lustig, "It was brutal, but you know, I loved it. It was the most fun I ever had ... it was a real family atmosphere." It was also an exercise in ingenuity. Lustig describes one of the film's most impressive scenes in which Tom Savini, who aside from handling the FX chores also had a minor role in the film, gets his head blown off by Spinell:

We shot it on location underneath the Verrazzano Bridge along the highway in Brooklyn. It's illegal to fire a live shotgun, of course, in the city. [laughs]. You can't fire a live shotgun, especially with a whole crew standing around. But the only way to achieve the effect where you see the windshield shatter and the head explode was by using a live shotgun. And the person who fired the shotgun at his own head was Tom Savini. What happened was, as soon as he fired the shotgun we grabbed the gun, stuck it in the trunk of the car, and sent a PA to drive to New Jersey. Get that shotgun out of town. Well, we needed this car so we could finish the scene. We needed a shot of the girl on the floor of the car. We needed all these other close-ups that we weren't able to finish that night. Remember now, we had put chicken salad and shrimp salad inside the head of the corpse to give it a brainy look, and tons of fake blood. So

here we have this car that was sprayed with blood and we didn't want to wash it because we needed the continuity. And we were shooting in the middle of the night. So we gave the car to a guy to drive to Staten Island, which was just over the bridge. Well, when you go over that bridge you have to go through the tollbooth. And here he's driving a car with a shotgun hole in the front and blood all over the inside of the car. So he goes through the tollbooth and he gives them the money. When he pulls out, six cop cars converge on him. There he is in the middle of the night trying to explain how this unregistered car has all this blood and a shotgun hole in the middle of it.

After *Maniac* had completed principal photography, Lustig needed a few pickups of Spinell. Spinell, however, was already well into production on *Nighthawks* (1981), a police thriller starring Sylvester Stallone and Rutger Hauer, and no longer looked the part of Frank Zito. He was clean-shaven and his hair was cut. Since he had been friends with Stallone for a long time, since their days on *Farewell My Lovely* (1975) and *Rocky* (1976), the *Nighthawks* makeup department fitted him with wig and mustache which allowed him to return to the role of Zito. But this wasn't the only production which helped out *Maniac*. The film was mixed in the same facility as *Dawn of the Dead*. For the shotgun scene, Lustig couldn't seem to get the sound of the blast right, so he lifted the effect from a scene early in Romero's film when a cop comes barging through a door and shoots a zombie.

During production, Spinell was the one who had the highest expectations for the film. Lustig kept telling him, "Joe, let's just make sure we can play on 42nd Street and Texas drive-ins," but Spinell kept saying, "Bill, you don't know what we're making, it's a happening. It's really going to be an amazing movie. You don't know how good this movie is turning out." Lustig had the normal insecurities of any young director and at one point, soon after the movie was finished, he even suggested they should have made it more violent. "I turned to Andy Garroni and said, 'We didn't put enough blood and gore in the movie.' I don't know why I would think that, but I really did. I honestly thought we should shoot some more blood and gore and put it in the movie."

According to Lustig, the moment at which *Maniac* came alive was when it was scored by Jay Chattaway, whom he calls a genius. At the Cannes Film Festival, the film's sales agent Irving Shapiro booked the film in a small theater for a midnight showing. The cinema sold out immediately and the producers had to turn people away. By the end of the festival, the producers had made deals which were worth at least a million dollars; the entire film was paid off and in profit without having even opened yet. *Maniac* looked and sounded so good, in fact, that Analysis Releasing, the distributor that Lustig finally settled on, had no idea it was shot on 16mm. Lustig can't say enough about the marketing savvy of Analysis, which was in the process of distributing the equally problematic *Caligula* (1980):

> The advertising created by the U.S. distributor was in your face. It was undeniably perverse. I sat at meetings with these two lunatics at Analysis Films, and I say that with affection because I think both those guys are amazing, Paul Cohen and Bob Kaplan. And these guys would be telling me, honest, to add more shadow in the crotch so it looks like he [the figure on the film's one-sheet] has a hard-on. And I go, "My God, I couldn't have picked a better couple of guys to handle this movie." It was so totally perverse it was amazing. These guys just went for it. They took this movie and threw it in the faces of everybody and said we are coming out with the *Gone With the Wind* of gore.

Maniac was released in January 1981 to unanimously bad reviews. Lustig had a good sense of humor about the whole thing and said to Spinell, who took the *Times* review personally, "Joe, listen, don't get upset about this review from Vincent Canby. Our audience for this movie either lives *on* or *under The New York Times*." The *Los Angeles Times* didn't share Lustig's sense of humor and, in a blatant act of censorship, banned the entire existence of the film in their newspapers. They didn't just ban the ad or decline to review the film, they refused to print its name in the paper. For the theaters in which *Maniac* was playing, the listing cryptically instructed readers to call the theater for information. Seeking to capitalize on the film's notoriety, Analysis plastered posters all over L.A. saying: *Maniac. The film the **Los Angeles Times** refuses to advertise*. It became something of a cause, albeit a minor one, within the film community, which wasn't exactly pleased with the *Times*' stance. William Friedkin even wrote a letter to the paper, chastising them for their attempt to stifle artistic freedom. In the end, the *Times*' tactics failed miserably. If anything, they succeeded in attracting more people eager to see what all the fuss was about.

Maniac is often a tough film to take. It *is* disturbing, unrepentant and gleefully violent. It is also well-crafted, suspenseful, gutsy (no pun intended) and visually striking, especially the remastered prints—the only way this film should be seen—which are available on VHS, laserdisc and DVD. While *Maniac*'s absence of any humor is sometimes seen as tacit approval toward Zito's dirty little habit, never does the film condone or celebrate the murders. It doesn't, however, gloss them over by treating murder as a game, like many of the other slasher films which tried to satisfy both their core audience and the implacable censors. *Maniac* is a far cry away from

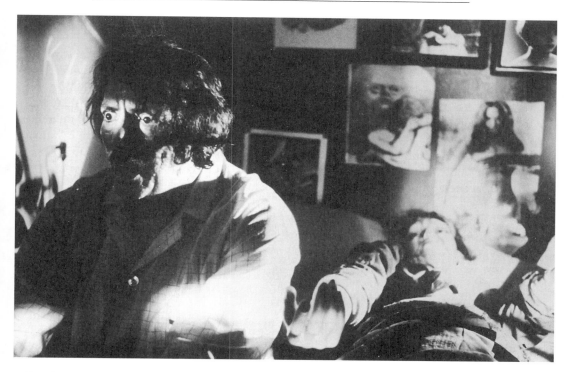

Frank Zito (Joe Spinell) is a deeply disturbed loner who can't break his compulsion for slaying and scalping young women in Bill Lustig's unfairly maligned *Maniac* (1981).

a film such as *Combat Shock* (1986), an exercise in *real* sleaze to which it has been compared. Rather, it is the film that *Taxi Driver* (1976) didn't have the guts to be—a dark examination of psychosis and death on the mean streets of New York City.

In the early '80s, producers John Dunning and Andre Link were running Cinepix, a Canadian production company. They knew that the only way they could compete with the majors was with low-budget exploitation films. They also realized that the horror climate was, as Dunning puts its, "once again ripe for the psychopath." The Motion Picture Association of America was beginning to realize that the slasher film was not a passing fad. It tried to discourage the studios from getting involved in such garbage by drastically cracking down on the amount of on-screen sex and violence. Therefore, the task of supplying such films fell to inde-

pendent producers like Dunning and Link. Both had experience with horror films; they had recently produced David Cronenberg's *Rabid* (1977) and had executive produced William Fruet's disturbing *The House by the Lake* (1976).[5] Since everyone was choosing a holiday as the backdrop for their film, Dunning and Link settled on Valentine's Day.

John Beaird was hired to write the script which eventually became *My Bloody Valentine* (1981) and George Mihalka, who had recently directed a low-budget action film, was slated to direct. Both were relative novices at the time. Dunning and Link then went to Paramount's Frank Mancuso, with whom they had worked the year before on the hysterical summer camp comedy *Meatballs* (1979). As furious as the MPAA was about *Friday the 13th*, Mancuso was not about to pass up another potential cash cow and promised to come take a look at *My Bloody Valentine* once it was finished.

Paramount was trying to keep its hands clean for as long as possible, however, and with only the possibility of a distribution deal, Dunning and Link were forced to solicit outside financing for the film. *My Bloody Valentine* was budgeted between $1.5–2.5 million and was shot between late September and early November of 1980, in and around Nova Scotia's Sydney Mines.

Dunning good-naturedly calls *My Bloody Valentine* a "horrendous shoot." The Sydney Mines were in use at the time and the crew only had a few abandoned mine shafts in which to film. Along with the inherent problems of shooting in a working mine, the production was fraught with other difficulties. In addition to spending $30,000 to repaint a part of the mine which an art director erroneously defaced in an attempt to create a dingy look for the set, the production was threatened with a lawsuit by an artist whose uncredited work is briefly shown in one scene. This minor fiasco cost them $15,000 to settle out of court. One of the more comical on-set stories involves an actor whose driving skills left much to be desired. As Dunning tells it:

> One of our lead actors said he could drive a car. Well, he couldn't drive a car. In Canada, you can drive a car without a license as long as you're on private property. Well, this guy went crazy. He hit another car because he had never driven and injured his foot. He also hit one of our electricians, who went to the hospital. So he [the driver] shows up the next day with a cane and was giving the crew a hard time. The prop man who was in charge of his cane was slowly cutting a half inch off everyday. So the cane was getting shorter. He didn't realize it though so he thought his limp was getting worse, because his back was hunching when he leaned on the cane. Those are the kind of things a crew will do if they want to put you off.

The electrician who was hit eventually sued and the police desperately wanted to arrest the reckless driver, but perhaps the biggest threat to the production came from the locals themselves. Eventually, the actual mine workers got fed up. They worried that the powerful lights which were being used to illuminate

Peter Cowper is Harry Warden, a crazed miner who returns to the small town of Valentine's Bluff to mete out his own brand of justice in George Mihalka's *My Bloody Valentine* (1981).

the mine's dark shafts would somehow cause an explosion and gave the production 24 hours to vacate the premises. Since the film was not done, the production went into "triple golden time"—the film industry's version of overtime—a nightmare for cost-conscious producers and especially devastating to low-budget productions. Mihalka was racing to finish and had not slept in over a day, but as Dunning says, "The result it great ... he did a helluva job."

Mihalka did do a helluva job, as did the rest of the cast and crew, for *My Bloody Valentine* is easily one of the best and most polished slasher films. It is set in the appropriately named small mining town of Valentine's Bluff, where the annual Valentine's Day dance has been resurrected after a 20—year hiatus. While the town's young miners and their girlfriends prepare for the celebration, an insane miner armed with a pickax begins slaughtering the town's unlucky residents. He sends one victim's heart to the mayor and sheriff, accompanied by a prophetic warning instructing them to cancel the dance. The mayor takes the threat seriously, but despite his pleas, a group of young townies decide to hold their own party. His warning unheeded, the miner pays them a visit. In a deliciously sinister open ending, the killer escapes into the belly of the mine.

Paramount released a heavily edited version of *My Bloody Valentine* on February 11, 1981, a few days before Valentine's Day. As Dunning says, the film "was cut to ribbons." After initially screening *My Bloody Valentine* in Canada with some other Paramount executives, Mancuso had left numb, shocked by the graphic and realistic murders which even Dunning admits they may have been a bit "overenthusiastic" about. Jack Valenti was even more incensed and kept demanding that further cuts be made to the film. The version which the MPAA finally approved may be devoid of some of the bloodier scenes but this in no way lessens the film's effectiveness. Mihalka did a masterful job utilizing the claustrophobic confines of the abandoned mine shafts and managed to draw out fairly realistic performances from his young cast. He clearly understands the conventions of the slasher film and shrewdly exploits the natural eeriness of the setting. The scene in which the miner methodically smashes each lamp, plunging the mine into darkness, is one of the most suspenseful in any slasher.

My Bloody Valentine made Paramount close to $6 million, although Dunning insists that the producers "never saw a nickel for the film." He does, however, hold a trump card in the form of six minutes of lost footage which he recently unearthed during an inventory of his office. Paramount has expressed some interested in an unexpurgated director's cut and Dunning is anxious for audiences to see the film as it was meant to be seen—in all its bloody glory. Recently, there have been some rumors about a sequel, logical since *My Bloody Valentine*—with its ambiguous ending—is one of the few slasher films which inherently lends itself to one. Whether Paramount, who has first rights to a sequel, will want to revisit a slasher classic instead of developing new projects remains to be seen.

After *The Texas Chainsaw Massacre*, Tobe Hooper was prematurely anointed the patron saint of gore—despite the fact that *Chainsaw*, while terrifying, was far from gory—an honorary position he had little desire to hold. His follow-up to *Chainsaw*, *Eaten Alive* (1976), a disappointing film about a motel owner who feeds his guests, employees and whomever else he can get his hands on, to his pet crocodile, was a huge flop at the time of its release but has recently begun to receive some undue praise. He then directed the miniseries *'Salem's Lot* (1979), based on

Sylvia (Helene Udy) is surprised by Harry Warden (Peter Cowper) in *My Bloody Valentine* **(1981).**

Stephen King's best-selling novel. Made for TV, *'Salem's Lot* is naturally less graphic than both *Chainsaw* and *Eaten Alive* and was generally well-received by both critics and fans. This stymied those who said that Hooper was only effective when working in some desolate Texas outback-like milieu.

Tucked away on his résumé, between these raw early works and the *Poltergeist* debacle, is *The Funhouse* (1981), a restrained and intelligent slasher-monster movie amalgam.[6] Proving that he can be just as self-conscious as Joe Dante, Brian De Palma and John Carpenter, his fellow "movie brat" contemporaries, Hooper starts *The Funhouse* off with a bang—a double reference to both *Psycho* and *Halloween*. As the film's star, Amy Harper (Elizabeth Berridge), showers in preparation for her upcoming date, a familiar

presence approaches the bathroom. The scene is shown as a point-of-view shot from the two eyeholes of a mask. The curtain is flung away, and the masked knife-wielding fiend drives the blade into her stomach. She screams in terror, as the blade ... bends on contact with her soft flesh. Such is sibling rivalry in suburbia, as Amy's younger brother—mask and rubber knife in hand—makes a beeline out of the bathroom with his livid sister close behind.

But the Harper "funhouse" is only an appetizer for the local carnival which Amy attends with her date, Buzz (Cooper Huckabee), a guy from the wrong side of the tracks, and their two friends, the annoying Liz (Largo Woodruff) and Richie (Miles Chapin). The group takes in the usual carnival staples, including an animal freak show which boasts such oddities as a cow with a cleft palate and a six-legged horse, before Richie comes up with the bright idea to hide out and spend the night in the funhouse.

But their romantic rendezvous is short-lived when they witness the son of the carnival barker (the barker is played by a wonderfully fried Kevin Conway) murder the fortuneteller (Sylvia Miles) because he is unable to perform after paying her for sex. The barker's son, played by mime Wayne Doba, wears a Frankenstein mask to conceal his hideous deformity. The face of this pale, drooling mutant was designed by Rick Baker (and carried out by Craig Reardon), whose effects in *An American Werewolf in London* of the same year raised the bar for monster movie transformations. Once the barker and his son get wind of the group's presence, they

realize there's only one way for them to conceal the crime, and the funhouse is turned into a beeping, whirring, screeching, buzzing, humming house of death.

When only Amy is left alive, she faces off with the monster in a final confrontation. Not nearly as headstrong or effective as most Final Girls, she basically just stands there screaming while the monster manages to electrocute himself, gets caught on a metal ceiling hook and is finally crushed to death between two gigantic cogs in the bowels of the funhouse. As he stands there shrieking, trying in vain to free himself from the gigantic gears, the sheer ferocity of his death throes recalls Leatherface's chain saw ballet in the final scene of *The Texas Chainsaw Massacre*. This scene also showcases Mort Rabinowitz's impressive production

In the first scene of Tobe Hooper's *The Funhouse* (1981)—an homage to both *Psycho* and *Halloween*—Joey (Shawn Carson) terrifies his sister Amy (Elizabeth Berridge) as she showers.

design—the funhouse was completely con- structed on a Florida soundstage—and re- inforces Hooper's talent for authenticating marginalized environments.

Yet despite the savagery of the mon- ster, he is not an altogether unsympathetic creature, a point which Hooper forces by having him wear a Frankenstein mask, but one which was lost on many critics anyway. Like Frankenstein's monster, he is the less- than-human spawn of the film's real vil- lain, the cruel barker (although a strong argument can be made for the four teenagers since they are the ones whose thoughtless actions set the events in mo- tion). Seeking love and affection—no mat- ter how artificial—in the only place avail- able, the monster is more accidentally or impulsively deadly than truly evil. Still, like Frankenstein's Monster, it is impossi- ble for him to fit into "normal" society, even one as self-contained as that of the carnival, and his fate is practically sealed the moment he is revealed to the outside world.

The Funhouse was released on March 13, 1981, and grossed almost $8 million. Although it was distributed by Universal Pictures, a major studio which could afford an extensive publicity campaign, the com- bination of slasher film and classic mon- ster movie never struck a chord with au- diences. It managed to get somewhat lost in the shuffle between the straight slash- ers of the time and films like *An American Werewolf in London*. Like many of Hooper's films, *The Funhouse* was rumored to be a troubled production, with the director constantly clashing with producers. If this is true, and it probably is, this friction is certainly not evident in the finished film. Low-budget to be sure, *The Funhouse* is still a slick-looking work. There were those who admired the restraint and com- plexity which a more polished Hooper brought to the film, while others were sorely disappointed that it lacked anything close to the random mayhem which had become synonymous with the director since *The Texas Chainsaw Massacre*.

ʔ

CHAPTER 7

Campus Killers, Slashing for Laughs and One Human Brain

While producers continued to use *Halloween* as a template for how to make an effective slasher film, the success of *Friday the 13th* had Paramount laughing all the way to the bank. The studio shrugged off the negative publicity it had received from those who thought a major company should pay more heed to the type of product it was promoting. This was a minor nuisance in light of the jaw-dropping profits the film had earned, and once the box office tally was counted, there was never any real doubt that a sequel was in the works.

The task of continuing the *Friday the 13th* saga fell to Steve Miner. Miner had been a production assistant on *The Last House on the Left* and had worked with Sean Cunningham again on both *Here Come the Tigers* and *Manny's Orphans*, before earning an associate producer credit on the original *Friday the 13th*.

In many ways, *Friday the 13th Part 2* is a much better film than its predecessor. It is sometimes assumed that the reason it looks so much more professional than the original is because it had the backing of Paramount, when in fact the studio acquired it as a negative pickup for $2.5 million. Because Miner was intimately familiar with the original, he already had a firm grasp of what needed to be done. Throughout the course of the film, he implements almost every horror cliché—the ringing phone with no one on the other end, the cat jumping through the window, the crazy local prophet of doom, the head-in-the-refrigerator gag—but because he knows exactly when and for how long to use these bits, they never lose their power to shock and delight.

Miner and writer Ron Kurz knew better than to tamper with a successful formula. Consequently, *Friday the 13th Part 2* is less a sequel than a remake of the original. A new group of counselors have arrived to open a camp near the site of the first massacre. But this time they are killed not by Mrs. Voorhees, but by Jason himself, the drowned boy who, in five short years, has grown from a small child into a hulking man. In the film's first scene,

Camp counselors Mark (Tom McBride, in wheelchair), Vickie (Lauren-Marie Taylor), Paul (John Furey) and Ginny (Amy Steel) huddle around a campfire to hear the legend of Jason in Steve Miner's *Friday the 13th Part 2* (1981).

Miner surprised many by having Jason kill off Alice, the lone survivor from the original. This set the stage for the "anything goes" mentality of the rest of the film in which Jason kills, among others, a paraplegic and a couple in the throes of lovemaking. This lovemaking scene is the source for a frequent accusation that *Friday the 13th Part 2* is a blatant imitation (read rip-off) of Mario Bava's *Twitch of the Death Nerve*. While there are some striking similarities between the films, especially in the murder sequences, even if Miner was keenly aware of, and influenced by Bava's film, it was more of an homage than anything else. After all, the *Friday the 13th* series does not need any help in coming up with creative ways to kill people.

   Friday the 13th Part 2 was released on April 30, 1981, to millions of awaiting fans.

Somewhat embarrassed by what had slipped past them a year before, the MPAA was ready this time, scissors in hand. The cuts "suggested" by Valenti's organization reached such ludicrous extremes that, in a rather funny slip-up, the back of the film's VHS cassette box, which any impressionable youngster could get a-hold of, depicts a scene deemed too graphic for the film itself. *Friday the 13th Part 2* made over $21 million, not nearly as much as the original, but enough to suggest that the series was far from over.

   All too often dismissed as a *Friday the 13th* imitation, *The Burning* lays claim to the most impressive collection of future talent ever assembled in a slasher film. It stars Jason Alexander as a wise-cracking counselor, sporting a full head of hair and far removed from his character of *Seinfeld*'s neurotic George Costanza, and Brian

Paul (John Furey) and Ginny (Amy Steel) make their way back to camp, mistakenly thinking that they have killed Jason Voorhees once and for all in *Friday the 13th Part 2* (1981).

Backer, even more unsuccessful with women than he was a year later in *Fast Times at Ridgemont High* (1982). Both Holly Hunter and Fisher Stevens have smaller roles as campers. Jack Sholder, who would go on to helm *Alone in the Dark* (1982), *A Nightmare on Elm Street 2: Freddy's Revenge* (1985) and *Wishmaster 2: Evil Never Dies* (1999), cut the film, while Tom Savini, who chose to work on *The Burning* instead of returning to the *Friday the 13th* series for *Part 2*, did the special makeup effects. *The Burning* was produced by Harvey Weinstein and written by his younger brother, Bob. While today the duo is best known as the founders of Miramax, the most successful independent production company in history, back in 1981 they were busy racking up slain campers, not Oscars.

The Burning begins with a prologue at Camp Blackfoot, where a group of campers play a prank on Cropsy, the despised caretaker. The joke goes horribly awry when Cropsy accidentally knocks over the burning skull which was placed on his window, setting himself ablaze and disfiguring him forever. Miraculously, he survives, and after five years of hospitalization and unsuccessful skin grafts, he is released back into society. He returns to the nearby Camp Stonewater (camp Blackfoot was closed after "the burning") to get his revenge. With his trusty garden shears he succeeds in depleting the ranks of campers before being killed—immolated again, then axed in the face in case there was any question—by one of the original pranksters, who is now a counselor.

The Burning was shot in upstate New York in the late summer of 1980 for approximately $1.5 million. It is an extremely

After some moonlight skinny dipping—a no-no in the slasher film—Karen (Carolyn Houli-han) is surprised by Cropsy (Lou David) in *The Burning* (1981).

entertaining entry which deviates from the typical slasher, in part, by making the Final Girl a man (Brian Matthews). As one of the adolescent pranksters, he bears some responsibility for the subsequent massacre, an interesting plot point whose significance is unfortunately obscured by Cropsy's indiscriminate murders.

The film's highlight, a terrifying attack on a group of campers who are trying to paddle a makeshift raft to safety, was unforgivably butchered to secure an "R" rating. Among Savini's effects which were cut (no pun intended) is the particularly effective shot of Cropsy's shears snipping off Woodstock's (Fisher Stevens) fingers. These gruesome touches have never been officially restored; both the U.S. theatrical and video release leave out the footage, a

more unfortunate casualty than the obnoxious campers who meet their gruesome end in this scene.

John Dunning and Andre Link's second famed slasher production, *Happy Birthday to Me*, was actually filmed immediately before *My Bloody Valentine*, although it was released three months later, in May 1981. *Happy Birthday to Me* is a complicated and confusing film. The plot, which is often hard to follow, involves a teenage girl, Virginia Wainwright (Melissa Sue Anderson), who sustained a terrible head injury in a car accident which killed her mother. Having undergone apparently successful, albeit experimental brain surgery, she is admitted back to a prestigious boarding school. A series of six of the most bizarre murders you will ever see

Cropsy, the horribly burned killer in Tony Maylam's *The Burning* (1981), an early production from the Weinstein brothers, approaches the hiding place of one potential victim.

follows (or so the promotional ads promise), including one involving a shish kebab skewer. Although we see Virginia commit the murders, in *Happy Birthday to Me* nothing is what it seems, and the true killer is revealed in an entertaining, however unlikely, climax.

The genesis of *Happy Birthday to Me* was similar to that of *My Bloody Valentine*. "We sat around and brainstormed for awhile and came up with the idea that it should be a birthday because no one had done a horror film with birthdays," said Dunning. Signing J. Lee Thompson was a minor coup, since the director had done such classic films as *The Guns of Navarone* (1961) and *Cape Fear* (1962). On a whim, Dunning called up Thompson's agent and asked if Thompson would be interested in

coming up to Canada to shoot a thriller. As it turned out, Thompson was fascinated by the story and, since he had never directed a true horror film, he took it as a challenge.

Dunning has nothing but praise for his director, whom he calls, "a great guy … one of the nicest men I ever met." Instead of looking at the film with disdain, as a blemish on an otherwise impressive career, Thompson was the consummate professional. He had editing experience and, like Hitchcock, cut the film in his head, so there was no need for the normal amount of pick-up shots. "With J. Lee, I never had to ask for anything," remembers Dunning. "The film cut like butter."

Nothing illustrates Thompson's proficiency and experience better than the

The past comes slowly creeping back to a disturbed Virginia Wainwright (Melissa Sue Anderson) in *Happy Birthday to Me* **(1981).**

film's large dance scene which was shot at McGill University in Toronto. To this day, Dunning is still amazed how well Thompson managed to pull off the feat:

"When they did that dance sequence, [Thompson] was setting up and I got a call. It was ten to five and not one shot was made and we had to get out at six o'clock. J. Lee had spent the whole day setting up the shot. And I got there and I rushed down and said, "J. Lee, we only have an hour and a half and have a whole scene to shoot. There's four pages!" He says, "John, don't worry. I'm doing it in one shot. We'll be out on time." I said, "J. Lee, how can you do that?" But he tracked all through the dance on a crane and did the whole thing and got out. Boy, I was amazed. I'm used to younger guys taking all day to do little bits and pieces and he just banged it out."

If Thompson was largely responsible for what Dunning calls "a good shoot, one of the more comfortable ones," then a contemporary of his, actor Glenn Ford, was responsible for some of the tensest moments. The irascible Ford was a veteran of Old Hollywood. He had been in the business for over 40 years and was best-known for his roles in *The Big Heat* (1953) and *Blackboard Jungle* (1955), as well as some lesser-known Westerns in the '40s and '50s. In *Happy Birthday to Me,* he plays Virginia's avuncular psychiatrist. While Dunning can now look back and laugh at the actor's antics, they were undoubtedly not as funny during the production:

The stories with Glenn Ford, oh, boy, they were terrific. One time Glenn punched out our second assistant director. I got a call while I was having supper at home. J. Lee called me and said, "The shoot's down. Glenn is in his dressing room and won't come out and the second AD has been hit and he's called the police and is having Glenn up for assault." So I ran over to the set and I found out what had happened. This second had called a meal break right in the middle of a shot with Glenn, and Glenn had been working himself up for this. He just blew a stack and punched the guy.

So I got him to calm down but Glenn still wouldn't come out until the second AD apologized. So he was locked up with his latest girlfriend and I said, "Glenn, will you come out?" And he said, "No, John, I won't come out until he apologizes." So I went back to the guy and I said, "Look, you have to bloody well apologize. You did make a mistake. You should have let him run the scene." He was a young kid, so he said, "All right, I'm sorry, Glenn." Then Glenn came out and we finished.

Another time, while shooting at McGill, a bystander whistled at Ford's wife. Infuriated, Ford refused to leave his limousine until the police removed the guy from the premises.

Although he was the most notorious, Ford wasn't the only celebrity involved with the film. For ten seasons, Melissa Sue Anderson had played Mary Ingalls on television's beloved family drama *Little House on the Prairie*. Dunning, however, was looking to cast against type, and Anderson's role as the disturbed Virginia Wainwright in *Happy Birthday to Me* was a huge departure from the kind of character audiences were accustomed to seeing her play. Today, this type of casting is not uncommon, and television actresses in hit series, such as Neve Campbell and Jennifer Love Hewitt in Fox's *Party of Five*, have made their move to the big screen courtesy of slasher films.

Happy Birthday to Me, which cost over $3 million to make, was an exceptionally expensive slasher film. It wasn't just the salaries of Thompson and Ford

which were responsible for the inflated budget, but the magnificent special effects, which Dunning says "cost an arm and a leg." The most impressive sequence is easily the "bridge jump," in which cars are launched over an opening draw bridge in an especially dangerous variation of "chicken." Dunning describes the filming:

> We got some stunt guys to come up from Hollywood to do this. There was a little town in New York that would let us use the lift bridge. The bridge man had to lift it at exactly the same time, otherwise there was an imbalance. The first time we did the stunt, the stunt guy roars over but the other arm lifted ahead of it. And he smashed right into the lifting part. Totaled the bloody car. Broke his ankle and they took him to the hospital. An hour later he comes back in plaster and insists on doing the stunt again. These guys, you have to take your hat off to them.

When the film was completed, Columbia Pictures expressed strong interest, based mainly on Thompson's involvement. They made such a good offer that Dunning and Link sold the film outright and were able to make an immediate profit. Although Paramount had enormous success with both *Friday the 13th* and *My Bloody Valentine*, they were being constantly harassed by the MPAA and were in no position to make a serious bid for the film. Because of Thompson's stature, *Happy Birthday to Me* was not subjected to the same scrutiny. It was released virtually uncut and managed to scare up $3 million in its first week of release, proving that a once great director still had a few tricks up his sleeve.

Hell Night, a fairly restrained slasher film which takes place during the final (and traditionally wildest) night of a fraternity or sorority initiation, benefits from the experience of a couple of horror veterans. It was executive produced by Irwin Yablans and stars Linda Blair, who will be

A far cry from her role as Mary Ingalls on *Little House on the Prairie*, in *Happy Birthday to Me* (1981) Melissa Sue Anderson plays Virginia Wainwright, a victim of a traumatic car accident who just may be responsible for a series of gruesome murders. Here, in the film's final scene, her father (Lawrence Dean) learns the unspeakable truth.

forever remembered as Regan, the possessed pea soup—vomiting girl from *The Exorcist*.

Hell Night was directed by Tom DeSimone, who had made his debut with the 1977 film *Chatterbox*, a low-budget, adult exploitation picture about a woman who possesses a talking vagina.[1]

DeSimone developed his love for cinema at an early age. When he was ten years old, he was stricken with rheumatic fever and was confined to bed for several months. To boost his spirits, his father bought him a film projector and DeSimone would spend hours in bed watching various cartoons and movies. He started making his own films as a teenager and studied dramatics at Emerson College. After completing his master work at

UCLA, DeSimone worked as an editor and cinematographer on a variety of extremely low-budget projects.

At a New Year's Eve party, DeSimone met Bruce Cohn Curtis, who went on to produce *Chatterbox*. It was a successful collaboration, and DeSimone expressed his interest in eventually directing a horror film. A few years later, DeSimone received a call from Curtis, who had a script called *Hell Night* which was written by Randy Feldman and had Linda Blair attached. Curtis had worked with Blair on the 1974 television movie *Born Innocent*, which had received a great deal of publicity—much of it negative—for its intense broomstick-rape scene. Although Blair was skeptical of doing another horror film after *The Exorcist* and *The Exorcist II: The*

Heretic (1977), she was looking for work and finally agreed to star in the film.

Hell Night follows the titular ordeal of four pledges—the smallest and only co-ed pledge class I've ever seen—who are locked in an old abandoned mansion overnight. According to the legend, Raymond Garth, the family patriarch and last resident of Garth Manor, slaughtered his deformed family before committing suicide. As the pledges soon find out, not only is the homicidal Garth very much alive, but his youngest son, Andrew Garth, has also survived. One by one, the Garths kill both the pledges and the mischievous fraternity brothers (and one sister) who have remained at the house to try and frighten the pledges with elaborate practical jokes. The lone survivor, Blair, who

is well prepared to handle the ghoulish patriarch—having escaped the clutches of Lucifer himself eight years earlier—impales her adversary on a razor-sharp wrought-iron fence, effectively ending the Garth line forever.

Except for the few scenes for which sets were built, *Hell Night* was shot in two locations.[2] The exterior of Garth Manor was shot in Redlands, California. The owner of the mansion had just died and the town was in the process of turning his home into a museum. Since town officials refused to grant the crew entry into the mansion, they were forced to shoot the interiors in a Pasadena home which was inhabited at the time. The owners, however, allowed the crew to come in and redecorate the house. This was perfect for DeSimone, who had always envisioned a strong Gothic element, evidenced by his decision to combine the traditional Greek hell night with an old-fashioned costume party:

I wanted a classic Gothic look. I don't like these horror films where people are walking around haunted houses wearing jeans and T-shirts. So we threw our heads together and I said I wanted Linda in a Gothic kind of wardrobe. And we came up with the idea to make the hell night party a costume party. And that way we were able to have everyone in those kinds of costumes that suited their personality.

Hell Night was filmed in a little over four weeks in the late fall-early winter of 1980. It was originally budgeted at approximately $1 million but the grueling shoot of six-day weeks—which went through Thanksgiving, Christmas and even New Year's—ended up going nearly $400,000

After battling Satan himself in *The Exorcist*, Linda Blair should have no problem with a family of deformed killers in Tom DeSimone's *Hell Night* (1981).

Denise (Suki Goodwin) and Marti (Linda Blair) prepare for their "Hell Night" initiation—a night in Garth Manor.

over. DeSimone remembers he and Blair spending Thanksgiving on the set, sitting in steel folding chairs and eating turkey off of paper plates. The first two weeks at Redlands, which were night shoots, were especially difficult. The entire crew was housed at a local Howard Johnson. Although they were supposed to sleep during the day to be ready for their 4 P.M. to 6 A.M. shoot, anybody who has ever worked nights on a film knows how physically draining this can be. You're exhausted during production but when the work day is finally over early in the morning it's nearly impossible to get a good night's sleep. To make matters worse, DeSimone's script was stolen during the first few days of shooting. Gone were his copious script notes detailing specific

camera angles and cast direction. It was months of hard work down the drain. So each day, instead of getting some well deserved sleep, DeSimone was forced to return to his room to try and remember what he had previously written. There were also the technical difficulties inherent in night shooting. In keeping with the plot of *Hell Night*, which makes a point to emphasis that Garth Manor has no electricity, only candlelight and the characters' flashlights provide any illumination. Cinematographer Mac Ahlberg, whose diverse career includes *Chained Heat* (1983), *Striking Distance* (1993), *The Brady Bunch Movie* (1995) as well as various episodes of *The Wonder Years* (1988–93), was forced to use a special lens suited for low-light situations. Unfortunately, this lens made the film more susceptible to sunspots which are apparent in a few of the scenes.

In comparison to its contemporaries, *Hell Night* is rather tame. Although DeSimone had no desire to make a film which relied more heavily on gore than thrills, he was also well aware that the MPAA was getting tougher and that the explicit murders which were shown in earlier slasher films had no chance of making it to the screen in *Hell Night*:

> We knew we were making a slasher film, however, we wanted to get away mostly from the gore and try to scare them with scares, rather than repulse them with guts. A lot of our murders, although they're kind of horrific, you don't really see that much. There isn't that much bloodletting in our picture.

DeSimone does express some frustration that *Hell Night*'s first murder— a graphic and elaborately constructed decapitation—was nixed by the producers before it even got to the censors. In the current version of the film, May (Jenny Neumann) has her head lopped off while waiting to scare the pledges. Almost immediately after the blade makes contact with her neck, there is a cut to another scene. DeSimone originally wanted the camera to linger on her head, held up by the killer, while her body collapses to the floor. Her eyes and mouth would remain open, as her brain would not yet have processed the shock of having its head separated from its body. The effect—which was extremely painful for Neumann, who was required to insert her neck through a faux wall at an unnatural angle—worked all too well. It was gruesome, shocking—and cut from the final print.

Hell Night's only sex scene, which was shot on New Year's Eve when everybody was preoccupied with the holiday, was a point of contention for both DeSimone and Vincent Van Patten, the actor who plays Seth, a good-looking, easygoing surfer. Apparently, Van Patten wasn't easygoing enough. He abruptly announced that he wouldn't do a sex scene with Suki Goodwin, the Lolitaish Euroslut who, in the film's longest running joke, keeps referring to Van Patten as Wes, not Seth. Goodwin was willing to do the scene topless, but Van Patten, who was worried about upholding his family's reputation, balked.[3]

Most slasher films had at least some nudity, and DeSimone knew that the audience, comprised mostly of teenagers, craved sex almost as much as violence. Van Patten won out in the end; his scene with Goodwin, including a goofy analogy

between surfing and sex, is as tame as they come.

(DeSimone was faced with the daunting task of creating an effective slasher film with little on-screen violence and no nudity, shot predominately at night on a tight budget while missing his script, and for the most part, he succeeds.) *Hell Night* didn't revolutionize the slasher film, but to this day it remains one of the classiest films of the cycle.

Made at exactly the same time as *Hell Night*, *Graduation Day*, an even lower-budget slasher, was neither bankrolled nor picked up by a major studio. The film, however, is virtually indistinguishable from the other studio-acquired slashers of the time.

Marti (Linda Blair) discovers the body of her fellow pledge Jeff (Peter Barton) in *Hell Night* (1981).

Graduation Day was conceived by writer-director-producer Herb Freed, whose circuitous career route makes him one of the most fascinating directors of the slasher film. Freed studied to become a rabbi at the Jewish Theological Seminary in New York City but left the rabbinate after only three years. He also dabbled in acting and dance, and worked as a choreographer. He figured the best way to make a living, however, was in advertising, and became a TV producer at BBDO before founding his own production company a year and a half later. Success and money never interested Freed, and although he worked on a variety of prestigious accounts—Pepsi, Revlon, Clairol—he yearned for a career where he could make a meaningful difference in people's lives. In the early '70s, he moved to California with his wife, the talented Broadway actress Anne Marisse.

Freed expresses no fondness for the horror genre. In fact, his attitude toward it is just short of loathing. In 1977, he had just finished directing *Haunts*, originally called *The Veil*, an underrated picture with May Britt and Cameron Mitchell, scored by Pino Donaggio, which Freed calls a "beautiful, sensitive film." It was, however, a lean time for restrained horror films, and *Haunts* didn't do as well as he expected. Freed's investors encouraged him to stay with horror for his next attempt, *Beyond Evil* (1980). When success again eluded him, Freed and Marisse decided to immerse themselves in the genre. They conducted an experiment to better understand how and why horror films worked. The two would screen films and Marisse would use a stopwatch to record the time between the killings, convinced that the secret to success lay in a specific formula.

Through *Haunts*, Freed became friendly with David Baughn, a local distributor. The two formed a partnership and, together with Marisse, they hammered out the script for *Graduation Day*, which was shot over the course of four weeks at a Los Angeles high school during the Christmas holiday of 1980. Without the backing of a major studio, Baughn and Freed decided the best way to finance the film was to go to various theater chains and obtain advances based on commitments to deliver a finished product. Since *Graduation Day* was essentially underwritten by the theaters themselves, they had an added incentive to insure that it played well.

Graduation Day opens at a high school track meet. After a lengthy, rather pointless montage of the event, star runner Laura Ramstead (Ruth Ann Llorens) drops dead from a freak medical condition in full view of hundreds of horrified onlookers. The film then jumps forward, to graduation day. Laura's sister Anne (Patch MacKenzie) has returned from a stint in the military to get to the bottom of Laura's death. At the same time, a killer has begun knocking off Laura's former teammates, right under the nose of an oblivious principal (Michael Pataki), a school security guard (Virgil Frye) and an apathetic detective (Carmen Argenziano) hired by the missing teenagers' parents. Anne eventually exposes the killer: It's Kevin (E. Danny Murphy), Laura's old boyfriend who was soon to be her fiancé, and who, in a nod to *Psycho*, has been keeping Laura's preserved corpse in his house. He blames Laura's death on her browbeating coach (Christopher George) and fellow teammates, but is killed by Anne before he can complete his grisly mission.

Like *Hell Night*, the bloodletting in *Graduation Day* is fairly restrained; the killings are far more creative than graphic, since Freed was especially fascinated by coming up with novel ways to kill people:

> We set about to find the most grotesque kinds of killing that one could do. So we

came up with a decapitation which upon reflection is scary as hell. When I saw the reaction of the audience on opening night, it scared the hell out of me. That's why I've never done another horror movie since. But when you're just doing it, you're involved in the process; it's such a fascinating process, making the latex masks and all that kind of stuff.

Freed, who was unaware of the slasher boom around him, manages to inject a few touches of originality into *Graduation Day*.[4] In an early scene, his subjective camera, already synonymous with the killer's point of view, further calls attention to the filmmaking process. As a victim's throat is slashed, blood spurts onto the camera lens, jolting the audience out of the story and actively reminding them that they are indeed watching a film. The murders in *Graduation Day* are not of the garden variety; one unfortunate jock is skewered after catching a football connected to a spear, while a pole-vaulter is impaled on a bed of spikes. For this sinister death, Freed was inspired by an actual Vietnamese booby trap. Perhaps *Graduation Day*'s most radical departure from the slasher formula is its depiction of the Final Girl. Like most Final Girls, Anne ultimately bests the killer, and like most Final Girls she embodies traditional "masculine" qualities, but, as an outsider returning home, Anne is not really part of the core group. Nor is she ever the direct focus of the killer's rampage. In fact, she is the one who actively seeks out the killer. In this way, her motivation, not the killer's, becomes the impetus of the film.

For the film's premiere at the Pacific Theater on Hollywood Boulevard, dozens of kids were sent out in caps and gowns with badges that read: **I Survived** *Graduation Day*. Thanks to Baughn's distribution experience, *Graduation Day* opened in nearly 200 theaters around Southern California, an astounding number considering that he and Freed alone were responsible for the film's theatrical release. Eventually, the film was sold to a few foreign territories and Columbia quickly nabbed the video rights.

Graduation Day is an above-average slasher, but more impressive than the actual film was Freed's ingenuity in getting it made. The fact that he managed to finance, produce, direct and distribute it himself is a tribute to his talent as both a

In Herb Freed's *Graduation Day* (1981), somebody has gone to great lengths to make sure the school's star pole-vaulter gets the point.

businessman and filmmaker. Although it was made at the height of the slasher craze, *Graduation Day* is not as famous as its contemporaries, but for Herb Freed, who never liked horror much in the first place, this isn't such a bad thing.

Critics are often fond of saying that the reason parodies of the slasher film don't work is because the slasher film—with all its excesses and silliness—unconsciously parodies itself. What they fail to consider is that when any genre, from the Western to the musical, proliferates rapidly within a fairly brief time period, the very conventions which define that genre are then thrust into the public eye. But an audience's familiarly with the genre should never be mistaken for self-reference by the film itself.

If parodies of the slasher film don't work, it is for the same reason that parodies of anything don't work—they're just not funny.

Student Bodies was released in August 1981, when the slasher film was at its peak. From its opening shot, which celebrates the most infamous slasher dates—Halloween, Friday the 13th and of course, Jamie Lee Curtis' birthday—it's clear that *Student Bodies* is not about to hold anything back. When it misses, it misses big, but when it hits, which is fortunately more often than not, the results are hysterical.

The film takes place at a typical American high school, where a maniac known only as "The Breather" has been killing sexually active students in ways far too gruesome to describe: by paper clip, eraser and, the most hideous of all, by eggplant. Within the film's first minute, it has effectively spoofed not only *Halloween* and *Friday the 13th*, but *When a Stranger Calls* and *Black Christmas* as well. Interestingly enough, it is the hilarious one-liners and fearless performances by the perfectly cast actors which are most effective. The running gags—the killer constantly stepping

in gum and the number of each victim flashing on screen upon the discovery of their body—tend to grow old quickly. While the entire cast is marvelous, it is Carl Jacobs as the unbalanced school psychiatrist Dr. Sigmund who really steals the show. Because the slasher film was already a fringe genre, *Student Bodies* was nowhere near as successful as other spoofs such as *Blazing Saddles* (1974) and *Airplane!* It was, however, the best of its kind, a cut above such liked-minded films as *Wacko* (1981), *National Lampoon's Class Reunion* (1982) and *Pandemonium* (1982).

By mid-1980, even before the release of *Friday the 13th*, producers were salivating for the next *Halloween*. Ruth Avergon, a stage director turned film producer, and her partner Larry Babb were shopping ideas around to various distributors. Naturally, most of them wanted something in the same vein as *Halloween* to attract the teenage audience, so Babb came up with, as Avergon puts it, "the idea of a guy running around Boston decapitating people." Avergon, however, wanted to make a horror film with some class to it. She was a trained pianist who cut her teeth writing sketch comedy before breaking into the film industry through a job at the Boston Film Board. After some research into the headhunters of Papua New Guinea, she turned Babb's idea into her first feature screenplay, *Night School*.

At Wendell College, a Boston night school, a leather-clad motorcyclist has been leaving the severed heads of his victims in different bodies of water (a duck pond, a bucket, etc.). Because of the ritualistic nature of the killings, suspicion falls on a charismatic anthropology professor (Drew Snyder) who has a habit of sleeping with his students. Rachel Ward, in her first starring role, plays his diligent assistant who just may know a bit more about the murders than she lets on.

Night School's $1.2 million budget was raised through private investors. Lorimar then acquired the film in a negative pickup deal, with Paramount releasing it domestically. It was shot entirely in Boston, except for an additional ending tacked on in New York, during a five-week stretch in the bitterly cold spring of 1980.

Although the film's original director walked off the production due to "major creative differences," his departure paved the way for two of *Night School*'s biggest assets. The first was Rachel Ward, who stepped into the starring role when the original actress, who had close ties to the former director, quickly followed suit. Ward was discovered at a New York City casting call by Avergon, who initially conceived the part as being played by an actress with a look entirely different from the tall, dark English beauty. In the end, Ward's talent and charisma prevailed, and her presence brings a sense of exotic danger to the role. The second was Kenneth Hughes, the veteran British director best-known for the beloved family classic, *Chitty Chitty Bang Bang* (1968). "We just called around and Ken Hughes happened to be available," said Avergon, who remained close friends with Hughes until his death in April 2001.

> Ken had enormous energy.... I just loved working with him. He was a joy to work with. He really knew what he was doing. There wasn't a lot of second guessing. He knew what shots had to be taken for our budget. The production value that he gave us, along with Mark Irwin [cinematographer], was wonderful. I thought they really captured a nice look for the film.

Along with *My Bloody Valentine*, *Night School* is one of the slickest looking slashers and appears far more expensive than it was. It practically drips with atmosphere and makes impressive use of Boston's stately Beacon Hill. According to Avergon:

> We wanted a certain look for it. We had a wonderful setting; Beacon Hill is just incredible. We had done a lot of location scouting beforehand so we knew the look we wanted for the film. And we wanted to juxtapose this elegant, gorgeous Old World look with this horrible thing that was going on. That was very much part of the design of the film. I think the combination of Ken and Mark Irwin [cinematographer] being extremely fast and good enabled us to get what we wanted.

In sharp contrast to its aesthetic beauty, *Night School*'s murder sequences are especially violent, a fact which did not go unnoticed by those who find every female death misogynistic. The camera never shrinks from the victim's pain and tends to linger a bit longer on their death throes than is usual in most slashers. *Night School* sidestepped drastic MPAA cuts by focusing on the victims' faces rather than the wound, unconsciously making the killings all the more unnerving.

Although a female scribe working in the slasher film was a rarity, Avergon was not trying to make a statement either in the choice of the victims or in the gender of the killer. Despite the anatomical impossibilities of the helmeted killer actually being played by Ward herself, by the end of the film there is never any doubt that she is responsible for the murders.[5] Even this twist of a female killer, however, was used more for shock value than for any relevant social commentary.[6]

In fact, no one was more surprised by the backlash against a homicidal female than Avergon. "It was only after the film was done that that even occurred to me," she explains. "To me this was such a fantasy. It was like me standing in the hallway behind the door and yelling *boo*. It didn't occur to me that anybody would take this thing seriously."

In Kenneth Hughes' *Night School* (1981), a leather-clad motorcyclist relieves co-eds of their heads. A rather grim slasher, *Night School* was a far cry from Hughes' best-known film, *Chitty Chitty Bang Bang* (1968).

Night School was released on September 11, 1981, just in time for the fall semester, and quickly shot to the top of *Variety*'s box office chart. It won an award at the Avoriaz Film Festival in France, putting it in the distinguished company of other winners such as David Lynch's *The Elephant Man* (1980), *Fade to Black* and *The Howling*. After *Night School*, Hughes retired from directing, having capped his career with a quality, however underappreciated, slasher film. Avergon continued writing screenplays—a few of which were optioned but never produced—and made two documentaries about football for the Video Sports Network.

How much of an introduction is necessary for a film whose video distributors trumpeted its release with a contest where

people had to guess the weight of a human brain preserved in a glass jar?

What celluloid atrocities could be so revolting as to warrant the film's British video distributor being jailed for six months for releasing a version which was 60 seconds longer than the BBFC approved version?

Romano Scavolini's *Nightmare* (released on video as *Nightmares in a Damaged Brain*) opened in New York City on October 23, 1981, on the very same streets on which the film's seriously disturbed protagonist with a nasty homicidal habit roams. Before *Nightmare*, the American slasher film had fallen into a comfortable rut. Always somewhat formulaic, the slasher now seemed reluctant to push the envelope, content to trot out a host of young good-looking actors, place them in an identifiable situation—prom night, graduation, fraternity hell night—and then have them killed in ways which were becoming less and less interesting. Some would even say that the slasher film had grown soft. Then came *Nightmare*, a film which had no financial expectations, no studio to appease and, most of all, nothing to lose.

For David Jones, a young New York broker who had made a small fortune on the gold market, *Nightmare* (then titled *Dark Games*) was the perfect vehicle for his newly formed company, Goldmine Productions. If it made money, it would be just another success story in his rapidly expanding portfolio; if not, the $400,000 it cost to make could be used as a tax write-off. *Dark Games* was conceived by Italian filmmaker Romano Scavolini, who had worked as a freelance photographer in Vietnam and had made numerous short films and documentaries in Italy. He was inspired by an article he read in *The New York Times* about how the CIA had been using schizophrenics as guinea pigs for a series of drug experiments. Scavolini then took this disturbing premise and used it as the plot of *Nightmare*: George Tatum (Baird Stafford), a psychotic inmate of a New York City mental institution who is haunted by a gruesome nightmare, escapes and travels to Florida to track down his ex-wife and young son, leaving a trail of bloody corpses in his wake.

Nightmare's most notorious scene—as well as its greatest achievement—is Tatum's reoccurring nightmare which is shown in multiple fragmented flashbacks throughout the film. After Tatum's death at the hand of his son C.J. (C.J. Cooke), the entire flashback is played out and we learn the reason for his madness. As a child, Tatum came home from school and surprised his parents who were engaged in some light bondage sex play. Something snapped, and he decapitated his mother

before burying the ax in his father's skull. This bloody massacre, shot with two different cameras, took an entire day to film. As disturbing as it is—and believe me, a writhing headless body spurting blood while still straddling her lover *is* disturbing—Scavolini took tremendous care in planning the scene, even going so far as to put plastic supports behind the fake head so the ax's impact would provide a greater jolt. His insistence on realism throughout the film, which includes numerous shots of gurgling wounds, was much appreciated by gore fans.

These grisly but brilliant effects were a matter of much contention which, surprisingly, had nothing to do with their explicitness. They are the source of a major dispute between Scavolini, who credits the film's effects to Tom Savini, and Savini, who categorically denies ever working on the film. What makes the situation so strange is that the "argument" is gentlemanly. In fact, Scavolini insists that Savini's denial is a tribute to his professional courtesy. This issue has been well-documented in two excellent interviews, one with Savini and one with Scavolini, conducted by Luca M. Palmerini and Gaetano Mistretta for their book on Italian horror, *Spaghetti Nightmares*. It has been so well-documented, in fact, that there is no way the situation can be construed as a simple misunderstanding. Unfortunately, the one undeniable fact is that someone must be lying.

According to Savini, in the early stages of the project, when it was still known as *Dark Games*, he was approached to do the special effects. However, no one ever followed up with him and he went off to work on George Romero's *Creepshow* (1982). When *Nightmare* was released, he discovered that the effects were credited to him. Although he threatened to sue, the producers asked him to first take a look at the finished film before deciding whether or not to remove his credit. But quality wasn't the issue. Savini didn't want anybody capitalizing on his name, even after the producers offered him a substantial fee. In the end, Savini never went forward with his lawsuit. Nor did the producers keep their word and remove his name. For even today, *Nightmare*'s opening credits still read: Makeup by Tom Savini.

Scavolini has a drastically different version of the story. He maintains that Savini was not only on set, but closely supervised most of the effects. The original effects man on *Nightmare* was Lester Lorraine, the person to whom Savini credits the work and who tragically took his own life soon after the film was released. Lorraine's work was excellent, so good in fact that the producers made a decision to showcase these effects. They also called in a resident expert, Savini, who could act as a supervisor. By this time, Savini had already become something of a star in his own right. In order to generate more publicity, the producers wanted to exploit his involvement, but out of fairness to Lorraine, Savini downplayed his contribution to the film to the point of disavowing it.

Whoever was responsible for the special effects, whether it was Savini or the late Lester Lorraine, can take comfort in knowing that they were a big reason, if not *the* reason, the film was such a success. This is not, however, to discount Scavolini's direction. Through all the gore and gristle he manages to create a few incredibly suspenseful sequences. The best of them is when Tatum's ex-wife (Sharon Smith) and her lover (Mik Cribben) are taking Polaroids of her house and notice a strange figure in the window. Is it a shadow? Their eyes playing tricks on them? Or just an insane ex-husband? There is also a beautifully composed shot in the flashback of the mother bending down to reveal the young ax-wielding Tatum behind her. This same shot was used just as effectively by Dario Argento a year later in *Tenebrae*.

Scavolini never again made a film which came close to *Nightmare*. As easy as it is to dismiss the film as simple exploitative trash, *Nightmare* is not the mindless film it is often made out to be. It was a backlash against the "safe" slasher, where audiences went in expecting to be scared but never believing they would be witness to something truly horrifying. Films like *Maniac* and *Nightmare* proved that the slasher film was still the bad boy of cinema and seemed to delight in their assertion that any horror, no matter how deviant, could be realistically translated to the screen.

After the success of *Halloween*, the question became not *if*, but *when*, there would be a sequel. Although it took a full three years for *Halloween II* (1981) to reach theaters, the horror climate was such that producers were not yet compelled to churn out a sequel even as the first film was still playing. John Carpenter was grateful for the exposure which *Halloween* had brought him, but he was also afraid of being pigeonholed as exclusively a "horror director," and wisely decided to hire Rick Rosenthal, a young director whose short film *The Toyer* had impressed him. He didn't relinquish all control, however. He and Debra Hill not only co-wrote the screenplay but opted to stay on as producers.

Halloween II begins immediately after the first film ends or—more accurately, during its conclusion, as *Halloween*'s climactic scene is replayed during the first few minutes of the sequel.[8] Laurie Strode (Jamie Lee Curtis) is transported to the local hospital with Michael Myers in hot pursuit. But first, Myers stops off at the home of an elderly couple long enough to steal a kitchen knife. Not to be outdone by Carpenter's cinematic references—in *Halloween* the characters watched *The*

Thing—Rosenthal, an American Film Institute graduate, has Romero's *Night of the Living Dead* playing on the couple's television. Donald Pleasence returns as Dr. Loomis, Michael's manic psychiatrist who spends most of the movie chomping the scenery and trying to convince anyone who will listen that the carnage is far from over.

Rosenthal's decision to set the majority of the film in the hospital makes for some queasy scenes of needles piercing veins, eyes and temples, but one wonders why the place is conspicuously devoid of both patients and staff, aside from a small group of nooky-minded nurses who are knocked off in short order. Surprisingly, until *Halloween II*, the hospital, with its proximity to pain and death, had rarely been used as the setting for a slasher film. The following May, however, saw the release of *Visiting Hours* (1982), a Canadian slasher, and *X-Ray* (1982), both inferior films which effectively killed off the minor trend of hospital slashers.

Laurie Strode (Jamie Lee Curtis), hospitalized in *Halloween II* (1981) because of her ordeal from the previous film, is forced to contemplate the terrifying possibility that Michael Myers may not be dead after all.

Had it not been for its predecessor, *Halloween II* would have been considered a stylish successful slasher film. After all, it did make over $25 million. It was hardly, as Tom Shales of *The Washington Post* wrote, "a splashily bloody, tediously idiotic, doggedly inevitable sequel...." One person who was extremely happy with the result was legendary producer Dino De Laurentiis, who immediately wanted to begin work on the next sequel. Unfortunately, the decision was made to move in a new direction and go with a wholly original premise for *Halloween III: Season of the Witch* (1982). No Michael. No Laurie. No Loomis. Not even a Haddonfield. Instead, Dan O'Herlihy stars as a sinister Halloween mask maker whose creations are the cause of a series of gruesome deaths in the small California town of Santa Mira. Whatever *Halloween III* was—and in all fairness, the film does have its admirers—it wasn't a slasher.

After only two entries, the future of the original slasher franchise looked bleak.

CHAPTER 8

Prowlers, Spaghetti Slashers and the Joys of Summer Camp

During the feeding frenzy of the early '80s, when every independent low-budget slasher was another chum bucket for the circling producers, almost all of the slasher films which were worthy of national distribution were quickly snatched up. *The Prowler*, a moody atmospheric film bolstered by some of Tom Savini's greatest effects, was one of the few deserving slasher films never to be released under the banner of a major company. Over the years, it has become something of a lost classic.

The genesis of *The Prowler* is the quintessential indie story, of which the major player, director Joseph Zito, is the quintessential indie helmer. Zito didn't have a movie pedigree. As he says, "The closest I came to knowing somebody in the business was the projectionist down the block." At the City College of New York, where he studied economics and psychology, the ambitious and industrious Zito started making some "little films" with money he raised by hitting up friends, family members and even his dentist. Eventually, he went to the Cannes Film Festival with a short ten-minute

product reel he planned to use as his calling card. He also had a screenplay called *Quarantine*, about the government's response to an outbreak of a strange disease in an American city.

In Cannes, while Zito was showing his reel to a foreign distributor, he attracted the attention of an attorney who was hanging around the office. The attorney, who with his blue seersucker suit looked more like a bum than a lawyer, was extremely impressed with what he saw and told Zito he wanted to introduce him to a client of his who made movies. When Zito arrived back in the States and went to meet the mysterious client at his apartment on Central Park West, nothing could have prepared him for what happened next. The man came to the door wearing only boxer shorts and sporting a long gray beard, looking like Howard Hughes in his *Ice Station Zebra* days. He invited Zito in, told him to take off his shirt, and began raving about the script which at this point nobody other than Zito had even read. Zito left the guy's apartment, shirt intact but minus his script, only to receive a phone call several hours later. "Come on over," said the guy, "we're going to make this script."

Zito describes his reaction to the bizarre experience:

> I think, "wow, this is pretty easy. I meet this guy in Cannes who I think is a bum, we go to lunch, he makes a phone call to his client who calls me over, I hand him a script, and he calls me a few hours later and says he's going to make the film." I was just thrilled. Absolutely thrilled. I thought, "This is so great and so easy."

For the next few weeks, Zito began preparing *Quarantine*. Then, out of the blue, he received a phone call from the investor who said, "You know what, I'm not going to make that movie." Said Zito:

> I was crushed because I really believed everything 100 percent. It's very hard having this conversation today in the '90s, in 2000, many years after the naïve time when you could believe a phone call like that.... This kind of naïveté, I don't think can live any longer, but it lived just fine in me at that moment.

When Zito returned to the man's apartment, he was handed a script for *The Prowler*, written by Neal Barbera, son of Joseph Barbara, half of the legendary Hanna-Barbera duo, and Glenn Leopold. He read it on the spot and, although he thought it could use some polishing, was confident he could make it work. "It had this strange, dreamlike mood in it," said Zito of the script. "It wasn't trying to be very real, it was trying to be surreal in a way. It just had this misty feel to it." *The Prowler* was budgeted at around $1 million, a total investment from the peculiar financier in boxer

shorts. The film is set in Avalon Bay, California, and although it was originally slated to be shot there, Zito, who had always been fascinated by seaside communities in the off-season, felt the ghost town quality of Cape May, New Jersey, would be a more appropriate settings for the 36-day shoot:

> There was something about Cape May, it has strange culty people, and this voodoo hoodoo kind of thing.... That's the thing about a peninsula, it's sort of like these very, very weird people keep getting

Joseph Zito's *The Prowler* (1981) contains some of Tom Savini's most gruesome and realistic effects. It is one of slasher cinema's most brutal murders, the film's titular character drives a bayonet clear through the skull and out the throat of Carl (David Sederholm).

backed away and backed away and backed away and then they get to the coast and they start getting backed down until they're all jammed into this peninsula. You know, people who can't function anywhere else.

Although the six six-day weeks took their toll on the young and somewhat inexperienced cast and crew, there was a feeling of palpable excitement on the set which resulted in a level of professionalism not typically found in such low-budget slasher films. Veteran actors Farley Granger and Lawrence Tierney lent an air of respectability to the production. Assistant director Peter Giuliano, who also doubled as "the prowler," eventually became first assistant director on such blockbuster films as *Ghostbusters* (1984), *Twins* (1988) and *Bugsy* (1991). *The Prowler* also showcases Tom Savini's finest work, from an almost too realistic bayoneting to a grisly shower murder with a pitchfork, and ends with an exploding head sequence which rivals that of *Maniac*.

The Prowler begins in 1945 as jubilant GIs are returning home from the battlefields of Europe. As the voiceover explains, many were greeted not with thanks, but with Dear John letters which informed them that their estranged sweethearts had taken up with another man. Most accepted the letters as a casualty of war, but for one GI, the loss was too much to bear. In the small town of Avalon Bay, at a graduation dance, he takes his revenge on his ex and her new lover. As the couple necks on a small gazebo, oblivious to the danger around them, the now-crazed veteran impales them on a pitchfork.

Thirty-five years later, the Pritcher School is holding its first graduation dance since the tragedy. And wouldn't you know it, it's the exact same time the town sheriff

Otto (Bill Hugh Collins) learns the hard way that it takes more than bullets to stop "the prowler."

is about to leave for his vacation. As expected, the jilted GI returns and, believe me, for a guy who's at least in his mid-fifties, he packs a helluva punch. He slashes his way through the school's co-eds as Pam (Vicky Dawson), a spunky student who wrote an article on the postwar murders, and Deputy London (Christopher Goutman), a rather ineffective substitute for Sheriff Fraser (Farley Granger), try to stop him. Eventually, after the prowler has eliminated a good portion of the student body, he's finally unmasked by our plucky heroine. To no one's great surprise, unless you're one of few who hasn't already guessed his identity, the prowler is the vacationing sheriff.

When *The Prowler* was completed, the one semi-major distribution company that did express some interest in acquiring it was Avco Embassy. However, the deal they were offering wasn't satisfactory to the man in boxer shorts who ended up releasing the film himself through small regional distributors. Without national distribution, it was essential for the film to perform well in the few territories in which it did play and, unfortunately, that was not always the case. Although Zito laments *The Prowler*'s scarce distribution, especially since he was well-aware of the kind of business a quality slasher could do with a company like Avco behind it, he never let his frustration spoil his memory of working on the film. For Zito, it was just a great experience and an exhilarating time:

> It was extremely exciting, an absolutely wonderful time because what it did was it accessed audiences in movie theaters all over the world for very low-budget films that could be made by people without a great deal of experience. And that's a very very tough thing to accomplish today.

Fellow UCLA alums Stephen Carpenter and Jeffery Obrow's first collaboration, *The Dorm That Dripped Blood* (1981), is a bland uninspired slasher. It is set on a deserted college campus where five students have agreed to stay over Christmas break to close down a condemned dormitory. The film, released in the U.K. as *Pranks*, lacks any such practical jokes, or even any hormone-fueled hijinks which would be expected in such a setting. In fact, this bunch of rapidly-approaching-middle-age students is so well-behaved that the murderless portions of the film could easily double as a publicity video for the university. Carpenter and Obrow try to keep us interested in the uninspired killings by throwing in the most overused of all red herrings, the mentally challenged Peeping Tom. For the rest of this dark (as in underexposed, not sinister) film, we are forced to ponder the identity of the real killer who, when he is finally revealed, offers us absolutely no insight into his madness. *The Dorm That Dripped Blood* attempts one meager stab at originality by killing off the Final Girl in the film's last scene. This unnecessary, downbeat ending is actually a relief, for it signals not only an end to her annoying self-righteousness, but to the film as a whole.

An equally bad college dorm slasher released at approximately the same time is *Final Exam* (1981), the type of film you would get if you took all the generic conventions of the slasher film and proceeded to strip away any trace of originality or uniqueness. The film, which was shot in Shelby, North Carolina, steals every element from previously successful films and vigorously shakes them at the audience as if to say, "Now *this* is how you make a slasher film!", thereby reducing them to tired clichés with nothing new to offer. There is a homicidal maniac on the loose, but his lack of motivation and mysterious identity is less ambiguous than sloppy. There are killings galore, but all are virtually bloodless and most are embarrassingly

Joanne (Laurie Lapinski) gets a hand in Stephen Carpenter and Jeffery Obrow's dull and depressing slasher *The Dorm That Dripped Blood* **(1981).**

telegraphed. There is a clearly delineated Final Girl (Cecile Bagdadi), but her lack of distinction gives the climactic confrontation with the killer no real sense of urgency and danger. To make the entire experience all the more distasteful, the film's male lead (Joel S. Rice), a sweet bookworm with whom we are supposed to sympathize, expresses a fondness for serial killers and proclaims, in class, the "genius" of Charles Whitman's University of Texas massacre. You'll no doubt find yourself counting the minutes until the film is over, which you can accurately gauge since *Final Exam* plays like a primer on how to make a slasher film, albeit a bad one.

While the American slasher film was showing signs of fatigue, its Italian coun-

terpart was in excellent shape. *Tenebrae* marked Dario Argento's triumphant return to the *giallo*, the genre he had abandoned after *Deep Red* to work on the first two installments (*Suspiria, Inferno*) of his "Three Mothers Trilogy." In the Italian tradition of excess, *Tenebrae* is an über-slasher, a celebration of extremes which reaches an almost dizzying level of violence and insanity. Ironically, it is also one of Argento's most coherent films—which admittedly is like calling something the least bloody of Herschell Gordon Lewis'. Set in a cold and sterile Rome, absent of the warmth which cinema has traditionally bestowed upon the amorous city, *Tenebrae* is the story of American crime novelist Peter Neal (Anthony Franciosa), whose latest work, *Tenebrae*, may be acting as the template for a series of brutal murders. Even more unsettling than the film itself, is the story which inspired it. In 1980, Argento was in the United States pitching a project at MGM when a stranger called him at his hotel to discuss *Suspiria*. After more than two weeks of phone calls to Argento, the man finally confessed to the director that he was going to kill him. Although Argento returned to Italy unscathed, the episode affected him deeply and inspired him to write *Tenebrae*.

Over the course of writing this book, the question I am most frequently asked is, "So what's the goriest scene ever?" It's not an easy question to answer, for the slasher oeuvre is filled with many worthy candidates, from *Maniac*'s exploding head to *The Mutilator*'s (1983) "hooking," but the front-runner may very well be *Tenebrae*'s

murder of Jane (Veronica Lario), a downright gut-wrenching sequence made all the more shocking by its suddenness. Just as Jane sits down at her kitchen table, an ax smashes through the window and hacks off her arm. She leaps up in agony and paints the white wall with a swath of bright red blood which gushes from the stump. Mercifully, her attacker delivers the bloody deathblow seconds later. As graphic as the scene is, it is not without a certain artistic flair, and *Tenebrae*, being an Argento film, is filled with such flourishes. In the film's most visually and technologically impressive scene, Argento tracks from one side of an apartment building, over its roof, and enters a window on the opposite side—all without a single cut. To accomplish this feat, a special 360 degree, rotating camera was suspended on an oversized crane. The scene

Evidently, life does imitate art in Dario Argento's *Tenebrae* (1982), as crime novelist Peter Neal (Anthony Franciosa) watches both his plan and his sanity slip away.

is spectacle for the sheer sake of spectacle, pure Argento, a typical indulgence which consistently enthralls his fans and confounds his critics.

Argento has a rabid fan base, and because of this dedicated following he is one of the few foreign directors whose films are guaranteed to play well outside of Italy. Overall, *Tenebrae* was both a popular and critical success. The same cannot be said of his next film, *Phenomena* (1984, released as *Creepers* in the U.S.), which stars then-unknown American actress Jennifer Connelly. It is an unsatisfying hybrid combining elements of the *giallo*, the supernatural thriller and the nature-run-amuck films.

Argento's closest contemporary rival, the mercurial Lucio Fulci, made a career of taking various genres and stretching them to the furthest reaches of acceptable (depending who you ask) taste. His 1982 film *The New York Ripper*—an urban slasher with a mean streak a mile wide—seems to have been made for the type of person who found *Maniac* a tad light. A razor-wielding sadist who talks like a duck (yes, he literally goes "quack, quack") is roaming the city, murdering women and mutilating their bodies—not necessarily in that order—while taunting the police and promising he will continue. In typical Fulci fashion, the film wallows in graphic gore. We zero in on the killer's razor blade as he slowly slices through a young woman's abdomen, breast and eyeball. Any laughs, such as the atrocious dubbing of

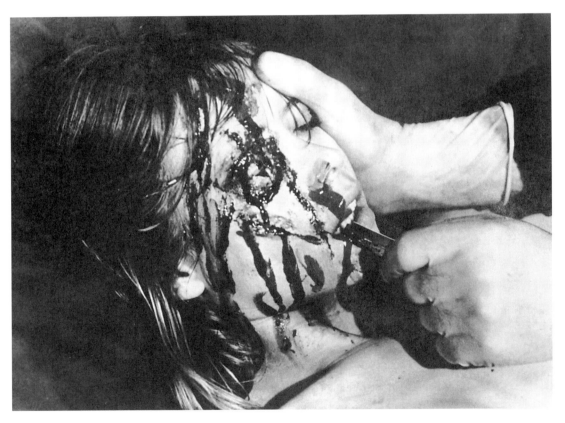

Lucio Fulci's *The New York Ripper* (1982), easily one of the most depraved slashers, wallows in the mutilation and humiliation of women. It is one of the few slasher films absent of any redeeming qualities.

the international actors' dialogue in the English language version, are purely unintentional. The explanation given for the killer's insanity makes little sense, and the "inspiration" for the murders, a beautiful blonde amputee, seems somehow inappropriate, even for a film as sleazy as *The New York Ripper*. When interviewed about the film's gratuitous sex scenes in *Spaghetti Nightmares*, Fulci offered this convoluted gem:

> I don't consider them gratuitous, I think they're fitting, because anyone who tries to kill beautiful women, whether they be loose ladies, professional prostitutes or just young girls, has got a problem which is possibly caused by having a daughter, who is not going to be a winner, in a country like America where being a winner is compulsory.

Let's be thankful *The New York Ripper*, as well as Fulci's candid opinion, went practically unnoticed by most critics.

Like most Fulci films, *The New York Ripper* is beautifully composed and stylishly shot, although at times, like Mario Bava in his later *gialli*, Fulci seems to think he's getting paid per unnecessary zoom. While Fulci has always had a die-hard fan base, he has also lingered in the long and bloody shadow cast by both Bava and Argento, never getting the same respect or notoriety as his better-known contemporaries. While he and Argento have taken mutual, however subtle, snipes at each other in the press, a long awaited collaboration was planned for the 1997 film *The Wax Mask*, which Fulci was slated to direct with Argento producing. Unfortunately,

Audiences had to beware of more than eyeballs in *Friday the 13th Part 3* (1982), which was filmed in 3-D. Here, a group of vacationing teenagers—Vera (Catherine Parks), Andy (Jeffrey Rogers) and Debbie (Tracie Savage)—stumble upon a bizarre vagrant (David Wiley) on the way to their lakeside destination.

Fulci's untimely death in 1996 ended the possibility of this joint production between two of Italy's greatest horror maestros.

Content to continue his role as the puppeteer of Jason Voorhees, horror's favorite new villain, Steve Miner returned to direct *Friday the 13th Part 3* (1982). The film tinkers a bit with the Jason myth; there is no mention of Camp Crystal Lake and Jason is treated not as some local legend, but as a singular flesh and blood boogeyman who had previously assaulted the film's heroine (Dana Kimmell).[1] The victims are no longer camp counselors but

Chris (Dana Kimmell) searches in vain for her boyfriend, Rick (Paul Kratka), who is about to have his head crushed in *Friday the 13th Part 3* (1982). This scene, in which Paul's eyeball pops out of his skull, was one of the film's 3-D highlights.

a group of young adults on vacation. In an enjoyable but somewhat lackluster sendup of *Friday the 13th*'s famous ending, the film concludes with Mrs. Voorhees—who somehow managed to find and reattach her head between *Part 2* and *3*—emerging from the lake to attack the lone survivor. Jumping on the bandwagon of a minor trend at the time, *Friday the 13th Part 3* was shown in 3-D, making for some mildly amusing shots of snakes, eyeballs and spears coming directly at the audience. More importantly, the film grossed over $36 million. Whether or not this was a result of the 3-D gimmick didn't matter. The series would continue.

Had *Slumber Party Massacre* (1982), a cheap but vaguely entertaining slasher more interested in showing breasts than blood, not been directed by a woman, or scripted by noted feminist writer Rita Mae Brown (*The Rubyfruit Jungle* [1973], *Southern Discomfort* [1982]), it would have quietly joined the ranks of such similar undistinguished later entries in the genre. The fact that it was directed by Amy Jones, formerly an editor for equal opportunity exploiter Roger Corman, gave it a sense of social purpose which while not deserved was certainly anticipated. However, those who hoped for some empowering feminist statement, a scathing critique on the blatant misogyny endemic in slasher films, were sorely disappointed. While Jones and Brown insisted *Slumber Party Massacre* was a parody, and despite the fact that in the film's climactic scene the killer is symbolically castrated as the tip of his phallic weapon is lopped off, sometimes a powerdrill is just a powerdrill, even if it is used to skewer a house full of half-naked teenage beauties. *Slumber Party Massacre* was no different from any other slasher film which provided some soft-core T&A along with a series of implausible murders. The fact that it panders to its target audience while pretending to be some sort of intellectual rallying cry for female solidarity makes it all the more reprehensible. After all, it's a weird brand of feminism indeed which equates a tawdry high school locker room shower scene with any liberation other than that from clothing.

Two years before New Line Cinema became a major player in the independent arena with the release of *A Nightmare on Elm Street*, it entered the slasher fray with *Alone in the Dark*, a highly intelligent and provocative film. Because it expertly combines horror with subtle touches of humor, it has mistakenly been called anything from a spoof to a satire.

The film begins with a surreal dream sequence in a roadside diner, a quietly disturbing scene which evokes the best of David Lynch. When a blackout shorts out the electricity at a mental institution, four psychotic patients—Frank Hawkes (Jack Palance), a former solider; Byron "Preacher" Sutcliff (Martin Landau), a pyromaniac ex-minister; Ronald "Fatty" Elster (Erland Van Lidth), an enormous child molester; and an anonymous character known only as "the bleeder"—escape and travel to the home of their new psychiatrist, Dr. Dan Potter (Dwight Schultz). The delusional quartet believes that Potter has murdered their beloved former psychiatrist, who actually took a different job in Florida. They proceed to terrorize the doctor, his wife (Deborah Hedwall), their young daughter (Elizabeth Ward) and Dr. Potter's teenage sister (Lee Taylor-Allan)—who is a bit unbalanced herself. Hot on their trail is the head of the institution, Dr. Leo Bain (Donald Pleasence), a charlatan who seems at least as crazy as the patients under his care. Eventually, the pacifist Dr. Potter must take up arms to defend himself and his family from the dangerous psychopaths.

In 1980, New Line Cinema was still predominately a distributor of cult movies, lost classics and obscure foreign films, but as the major studios and larger production companies began to take an interest in such fare, company founder Bob Shaye realized that to survive he would eventually have to move into production. Naturally, he believed that the easiest way to make money was with a low-budget horror film.

Shaye chose Jack Sholder, an editor who had a long association with New Line, to direct his company's first feature. Sholder had re-cut a lot of the films which New Line had acquired, including the famous *Street Fighter* films of Sonny Chiba. In fact, it was Sholder who suggested renaming the martial arts icon Sonny—he was originally named Shinichi Chiba—making him more accessible to American audiences and playing no small part in his rise to fame.

Sholder came up with an idea about a group of homicidal maniacs who escape from a maximum security mental institution and terrorize Little Italy until they are rounded up by the Mafia. Shaye liked the idea but didn't want to shoot the film in New York. Consequently, the besieged citizens of Little Italy became a wet-behind-the-ears psychiatrist and his family. Shaye then offered Sholder $10,000 to write the script and another $15,000 if he agreed to direct it. Sholder describes his state of mind before getting the assignment:

> At that point I was getting into my early thirties, and when 25 came and passed and I hadn't made *Citizen Kane* yet, I was getting worried. I was really starting to wonder if I was ever going to get to make my feature. I'd worked as a film editor but I never really approached it as seriously as other people because I always felt I was going to direct a movie.

After Sholder turned in his draft of the script he went off to edit *The Burning*,

ironically, an early production of the Weinstein brothers who, over a decade later,
would become Shaye's main competitors
for supremacy over the New York independent film industry. When Sholder returned, Shaye informed him that *Alone in
the Dark* was a go. Although the film was
originally budgeted at $800,000, the deci-
sion to cast such esteemed actors as
Palance, Pleasence and Landau pushed it
closer to $1 million.

For a first-time director, Sholder was
saddled with an enormous chore: successfully meld horror and comedy to the sat-
isfaction of a demanding producer while
overseeing a rather inept production team
on a nearly impossible shooting schedule
while stroking the egos of three aging veterans whose best years were clearly behind
them.[2] It was a challenge he was more
than up to.

Even before shooting began, Sholder
was well-aware that working with the notoriously cantankerous Palance was going
to be difficult. He had heard all the horror stories and Shaye, who should have
been reassuring his freshman director, did
little to assuage his trepidation. "Oh, I met
Jack Palance today," Shaye told Sholder
offhandedly. "He's out of his mind. He's
the meanest man I've ever met and he's really pissed off."

As it turned out, Palance was less
than thrilled to be working on the film and
didn't hesitate to voice his displeasure. Sholder explains the main source of Palance's
resentment:

> We had cast him and what had happened
> was that he was doing a series, *Ripley's
> Believe It or Not*. He'd done a pilot and it
> got picked up and they wanted him to go
> to Florence. Instead, we held him to his
> contract and forced him to go to New Jer-
> sey, so he wasn't that happy. And some-
> how the producer who had made
> Palance's deal had informed him that he
> was playing the Donald Pleasence role.

Then he found out that he was playing
the villain instead, which he wasn't happy
about either. He also claimed he had been
told that there would be no night shooting. It's called *Alone in the Dark* but there
won't be any night shooting, don't worry
about it *[Sholder laughs]*.

Although Sholder was initially
terrified of the volatile actor, he knew that
if he gave in to Palance's sometimes
ridiculous demands that his authority
would be usurped for the entire production. One instance where he did acquiesce
and defer to Palance's judgment, however,
was in the scene where the patients break
out of the institution. Originally, it was
Palance, not Erland Van Lidth, who was
supposed to kill the guard on duty, but
Palance maintained that he did not believe
in violence and balked at having to do the
scene. When Sholder explained that it was
necessary for the audience to understand
that his character had a capacity for violence, Palance stared at him, steely-eyed,
and said, "I think they'll know."

Despite their many disputes, Sholder
looks back fondly on his time spent with
Palance, who beneath his gruff exterior
was not only a "very interesting actor but
a very cultured guy." Sholder is an accomplished musician and both he and Palance
shared a love for classical music and high
culture, which made it all the more ironic
that for his first film he found himself "in
the middle of the night telling people how
to stab each other." But the violence in
Alone in the Dark is never gratuitous, even
in the film's most memorable scene in
which a terrified babysitter, who has just
witnessed her boyfriend's murder, is
trapped on a bed while the maniac hiding
underneath tries to stab her through the
mattress. Explains Sholder:

> I was never a hard-core slasher kind of
> guy.... I never wanted to humiliate peo-
> ple or inflict pain just for the sake of

Ronald "Fatty" Elster (Erland Van Lidth), an escaped mental patient, pays a surprise visit to the daughter (Elizabeth Ward) of his psychiatrist, Dr. Potter, in Jack Sholder's *Alone in the Dark* (1982). This darkly comedic, intelligent slasher was an early production of New Line Cinema.

inflicting pain, or do horrible effects just to see how gross I could possibly be. That never really interested me that much.

Instead, he dilutes the violence with equal parts black humor. "I've always had a cynical outlook on life," Sholder admits. "Odd things strike me as funny. I'm the sort of person who'd laugh at a funeral under the right circumstances."

Alone in the Dark was shot over the course of 35 days in the fall of 1981. For Dr. Potter's house, the crew used the home of an actual psychiatrist in Sneeden's Landing, a small town in upstate New York, while the scenes at the disco and shopping center were shot in Bergen County, New Jersey. Tom Savini, with whom Sholder had worked on *The Burning*, was flown in for one of the film's biggest jolts. He de-

signed the decomposing corpse which Dr. Potter's sister hallucinates.

A year later, in November 1982, *Alone in the Dark* opened in Bob Shaye's hometown of Detroit, Michigan. New Line made about 25 prints of the film which Shaye planned to open region by region across the county. While *Alone in the Dark* was far from a financial failure, especially as the first offering from a start-up production company and a first-time director, it was much too cerebral a film to really have the mass appeal of a *Halloween* or a *Friday the 13th*. In fact, the film to which it is most often compared—not just because of plot similarities, but because both explore the breakdown and subsequent defense of the nuclear family in the face of some primitive threat—is Sam Peckinpah's *Straw Dogs*.

Shaye would go on to produce *A Nightmare on Elm Street*, effectively jettisoning New Line Cinema as Gotham's premier independent production company. Sholder would eventually direct *A Nightmare on Elm Street 2: Freddy's Revenge*, the second installment of the *Nightmare on Elm Street* series, before moving on to *The Hidden* (1987), an extremely popular cult film about malevolent alien creatures which take control of the Los Angeles populace. As a director, he has distinguished himself by his ability to successfully meld elements from different genres in a single work. While he looks back fondly on his first feature film experience, apparently not everybody harbored such good memories. According to Sholder, a few years after *Alone in the Dark*, Shaye ran into Donald Pleasence at a European film festival. Initially, Pleasence didn't remember the producer. "Come on," Shaye joked good-naturedly, bringing up the film, "You must have had worse experiences than that." The actor thought for a moment. "Yes," he said quietly. "Once, in Italy."

There is no one, perhaps, more thankful for the obscurity of *The Slayer* (1982) than Wes Craven. J.S. Cardone's little-seen film predates Craven's masterpiece *A Nightmare on Elm Street* by at least a few years. While the quality of the two films is obviously far different, their central premise is strikingly similar—a woman is terrorized in her dreams by a killer whose dastardly deeds manifest themselves in reality. She agrees to accompany her husband, brother and sister-in-law on a vacation to a deserted island resort, only to discover that "the slayer" of her nightmares is more than a figment of her imagination. Overshadowed at the time of its release by other high-profile slashers, *The Slayer* is a straightforward, sophisticated and unexpectedly well-acted film. It is devoid of the typically asinine

teenagers endemic to many of these films and creates complex and sympathetic, if not totally believable, adult characters. The special effects—a painfully extended decapitation in an elevator shaft and a pitchfork impaling—are particularly impressive, especially considering the film's tiny budget. Like so many other films of its kind, *The Slayer* suffered from a lack of distribution, a raw deal for horror fans but one which ultimately saved Craven from having to answer questions about the inspiration for his own film.[3]

After *Prom Night*, producer Peter Simpson did what so many other like-minded producers did in the wake of their own overnight success—he again attempted to capture lightning in a bottle. In late 1980, he began production on *Curtains*, but instead of another *Prom Night*, he got a two year-plus headache. The Toronto-lensed film took over a year to shoot and wasn't released until March 1983. Director Richard Ciupka, who, depending to whom you speak, was either fired or quit in mid-shoot, opted for the pseudonym Jonathan Stryker, the name of the tyrannical director within the film. His departure was far from amiable, as his entire biography is blatantly omitted from the *Curtains* press kit. Because of uncertainly with the film's ending, the screenplay was still being revised during shooting. In the juiciest behind-the-scenes incident, actress Celine Lomez was replaced by Linda Thorson after allegedly refusing to do full-frontal nudity. Ironically, there is no nudity, full-frontal or otherwise, in the finished film.

What makes this all so unfortunate is that *Curtains* could have been an excellent slasher film, a more mature offering in the vein of *He Knows You're Alone* and *Alone in the Dark*, two "adult" slashers which don't derive their thrills from the stupidity of teenagers. *Curtains* begins with a premise that requires just a little bit of faith. In

Jonathan Stryker (John Vernon) tries to humiliate Samantha Sherwood (Samantha Eggar) by forcing her to don an old hag mask in the problem-plagued Canadian slasher *Curtains* **(1983).**

order to win the starring role in director Jonathan Stryker's new film *Audra*, Samantha Sherwood (Samantha Eggar) feigns madness and has herself committed to an asylum, all in the name of research, of course. But the megalomaniac director has other plans. He decides to leave her to her own devices while he auditions six young actresses at his country estate. With the help of a friend, Samantha learns of his plan and manages to escape. Once she arrives at the house, the fun really begins; someone wearing an old hag mask and wielding a scythe begins narrowing the field of beauties for Stryker to choose from.

The highlight of the film is an unexpected sequence in which one of the girls (Lesleh Donaldson) is murdered in broad daylight while ice skating on a pond. She is distracted during her routine by a small doll buried in the snow. As she tries to excavate it, the hag, scythe in hand, begins

skating towards her in slow motion. Scenes like this, where the discovery of the creepy ceramic figurine precipitates the murder, are used all too infrequently. In fact, this doll, the killer's wonderfully effective calling card, is never used again. Could this have been an oversight on the part of the director, or are these scenes the last remaining vestige of Ciupka's vision? In either case, the victim of all this infighting was clearly the film itself. *Curtains* is still a decent slasher, but one that occasionally hints at greatness that could have been.

Considering the inability of film critics to discuss the work of Brian De Palma without giving in to their compulsion to make comparisons to Alfred Hitchcock, it is not surprising that *The House on Sorority Row* (1983), the debut feature of former De Palma assistant Mark Rosman, was needlessly and ridiculously compared to the films of De Palma, and, by proxy, to Hitchcock himself. But if his sometimes

Brooke Parsons (Linda Thorson) comes to the realization that the role of Audra in Jonathan Stryker's new film may entail more than she bargained for. The actual production of Richard Ciupka's *Curtains* was just as dysfunctional and unpleasant as *Audra*, the fictional production it portrays.

uneasy relationship to Hitchcock has been the bane of De Palma's career, his protégé seems unconcerned of the same fate; within the first ten minutes of this sorority house slasher, Rosman implements montages, lingering close-ups and meandering tracking shots, all stylistic techniques favored by De Palma. With its premise—the old "killer in the attic" bit—and open-ended finale, *The House on Sorority Row* is vaguely reminiscent of *Black Christmas*, with dabs of *Hell Night*, *The Funhouse*, *Silent Scream* and *To All a Goodnight* thrown in. The story is nothing new: a group of party-minded co-eds who are planning one last sorority bash before graduation, much to the displeasure of their humorless house mother Mrs. Slater

(Lois Kelso Hunt), accidentally kill the woman in a thoughtless prank gone awry. Of course, calling the authorities, the only sensible and least likely course of action, is debated long enough for the woman's deformed son to come down from his attic lair and begin murdering the guilty. Despite some suspenseful touches which really are Hitchcockian—the girls' growing fear that somebody will turn on the swimming pool lights, thereby revealing the corpse of their house mother, and the darkly comedic scene in which they push a Dumpster containing the body into a parked police car—*The House on Sorority Row* is little more than a run-of-the-mill slasher film clearly made by someone with much higher aspirations.

Morgan (Jodi Draigie) is about to find out that this kitschy little jack-in-the-box is a bit more than an innocent childhood relic in Mark Rosman's *The House on Sorority Row* (1983).

But if one was to truly aspire to continue the legacy of Hitchcock's influence on the slasher film, there was really only one option—a sequel to his masterpiece. Producing a sequel to *Psycho*—whose story doesn't particularly lend itself to a continuation—was one of the most daunting tasks in the history of cinema. The project, conceived by executive producer Bernard Schwartz, was both galling and courageous. No one expected the film to approach the greatness of its progenitor, and critics, some of whom had hastily panned the original at the time of its release, were waiting with poisoned pens ready to do the same to its unwanted son.

Psycho II (1983) takes place 22 years after the original. An older, less jittery and supposedly rehabilitated Norman Bates is released back into society. To start anew, he returns to his old slashing grounds, the Bates Motel. However, in 1960, nobody could have anticipated a sequel and in the years that passed the *Psycho* house had been moved from its original location and the motel had been demolished. As a result, the producers were forced to find a new location which was landscaped to resemble the ominous bluff in the original film. They then transported the house there. The new motel was partially built by production designer John W. Corso with the rest added optically by matte artist Albert Whitlock. Vera Miles reprises her role as Lila Loomis, sister of the slain Marion Crane, who will do, and does, everything in her power to see that Norman is sent back to the institution. She enlists the aid of her daughter Mary Loomis (Meg Tilly) for an elaborate and cruel-hearted plot to once again drive Norman insane. But someone else has returned to the Bates Motel, someone who will stop at nothing to see that Norman is

Twenty-two years later, Norman Bates (Anthony Perkins) has arrived home in Richard Franklin's *Psycho II* (1983), a decent sequel for a film which never needed one.

left alone. The avenging killer is Ms. Spool (Claudia Bryar), a kindly waitress from the local diner who is Norman's true mother.[4] Ironically, in an effort to protect her son, she succeeds in turning him back into a murderer. Ever grateful, Norman thanks her for her efforts by killing her with a brutal blow to the head with a shovel. The demons in his mind have indeed returned.

While comparisons to the original, while inevitable, are ludicrous, *Psycho II* was not the embarrassment most had predicted. It's well-directed by Richard Franklin, whose 1980 thriller *Road Games* has been called Hitchcockian by some. Dean Cundey, Carpenter's cinematographer on *Halloween*, shot the film in a staid and mournful style which beautifully compliments the stark black and white photography of the original. Tom Holland's script, while containing some glaring plot holes, is strong on character, and

was instrumental in getting Anthony Perkins—a magnificent versatile actor forever typecast—to return to the role of Norman Bates. Perkins himself directed *Psycho III* (1986), a good-enough sequel in which a suicidal nun with the initials M.C. awakens Bates' homicidal tendencies. *Psycho IV: The Beginning* (1990), which hinges on the unlikely premise that Norman would call up a radio talk show to discuss his past, was a huge disappointment, considering that it was scripted by Joseph Stefano, writer of the original.

By the time *Sleepaway Camp* was released in November 1983, *The Burning* and *Friday the 13th*'s first two sequels had effectively wrung the life out of overnight camp slashers. Although *Sleepaway Camp* is inferior to the films which preceded it, it managed to attract a fair amount of attention due to its realistic depiction of teenagers, hilarious over-the-top performances and legendary ending. Through the years, the film has developed somewhat of a cult following. The proliferation of Internet sites—some solely devoted to the film and loaded with the most esoteric facts—is evidence of its enduring popularity.

After a brief prologue in which a man and one of his children are killed in a boating accident, the film jumps forward eight years. Ricky (Jonathan Tiersten) and Angela (Felissa Rose) are getting ready to leave for sleepaway camp. Angela is presumably the lone survivor of the accident and has been adopted her aunt, Ricky's clearly unstable mother (Desiree Gould). Gould's turn as the doting Aunt Martha is the highlight of the film. As she obsessively fawns over her son and niece, director Robert Hiltzik allows her performance to veer dangerously close to high camp be-

fore reining her in. Rose, only 13 at the time, is equally impressive as the near-mute Angela. Her mother, who accompanied her on set, displayed some refreshing parental concern by forbidding her daughter's hands to be used in the murder sequences. Jonathan Tiersten's hands, which were small enough to preserve continuity, were used instead.

Once at Camp Arawak, the precocious, athletic Ricky—who unofficially wins the award for dirtiest mouth on a teenage actor—fits right in with the other campers, while Angela keeps mainly to herself, refusing to speak to anyone. This doesn't go over well with the spoiled brats whose main summer activity seems to be harassing the shy girl. Revenge is forthcoming, as everyone who crosses Angela is

Mel (Mike Kellin) realizes that his summer camp has become a slaughterhouse in Robert Hiltzik's *Sleepaway Camp* (1983). A horrifying realization indeed, though not half as horrifying as Angela's secret.

soon killed in a variety of unpleasant ways: one girl is stung to death when a hornets' nest in placed in her bathroom stall, another is slit in half with a hunting knife and, in an especially stomach-churning scene, the most unrelenting of Angela's tormentors is strangled while being violated with a hot curling iron. All fingers point to Angela, and when it is finally revealed that she is, in fact, the killer, any disappointment at this seemingly suspenseless revelation will have long since vanished after *Sleepaway Camp*'s final shock. The film ends on a naked, very obviously male Angela, whose gender had been repressed for years by Aunt Martha, who had always wanted a daughter. Two grislier sequels—*Sleepaway Camp 2: Unhappy Campers* and *Sleepaway Camp 3: Teenage Wasteland*—starring Bruce Springsteen's sister Pamela as a post–sex change operation Angela, followed in 1988 and 1989.

As the American slasher floundered, the Italian *giallo* sailed for calmer bloodier seas with Lamberto Bava's *A Blade in the Dark*. Bava's pedigree was impeccable; he was the son of Mario Bava and protégé of his father's heir apparent, Dario Argento. He had made his directorial debut with 1980's *Macabro*, the bizarre story of a woman's relationship with a severed head, and had been Argento's assistant director on both *Inferno* and *Tenebrae*.

According to Bava, *A Blade in the Dark* was originally shot for television in four 25-minute episodes. For theatrical release it was blown up from 16mm to 35mm. Apparently, Italian television standards are far more lenient than American ones, for it is laughable to think that the film, in any incarnation, would have ever aired on American network TV.

A Blade in the Dark is the story of a composer (Andrea Occhipinti) who is hired to score a horror film. To capture the mood of the film, he retreats to an isolated villa where he slowly begins to suspect that a murderer is killing off the strange and beautiful women who have been visiting him. Despite some painfully slow stretches and a dreadful dubbing job, *A Blade in the Dark* manages to create a decent claustrophobic atmosphere within the confines of the spacious villa. Similar to other *gialli*, the mystery behind the killer's identity, as well as the explanation for his crimes, is a mixture of silliness and psychological babble—which is not to say it is not entertaining. After all, any slasher in which the killer's instrument of choice is an Exacto knife deserves some points for originality. Argento's influence is felt throughout, especially in the film's bloodiest scene—the brutal bathroom murder of Angela (Fabiola Toledo)—which recalls Jane's murder in *Tenebrae*. While *A Blade in the Dark* allowed Bava to make a name for himself independent of his father and Argento, it was not until *Demons* (1985) and *Demons 2: The Nightmare Returns* (1986) that he really hit his stride.

Released in 1983, when the slasher film was clearly on the decline, *The Initiation* makes a noble attempt to drum up some attention; it casts an aging Vera Miles, who puts in a respectable performance in a lead role, and "introduces" a fresh-faced Daphne Zuniga, who just happened to have been "introduced" two years earlier in *The Dorm That Dripped Blood*. The film is an odd mix of elements borrowed from better-known slashers. During a sorority prank, a group of pledges (led by Zuniga) break into a shopping mall where they are terrorized by an unknown assailant. Meanwhile, Zuniga is undergoing some sort of half-baked dream therapy for a reoccurring nightmare she has been having since childhood. Throw in a breakout at the local sanitarium and you have the plot of this Charles Pratt, Jr.—scripted potboiler, which, despite its proclivity for laughable dialogue and silly plot twists, manages to be a fairly entertaining and occasionally frightening film. Pratt and Zuniga were reunited nearly a decade later on the prime time soap opera *Melrose Place* (1992–99), which Pratt executive produced, wrote and directed. Ironically, *Melrose Place* guest star Hunter Tylo, who also appeared in *The Initiation*, ended up suing television mogul Aaron Spelling after he fired her from the series, essentially for getting pregnant. Tylo was awarded nearly $5 million for her troubles.

As the few original slashers which were now dribbling out of a once overflowing spring attempted to grab their own little piece of the rapidly deteriorating pie, the old stalwarts were carrying on.

Friday the 13th—The Final Chapter (1984), which was hardly that, sets the action at an isolated lakeside community where a group of teenagers whose libidos are all in hyperdrive have come to spend the weekend. The film stars future teen heartthrob Corey Feldman as a miniature Rick Baker, who lives near the vacationing teens with his mother and Final Girl sister (Kimberly Beck). Tom Savini returned to work his magic, most notably in the final scene in which Jason, sans his trademark hockey mask, has his face slowly impaled on a machete. *Friday the 13th—The Final Chapter* was directed by Joseph Zito, who had worked with Savini three years prior on *The Prowler.* Although a novice to the series, Zito perfected the *Friday the 13th* formula— a carefully blended combination of shock, comic relief and suspense. Unfairly dismissed by critics, *Friday the 13th—The Final Chapter* is easily one of the most enjoyable entries in the series, proving with its $32 million box office take that

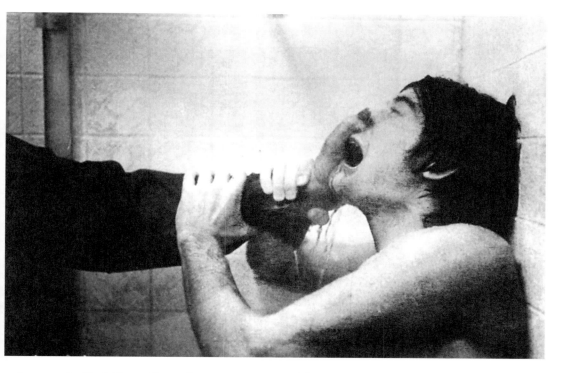

Apparently Paul (Peter Barton) never saw *Psycho*. This shower, in Joseph Zito's *Friday the 13th—The Final Chapter* (1984), is the last one he will ever take.

fans' appetite for Jason Voorhees had not yet been sated.

Towards the end of 1984, a low-budget film came out of nowhere to give the slasher a much needed jolt of adrenaline.

The film was *A Nightmare on Elm Street*. Along with reviving a dying genre, it spawned arguably the greatest, most popular and most profitable boogeyman of them all.

CHAPTER 9

A Nightmare on Elm Street, Sequels Galore and the Decline of the Slasher Film

In the early '80s, before New Line Cinema became the crown jewel of Time Warner's vast media empire, Robert Shaye's fledgling company was in dire straits. It hadn't released a film in months and was struggling to meet payroll. The market for esoteric art films was anemic and Shaye desperately needed a hit.

Born in Detroit in 1939, Shaye graduated from the University of Michigan in 1960. After receiving his law degree from Columbia University in 1964, he founded New Line Cinema, a small distribution company based out of his tiny Manhattan apartment. A passionate cinephile, Shaye handled an eclectic mix of films, from esteemed foreign offerings such as Lina Wertmuller's *The Seduction of Mimi* (1972) and Bertrand Blier's *Get Out Your Handkerchiefs* (1978), to Jean-Luc Godard's Rolling Stones documentary *Sympathy for the Devil* (1968) and campy cult favorites like the 1936 anti-marijuana film *Reefer Madness.*

As the 1970s—the decade which ushered in the modern Hollywood block-

buster—came to a close, the major studios began to covet a piece of the art film market. They formed their own specialty divisions, targeting the types of films on which New Line depended. Shaye had founded New Line as a labor of love and could never hope to match the amounts of money which the studios, with their bottomless purses, could allocate towards the acquisition of these films. The only way he could level the playing field was to position New Line as a bonafide production company, willing to take risks on the types of films the majors wouldn't touch.

His savior came in an unlikely form.

Wesley Earl Craven was born, like Shaye, in 1939, to a working class, fundamentalist Baptist family in Cleveland, where he was raised in a very religious environment. After studying literature and psychology at Wheaton College in Illinois, he received a Masters in philosophy from Johns Hopkins University. While teaching at Clarkson College, a small engineering school in Potsdam, New York, he bought a 16mm camera. With the help of some students, he made *The Searchers*, a 45-minute film inspired by the TV series *Mission: Impossible* (1966–73). Dissatisfied with the world of academia, Craven spent the summer of 1968 in New York City, trying in vain to break into the film business. Finally, one of his students, Steve Chapin, suggested that Craven contact his older brother, the soon-to-be-famous folk singer Harry Chapin. At the time, Harry was working as an editor, cutting documentaries, commercials and industrials for IBM. Although he was unable to offer Craven a paying job, he taught him the basic techniques of editing. Then, with his marriage in shambles, just as he was about to call it quits and return to teaching, Craven got a job synching up dailies on a film called *Together*, directed by Sean S. Cunningham. The rest, as they say, is history.

The idea for *A Nightmare on Elm Street* was gleaned from a series of articles which Craven had seen in *The Los Angeles Times*. They all involved people who had suddenly been wracked with what they described as "the worst nightmares they had ever had." They were terrified of going back to bed and, as it turned out, had good reason to be. When they eventually fell asleep, they died. Because this happened over the course of a year and a half, the paper had made no connection between the seemingly unrelated deaths.

Craven was fascinated by these stories and came up with the idea of a killer who reached his victims in their dreams. Even as a child, dreams had always intrigued Craven. In college, he had written a research paper on the subject and was well versed in the literature. He even kept a diary of his own dreams and claims that he became so adept at remembering them that he developed the ability to control them.

In an interview on New Line's remastered version of *A Nightmare on Elm Street*, Craven discusses the way he dealt with the question of how an omnipotent villain who only exists in the dream world could be defeated:

Wes Craven directs Tina (Amanda Wyss) in *A Nightmare on Elm Street*'s **(1984) first memorable murder sequence.**

Finally I hit upon the idea that the only way to deal with it was to somehow bring that being out into your world. So I struck upon the conceit that whatever you were holding in the dream at the moment you woke up would be brought back with you. That kinda completed the metaphor. That if you can bring this thing that is threatening you out into the light of day, you will have a way of coping with it. And in that sense, that's how humans deal with their nightmares.

A Nightmare on Elm Street's villain, Freddy, was named after Craven's worst enemy in junior high school. His last name, Krueger, is allegedly a variation of Krug, the sadistic villain from *The Last House on the Left*. In the original script, Freddy Krueger was a child molester—a fact which is alluded to in later installments of the series—because that was the most sick and evil pathology which Craven could imagine. The decision was made to turn him into a child murderer in order to avoid being accused of exploiting a spate of highly publicized child molestations which occurred in California around the time *A Nightmare on Elm Street* went into production.

If there is one thing, aside from his wicked sense of humor, for which Freddy Krueger is known, it is his weapon of choice. It was a conscious decision on the part of Craven, who recognized that the slasher film was becoming clichéd, not to have Freddy use a knife like his forerunners, Michael and Jason. But it was not until the third draft of his script that Craven hit upon his ingeniously cruel invention: a tattered leather glove with razor-sharp steel blades as fingers. As the glove sliced through the teenagers of Elm Street, it was forever securing its spot in the iconography of American cinema, the dark side of Dorothy's slippers and Chaplin's cane.

Even with his track record for turning an enormous profit with low-budget controversial films, Craven had a hard time attracting interest in his project. It was rejected by all the major studios who

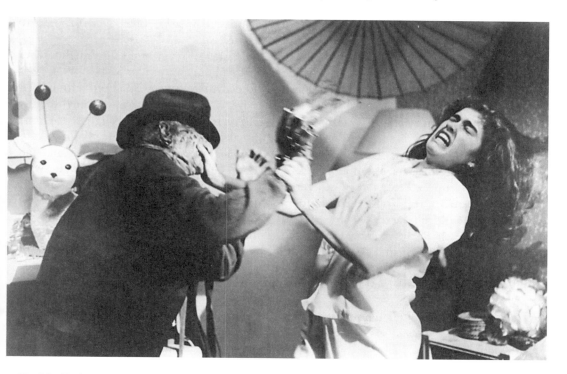

Freddy (Robert Englund) and Nancy (Heather Langenkamp) do battle in *A Nightmare on Elm Street* **(1984).**

failed to appreciate its blend of visceral horror—*à la* the smoldering remains of the slasher film—and the fantastic. Initially, as unbelievable as this seems today, Disney had toyed with the idea of turning *A Nightmare on Elm Street* into a children's film. Another early suitor was Paramount, who ultimately passed because of *Nightmare*'s similarity to *Dreamscape* (1984), a film they were developing at the time.[1] The whole *Dreamscape* affair has always been a bone of contention with Craven. "It's probably just one of those coincidences," Craven has said on record, although he often alludes to the fact that he finds the similarities between the two films fairly suspicious.

Finally, after all the majors had passed, Craven took *Nightmare* to New Line. Naturally, Shaye was familiar with Craven's previous work and quickly recognized the film's potential. He agreed to produce *Nightmare* despite the fact that New Line was hurting financially. Shaye was laying people off left and right and was up to his neck in bills. Still, he made the gutsy decision to pour all the money he had left into *Nightmare*. If it failed, however, New Line would go with it.

Now came the pivotal decision—the casting of Freddy Krueger. Previously, killers in slasher films had tended to be hulking behemoths devoid of any personality. Determined to buck this trend, Craven settled on Robert Englund, a slight-of-build character actor who had minor roles in *Big Wednesday* (1978) and *Bloodbrothers* (1978) and who was best-known for his portrayal of an alien in the 1983 TV mini-series *V* and *V: The Final Battle* (1984).

Said Jack Sholder, who directed Englund in *A Nightmare on Elm Street 2: Freddy's Revenge*:

One of the most brilliant things Wes did was cast Robert Englund because people always cast some lunk to play the killer … whereas Robert Englund is not a big scary guy. He's a guy with an interesting, almost funny face, but he's a terrific actor. And Wes made that choice; it was a brilliant choice.

Sholder goes on to describe a scene, in *Freddy's Revenge*, which personifies Englund's strange charisma:

There was just something about the way Robert Englund took over the scene, the way he walked, the way he stood, that had power to it because he's a wonderful actor.

The task of creating Freddy's horribly burned face fell to makeup man David Miller, who ironically had previously worked on *Dreamscape*. His initial sculptures were based on photos of burn victims which he obtained from the UCLA Medical Center. Then, under Craven's direction, he perfected the visage which would haunt the dreams of teenagers for years to come.

Craven fought for a 36-day shoot, but with a budget of under $2 million, he was forced to settle for 32. Production on *A Nightmare on Elm Street* wrapped in July 1984. It was rushed through the edit at breakneck speed to get it ready for its November release. It was a tense time, and both Craven and Shaye were well aware that their future careers were potentially dependent on the film's success.

A Nightmare on Elm Street begins on the comforting streets of suburbia, where the children of Elm Street are plagued by a series of similar nightmares. They dream they are being chased by a horribly burned maniac in a dirty red and green sweater who has knives for fingers.

The next day at school, one of the teenagers, Tina (Amanda Wyss), discusses her nightmare with her delinquent boyfriend Rod (Nick Corri); her best friend Nancy (Heather Langenkamp); and

Nancy's preppie boyfriend Glen (Johnny Depp). It is obvious from their uneasiness that each of them has had the same dream. That night, the group sleeps at Tina's to comfort her in the event of another nightmare. As soon as she and Rod fall asleep, Tina begins to thrash around in bed, as if she is having some sort of violent seizure. Rod wakes up, only to see bloody wounds being inflicted upon Tina by an invisible attacker. The mutilated girl is then dragged up the walls and ceiling until she collapses on the floor in a pool of blood.

Rod is arrested the next day by Nancy's father, Lt. Thompson (John Saxon), who jails him for the murder of Tina. Naturally, no one believes his innocence except Nancy, who is beginning to understand that the havoc which Freddy causes in their dreams is manifested in reality. After an episode in a sleep clinic in which Nancy pulls the hat off Freddy's head and brings it back from her dream, her mother Marge (Ronee Blakley), tells her the true story of Fred Krueger.

Years ago, a series of child murders had the neighborhood in a panic. No one could figure out who was responsible for the awful crimes. Finally, Fred Krueger was caught but was soon released on a legal technicality. A group of vengeful parents then tracked him down to his filthy boiler room—where he would take his victims—doused the place with gasoline, and burned him alive.

Nancy realizes that the only way to kill Freddy is to bring him out of the dream world. She constructs a series of elaborate booby traps around the house, falls asleep and, sure enough, manages to pull Freddy into reality, thereby stripping him of his powers.

The disagreement between Shaye and Craven regarding the film's ending has gone down as one of the great arguments in the annals of the slasher film. As is, *A Nightmare on Elm Street* ends with Nancy

and her mother—who Freddy had murdered in the previous scene—stepping out of the house into the warm hazy morning. Tina, Rod and Glen arrive in a convertible to drive Nancy to school. Just when it seems that the entire film has been nothing more than a bad dream, the top of the convertible—painted with red and green stripes—slams shut. Marge stands on the porch, smiling and waving, unaware that her terrified daughter is trapped in the car. Suddenly, Freddy's glove shoots through the window and pulls Marge to certain death.

Shaye had wanted the film to end with Freddy driving the car, a decision which was undoubtedly influenced by his hope for a sequel. Craven hated the idea, and simply wanted the film to end with Nancy turning her back on Freddy, a symbolic gesture of good triumphing over evil. "The ghost of *Carrie* haunts us all," said Craven derisively, referring to the way which many horror films, post-*Carrie*, tack on one last "shock sequence." Craven has said he agreed to compromise partly out of loyalty to Shaye for being the only producer willing to take a chance on his project, but later regretted it. However, according to Sara Risher, co-producer of *A Nightmare on Elm Street*, two endings were shot, Shaye's, which had Freddy driving the car, and the one actually used in the film, which she claims is Craven's.

Thankfully, the bickering behind the scenes was not reflected in the finished film. *A Nightmare on Elm Street* was brilliant, one of the last great horror films and a work of art which surpassed even the highest expectations. Dreams have always played an active role in films, but none have captured their elasticity and warped logic better than *Nightmare*, from the film's first sequence, in which a stray sheep wanders aimlessly around a boiler room, to Nancy's ascent up a flight of steps which suddenly turn to goo.

Theatergoers came in droves to see Freddy. *Nightmare* went on to gross nearly $26 million, propelling Craven into the limelight and transforming New Line into a major player in the industry, saddling it with moniker "The House That Freddy Built."[2] The series would become a cottage industry, spawning books, T-shirts, masks, gloves, a board game, buttons, trading cards, hats, key rings and countless other items of pop culture memorabilia. Over the next decade, six sequels followed as well as a short-lived television series, *Freddy's Nightmares* (1988), hosted by Englund, all decked out in his trademark hat, sweater and, most importantly, his fiendish glove.

A far more controversial film opened the same day as *A Nightmare on Elm Street*. The furor over its release is now legendary, and the story of the moral outrage which accompanied it has been well-documented by William Schoell in *Stay Out of the Shower*.

The film was *Silent Night, Deadly Night* (1984), an in-your-face slasher film whose protagonist is a homicidal orphan dressed as Santa Claus. At the Interboro Quad Theater in the Bronx, over 100 concerned citizens picketed the film and protested by singing Christmas carols. One Bronx parent told an interviewer, "I have a very impressionable three-year-old child"—evidently referring to the film's televisions ads which depicted Santa holding an ax, since it is impossible to imagine any three-year-old seeing the film in the theater. Various groups joined the crusade to uphold the image of Old St. Nick and one New York State assemblyman even began a campaign to boycott theaters showing the film. While *Silent Night, Deadly Night* immediately recouped its $1 million budget, no doubt aided by the free publicity, Tri-Star Pictures, the film's distributor, eventually succumbed to the pressure. The television ads were discontinued,

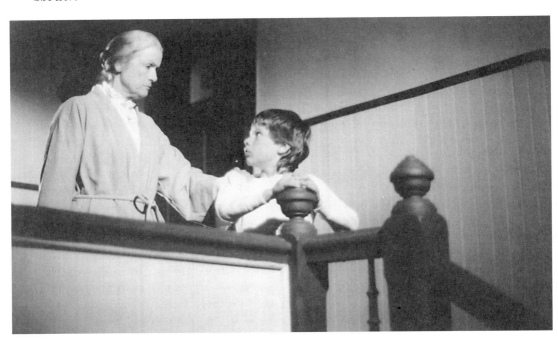

The sadistic punishments that Mother Superior (Lilyan Chauvin) metes out to young Billy (Danny Wagner) in Charles E. Sellier's controversial *Silent Night, Deadly Night* (1984) almost make us hope she'll be the first victim.

although Steve Randall, Tri-Star's Senior Vice-President of Marketing, said they were never planned to run past the first week anyway. Many theaters stopped showing the film entirely and Tri-Star even scrapped *Silent Night, Deadly Night*'s entire West Coast run.

What made this entire episode so confusing was that *Silent Night, Deadly Night* was only the latest in a fairly long line of similar films which depicted a killer Santa Claus. As early as 1972, Joan Collins was terrorized by Santa in the now-classic horror anthology *Tales from the Crypt* (1972). Although *Black Christmas* lacks the requisite jolly villain, it does set a series of disturbing murders on what is traditionally the most peaceful and joyous day of the year. *To All a Goodnight* (see Chapter 6) and *You Better Watch Out* (1980)—which not only features a psychotic Santa, but attempts to explain his psychosis with a scene of his mother getting it on with a visibly aroused St. Nick—were certainly as offensive as *Silent Night, Deadly Night*, but apparently were not well-known enough to rile the masses. *Don't Open Till Christmas* (1984), a British film made well before the controversy whose twist is that the homicidal killer is not Santa, but someone who is targeting Santa Clauses, was not released in America until after *Silent Night, Deadly Night*.

Lost in all of this righteous indignation was the film itself. While nowhere near as bad as its detractors made it out to be, the truth is, *Silent Night, Deadly Night* is more than a little distasteful. It's unquestionably mean-spirited and cruel, especially the scene in which young Billy witnesses the slaying of his parents by a robber dressed as Santa Claus. To watch a disturbed young man with a skewed sense of morality hack up promiscuous teenagers while dressed as Santa is one thing, but to watch the aforementioned robber brutally tear open a woman's blouse before

gleefully slitting her throat, all in plain view of her young son, is entirely something else. The film also spends an inordinate amount of time on the severe physical and psychological abuse which the cruel Mother Superior (Lilyan Chauvin) visits upon Billy. When he finally snaps and dons the Santa outfit, we can't help but think that the good mother may have had it coming.

Controversy aside, *Silent Night, Deadly Night* is not a bad film. It is well-acted—especially by Chauvin and Robert Brian Wilson, who plays the 18-year-old Billy—and nicely paced, with the gory slayings occurring at just the right moments. It was released at a time when the slasher film, although certainly on the decline, was beginning to *look* more and more professional, and Henning Schellerup's crisp cinematography gives the film a slick sheen which sets it apart from the faded grainy slashers of the early '80s. A few years later came a sequel (if you can call it that), *Silent Night, Deadly Night Part II* (1987) which mostly consists of footage from the original. Three more sequels—each getting progressively worse—followed: *Silent Night, Deadly Night 3: Better Watch Out!* (1989), *Silent Night, Deadly Night 4: Initiation* (1990) and *Silent Night, Deadly Night 5: The Toy Maker* (1991, sadly, with Mickey Rooney).

Splatter University (1984) was released by Troma, so you know it's going to be filled with bathroom humor, busty brainless co-eds and lots of bargain-basement gore effects. Fortunately, it wasn't produced by Troma, so you can cross your fingers and hope that the humor might be kind of funny, the actresses a tad professional and the special effects remotely believable. At the time of its release, given the fact that it was under the Troma banner, critics mistakenly called *Splatter University* a parody of the slasher film. But it is less a parody than a really bad movie,

Billy (Robert Brian Wilson) checks to see if a young girl has been naughty or nice. As expected in any film with an ax-wielding Santa, naughtiness brings more than a lump of coal in *Silent Night, Deadly Night* (1984).

and a mean-spirited one at that. However, like a train wreck, it forces you to keep watching, if only to see what foolishness director Richard W. Haines, who co-directed and co-wrote *Class of Nuke'Em High* (1986) with Troma founder Lloyd Kaufman, can come up with next. An escaped psychopath is terrorizing the students (mostly women) of Saint Trinians College, easily one of the most inept institutions of higher learning ever put on celluloid. The campus looks like the high school from *Welcome Back, Kotter* and the students— and I use this term as loosely as possible— don't seem as if they could pass a junior high spelling test much less a university exam. A completely unnecessary abortion subplot and one of the goofiest portrayals of the mental health profession in recent memory don't do much to help the film's cause. *Splatter University*'s lone high point

is its star, Francine Forbes, a decent actress and likable presence who deserves better than this silly film.

Evidently, producers of hit horror franchises don't share notes, nor do they heed the old adage about those who cannot remember the past being doomed to repeat it. It was only three short years before the release of *Friday the 13th Part V: A New Beginning* (1985) that *Halloween III: Season of the Witch* had decided to do away with Michael Myers in favor of an evil mask maker. Not surprisingly, fans didn't appreciate this attempt to alter the essence of the series. Nor did fans of the *Friday the 13th* series appreciate the fact that *A New Beginning*'s killer was not Jason, but an ordinary paramedic gone mad after his son's murder.[3] Apparently, the producers also forgot, or chose to ignore, how *Friday the 13th—The Final*

Pam (Melanie Kinnaman) and Jason (or is it?) do battle in *Friday the 13th Part V: A New Beginning* **(1985).**

Chapter ended; it all but assured us that Tommy, Jason's killer, would continue his work. But no, in *A New Beginning,* Tommy—who in the course of a year has grown from a young teenager into a fully mature 20-something-year-old—has been confined to a psychiatric institution with the best-looking mental patients you'll ever see. Despite a half-baked story and lack of continuity, the film has some of the most inventive and gory killings since the original, and managed to scare up $21.9 million at the box office. Now, the producers were faced with a dilemma. If the series was to continue, it needed a new villain. Didn't it?

The phenomenal success of *A Nightmare on Elm Street* guaranteed a sequel. Bob Shaye had handed the reins of the series over to director Jack Sholder and

nearly one year after the original film first hit theaters, *A Nightmare on Elm Street 2: Freddy's Revenge* (1985), was released. To the chagrin of some fans, *Freddy's Revenge* ignored the rules set forth in the original. It took Freddy out of the realm of dreams and brought him into reality through a conduit, high schooler Jesse Walsh (Mark Patton), who moves into Nancy's old house and finds her diary. Sholder deliberately pared down the film's violence and gore, refusing to make a run-of-the-mill slasher sequel. While many felt he went too far in the other direction, focusing too much on the psychology of the main characters instead of Freddy himself, *Freddy's Revenge* did have its admirers in the press. Janet Maslin, who had been notoriously quick to attack previous slashers, praised the film's direction, performances—especially

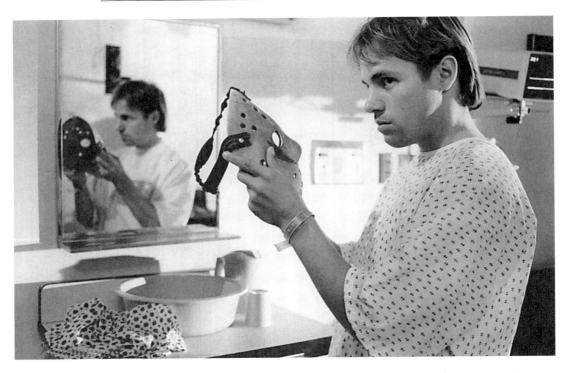

A severely traumatized Tommy Jarvis (John Shepherd) prepares to inherit the mantle as Crystal Lake's most infamous resident in *Friday the 13th Part V: A New Beginning* (1985).

that of the sarcastic Krueger (Englund)— and special effects, which were designed by Kevin Yagher, who had taken over effects duties from David Miller. Yagher was saddled with the unenviable chore of trying to duplicate Freddy's makeup from the original. Since New Line had no idea how prolific the series would become, and because Shaye wanted to maintain an air of secrecy about his villain, very few photographs of Freddy had been taken. *Freddy's Revenge* also began Freddy's metamorphosis from evil incarnate to a pop culture icon, increasing both his popularity and the profitability of the series.

By 1986, the end of the slasher film was in sight—that is, if you could wade through the glut of *Halloween*, *Friday the 13th* and *A Nightmare on Elm Street* sequels which were still trying to wring one last buck out of the dying genre. Out of this morass came a devilishly clever film which

was misunderstood, improperly marketed and all but overlooked at the time of its release. A victim of history, *April Fool's Day* should have heralded a new direction for the genre. Instead, it precipitated its decline.

To purposely distance himself from the film series which was both a boon to his bank account and blight on his résumé, Frank Mancuso, Jr., wanted to make a film which spoofed *Friday the 13th*—something classier, more fun and somewhat tongue-in-cheek. Danilo Bach, who would eventually be hired to write the screenplay, came to Mancuso with an idea he had read about in a Maine paper about a group of people who were planning a "mystery weekend." Mancuso liked the idea, and Bach was called in to meet with some Paramount executives, including Dreamworks co-founder, Jeffrey Katzenberg, who was then working at the studio. The

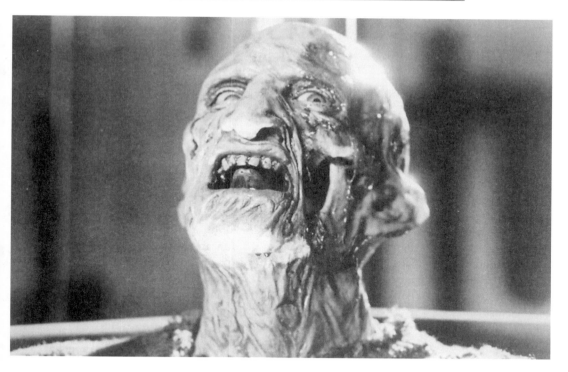

Freddy Krueger (Robert Englund) makes an unscheduled appearance in Jack Sholder's *A Nightmare on Elm Street Part 2: Freddy's Revenge* (1985), a special effects–heavy sequel to Craven's original.

project was soon greenlighted and Bach began working on the script, which took him only a month to complete.

Bach, who says the writing went "easy and well," describes the process:

My matrix was to take a younger version of *The Big Chill* [1983] and have fun with them. But it was very self-conscious. An attempt to take a lot of those traditional genre movies, *The Old Dark House* [1932], *Ten Little Indians* [1945], which as a kid I watched on TV, it was one of my favorites, the one with Louis Hayward ... and several others along the way.[4] In a sense to synthesize a lot of these films and a lot of these elements all the way up until the slasher. And then to have fun with it.

After interviewing various directors, Mancuso settled on Fred Walton, who had terrified audiences seven years before with *When a Stranger Calls*. Judging by Walton's recollection, however, their initial meeting was anything but smooth:

Mancuso almost didn't hire me. He told me, "I gotta tell you. Your whole attitude on this seems flaccid." That was that exact word he used. He says, "I've got other young guys coming in full of energy and excitement with just copious notes and stuff they want to talk about." Well, he hired me anyway. I've never been good at getting jobs for myself. Ever. I just don't make a good first impression. People think I'm weird, or flaccid, or whatever. But for me, your involvement in something has to deepen as you get into the project, as you start to hire actors and you're starting to look at locations. People would constantly say, "What's your vision?" I don't know what the hell my vision is. Let me work on it for awhile and

I'll tell you what my vision is. But I don't know now. It's idiotic.

For the role of Kit, one of the two female leads, Mancuso suggested Amy Steel, who had valiantly battled Jason Voorhees in *Friday the 13th Part 2*. Walton met with her at a Vancouver restaurant and, although she wasn't overly enthusiastic about the role, she eventually accepted. The critical part of Muffy/Buffy was played by Deborah Foreman, the star of the hit teenage comedy *Valley Girl* (1983), whose manager had arranged an audition with Walton and Mancuso. "She blew us away and won that part," remembers Walton. "She just had so much energy and so much charm. She's an interesting actress because she's very instinctive. Characters she's completed in the past never really leave her."

April Fool's Day was shot almost entirely on Vancouver Island. According to Walton, it was a "young, very talented group of kids that were having a lot of fun." The cast genuinely cared for each other and two of the leads even had a brief affair. Joel Schumacher, who was good friends with Mancuso, read the script and came up with one of the film's most chilling scenes.[5]

April Fool's Day begins with a group of college students, on spring break, arriving at the vacation home of their host and classmate, Muffy St. John. The week of sun, fun and practical jokes takes a sinister turn when the characters each find an item in their room which alludes to a personal secret: a painful reminder of an abortion, newspaper clippings of a car accident, drug paraphernalia and S&M restraints. Muffy begins acting strangely

Skip (center, Griffin O'Neal) explains how the events of the past evening have been nothing more than an elaborate ruse in Fred Walton's grossly misunderstood *April Fool's Day* (1986).

just as the guests start to disappear. At first, suspicion falls on Buck, a local worker who was horribly injured in a practical joke gone awry, but after learning that he had been in the hospital during the entire ordeal, the group realizes the killer must be one of their own. Muffy seems the obvious choice, until it is discovered that she has a crazy twin sister, Buffy, who may have indeed crashed the party. Just when it appears that Buffy will claim her final two victims, they stumbled into a room—filled with all their friends, drinking champagne and very much alive. The entire weekend was an elaborately constructed ruse, meticulously planned by Muffy (really, there is no Buffy) as a test for her "mystery weekend," which she hopes will provide her with the extra income necessary to retain ownership of her family estate.

There was initially an entire third act which was cut from the film. The way *April Fool's Day* ends, with all the guests celebrating and spraying each other with champagne, was originally the end of Act II. In the deleted act, the group gets back on the ferry the next morning and decides to give Muffy a taste of her own medicine. But someone, as Bach says, "now decides to do some serious damage. To kill someone. Since everything up to this point had been a joke, no one will come to anyone's help. It's like crying wolf." The culprit is Muffy's brother Skip, who wants the inheritance for himself. Paramount disliked this cut, however, and wanted the film to end after Act II, on a high note.

April Fool's Day was released over the Easter weekend, a notoriously bad time for films, but managed to gross a whopping $13 million. It was the perception of the film, however, not its actual gross, which was disappointing. Audiences, even fans, didn't know what to make of the film which blatantly flaunted the conventions of the slasher only to pull the rug out from under their feet. "Some people were very angry with the film and wrote that they disliked it because it was a joke ultimately," recalls Bach. "These people were basically slasher and horror groupies. I just think they didn't have much of a sense of humor."

Walton has a different take on the matter:

> The tragedy, I think, or the great disappointment, was that Paramount didn't know how to release it other than as a typical slasher picture. So most audiences came in expecting to see something that they weren't going to see and they were disappointed. It wasn't marketed as something fresh and hip and fun. That's why I believe it didn't do very well.

The failure of a fresh, exciting and original film like *April Fool's Day* didn't bode well for the future of the slasher film. Audiences had both tired of the old formula—that of a maniac decimating a group of teenagers—but were unwilling to support a new approach to their slagging genre. True, the film's marketing campaign could have been more focused and extensive, but poor advertising had never before prevented a slasher favorite from doing impressive business at the box office. These films lived and died by word of mouth, the most powerful predicator of a horror film's success. This time, however, the word of mouth was bad. The slasher film was clearly on its last legs.

The vile brilliance of William Fruet's overlooked 1976 rape-revenge classic *The House by the Lake* is nowhere to be found in *Killer Party* (1986), his rather innocuous but enjoyable slasher with supernatural undertones. At "Every Campus" University, naturally filled with all the elaborate pranks and hijinks which really occur nowhere except in the imagination of overzealous comedy writers, Jennifer (Joanna Johnson) and her two best friends pledge an elite sorority. At the big April Fool's Day bash, held in the house in which a pledge died in a tragic accident (a no-no for campus slashers), a killer dressed as a deep-sea diver begins slaughtering the guests. Just when it seems as if *Killer Party* is going to be an ordinary run-of-the-mill slasher, the killer is revealed to be Jennifer, who has been possessed by the vengeful spirit of the dead pledge. Thanks to some impressive effects and a delightful turn by Paul Bartel as an uppity professor, not to mention director Fruet's refusal to take the material too seriously, *Killer Party* was a cut above (no pun intended) the mostly uninspired slasher films of the time.

Friday the 13th Part VI: Jason Lives opened on August 1, 1986, to surprisingly restrained reviews, considering that most critics waited with bated breath to bash the next slasher, especially the hated offspring of *Friday the 13th*, a series they particularly detested. The series' sixth installment was also heralded by fans, most of whom had been extremely disappointed with *A New Beginning*. It was written and directed by Tom McLoughlin, the man responsible for 1983's *One Dark Night*. McLoughlin injected some well-received humor into the series, including a parody of the James Bond films' opening sequences, in which Jason strolls across the screen and slices his machete toward the audience as blood trickles down. Tommy Jarvis, still obsessed with Jason after all these years, returns to the grave of his nemesis to make sure, once and for all, that he really is dead. In a freak accident, Jason's corpse is revived when the metal stake which Tommy had plunged into his chest is struck by lightning. Refreshed,

In William Fruet's *Killer Party* (1986), Jennifer (Joanna Johnson), Phoebe (Elaine Wilkes) and Veronica (Alicia Fleer) wonder what horror awaits them in the basement of their sorority house.

invigorated and pretty pissed off, Jason returns to Crystal Lake, which has been renamed Forest Green in an effort to forget its bloody past. Unfortunately, the positive reviews didn't translate into box office success and *Jason Lives* only grossed approximately $19 million, even less than *A New Beginning.*

Obviously feeling left out of the race to see which slasher franchise could humiliate itself most thoroughly, *The Texas Chainsaw Massacre* threw its hat (or should I say chain saw?) into the ring. What followed was an unequivocal mess, but what was even more surprising than how badly Tobe Hooper disrespected his masterpiece, was the accompanying reaction. *The Texas Chainsaw Massacre 2*, which finds a severely demented former Texas Ranger (Dennis Hopper) out to avenge the death of his nephew and the torture of his niece (Franklin and Sally from *The Texas Chainsaw Massacre*), was seen by some as a take-no-prisoners satire on contemporary American society. John McCarty, who knows the genre as well as anybody, even called *Chainsaw 2* Tobe Hooper's best film. A more likely explanation is that the film is so bad that many critics, refusing to believe that Hooper could have actually made this poor excuse for a horror movie, needed some way to justify its existence. Three years later, in 1989, the equally bad *Leatherface: The Texas Chainsaw Massacre III* was released. The film is less a sequel than a rehashing of the original. It is quite grisly, although heavily edited, which possibly explains the gaping holes in its plot. An even more execrable sequel, *The Texas Chainsaw Massacre: The Next Generation* (1994), is only notable for starring both Renee Zellweger and Matthew McConaughey.

Had *Slaughter High* been made during the height of the slasher cycle, there is no reason it would not have been mentioned in the same breath as *Terror Train,* *My Bloody Valentine* and *Prom Night.* Alas, it was released in 1986, when the profits from original slashers were dwindling and no major distribution company was about to get behind a film which didn't star either Michael, Jason or Freddy. Yet it manages to distinguish itself from other slashers of the time by above-average performances, tight pacing by the directorial trio of George Dugdale, Mark Ezra and Peter Litten, and impressively gruesome special effects. The story is the standard faux high school reunion arranged as an elaborately constructed revenge plot. In this case, it is class nerd, Marty Rantzen—played by actor Simon Scuddamore who, with a name like that, must have endured some schoolyard taunting himself—who returns to settle the score with a clique of popular jocks and their girlfriends whose cruel practical joke left him burned beyond recognition. Similar to other class reunion slashers, the returning group doesn't find the absence of any other former students suspicious enough to warrant leaving. As long as there's beer, they seem content. The film's most illogical moment, however, occurs after one of the girls is splattered with blood from her friend's recently burst intestines; it seems someone slipped something a little stronger than a mickey into his drink. Rather than stay within the safety of the group, now that they know a killer is on the loose, she goes off by herself to an abandoned bathroom, takes off all of her clothes and runs herself a bath, which begs the additional question: What type of high school lavatory has a bathtub anyway? Her stupidity is short-lived; the water is not water at all, but caustic acid which reduces her to a skeleton within minutes. A nice creative touch, which some thought ruined the effectiveness of the entire film, is *Slaughter High*'s final sequence. We learn that Marty is still in the hospital and that the entire massacre has been his dream. When the attending physician arrives to calm him after the nightmare, Marty stabs him in the eye with a syringe, hinting that the film was less a dream than a premonition of things to come.

Return to Horror High (1987), a slasher spoof, was released at a time when many slashers were unintentionally spoofing themselves and features a pre–*ER* George Clooney and post–*Brady Bunch* Maureen McCormick (Marcia Brady). The plot follows a production team which is trying to shoot a low-budget horror film in Crippen High, where, five years earlier, a psycho who was never caught went on a killing spree. Why this ragtag bunch of filmmakers insists on using the actual location is never fully explained, but at least it allows for the killer to return to finish the job he started. The creative deaths of cast and crew members are intermingled with fictitious scenes of bloody mayhem so the audience is never sure if the murders are part of the film proper or the production contained within. All things considered—by this time, the slasher film was desperately trying to reinvent itself—the result could have been worse. Director Bill Froehlich manages to elicit a few genuine chuckles with his otherwise wooden performers and the murder scenes do have their tense moments. Maybe the most intriguing aspect of *Return to Horror High* is that not only is its plot vaguely similar to *Scream* (1996), but the killer's guise is almost identical to the now famous "Ghostface."

A Nightmare on Elm Street 3: Dream Warriors, directed by Chuck Russell, was released in February 1987. This time Freddy—again played by Robert Englund,

A dead body is never what it seems in Bill Froehlich's *Return to Horror High* (1987), a semi-parody of the slasher film.

This is easily one of Kristin Parker's (Patricia Arquette) worst nightmares. As a suicidal mental patient in Chuck Russell's *A Nightmare on Elm Street 3: Dream Warriors* **(1987), she'll soon meet the patron saint of bad dreams, the one and only Freddy Krueger.**

the only actor to ever don the glove—invades the dreams of a group of teenagers who have been committed to a psychiatric institution after a series of failed suicide attempts.[6] Hoping to recapture some of the magic of the original, *Dream Warriors* brings back two of its stars, Nancy (Heather Langenkamp) and her father Lt. Thompson (John Saxon). It also has memorable cameos by Dick Cavett and Zsa Zsa Gabor, the latter quickly dispatched by Freddy while on Cavett's talk show. By the end of the film Freddy had become a wisecracking caricature, in keeping with the darkly comedic tone the series was taking. His murders are more creative than bloody, preferring inventive methods to his traditional finger knives. While *Freddy's Revenge* had been a modest hit, earning $29 million, *Dream Warriors* took home a staggering $44.8 mil-

lion, guaranteeing the series would continue.

Inspired by his failed attempt to direct Giuseppe Verdi's *Rigoletto* for the Sferisterio Theater, Dario Argento began production on *Opera* (1987), which was, with a budget of $8 million, his most expensive film to date. Betty (Cristina Marsillach), a young and very talented understudy, inherits the lead in *Macbeth* when the opera's temperamental star Mara Cecova is injured in a automobile accident. Her instant fame comes with a price, however, a sadistic stalker who conjures up an ingenious way to torture her: Betty is bound and a row of steel needles is taped underneath her eyelids. She can't close her eyes at risk of tearing the tender flesh and is forced to watch as the stalker murders those close to her.

The entire *Rigoletto* experience left a

Freddy (Robert Englund) has finally reached the big time and guest stars with Zsa Zsa Gabor on Dick Cavett's talk show in one of *A Nightmare on Elm Street 3: Dream Warriors*' (1987) most bizarre dream sequences.

bad taste in Argento's mouth. His frustration is displaced, somewhat heavy-handedly, to his cinematic alter ego Marco (Ian Charleson), *Macbeth*'s director, a former horror movie director who at one point in the film is told to stick to horror films. Still, it is quite amusing to watch Argento, ostensibly the most humorless of directors, take digs at the pompous opera community. Like the film's cursed production of *Macbeth,* the set of *Opera* was besieged by problems. Vanessa Redgrave was signed to play diva Mara Cecova, but balked at the salary she was offered. Argento's response was to pare the role down to a bare minimum, eliminating the need for anything more than a stand-in. In addition, Argento's engagement was broken off and, most tragic of all, his father and longtime

collaborator, producer Salvatore Argento, passed away during shooting.

Opinion on *Opera* is sharply divided. Many felt the film was overindulgent and incoherent, a love letter to glossy but soulless filmmaking, a tendency Argento had narrowly avoided with *Tenebrae* but had fallen prey to with *Phenomena*. Others felt that despite the on-set turmoil, *Opera* was a fully realized, fiendishly clever film, on a par with the director's greatest works. After *Opera*, Argento took a hiatus from the *giallo*. He produced Michele Soavi's *The Church* (1988) and *The Sect* (1990) and directed a loose, ultra-grisly version of Edgar Allan Poe's "The Black Cat," the second half of *Two Evil Eyes* (1990), a collaboration with George Romero, a director whom Argento had always admired

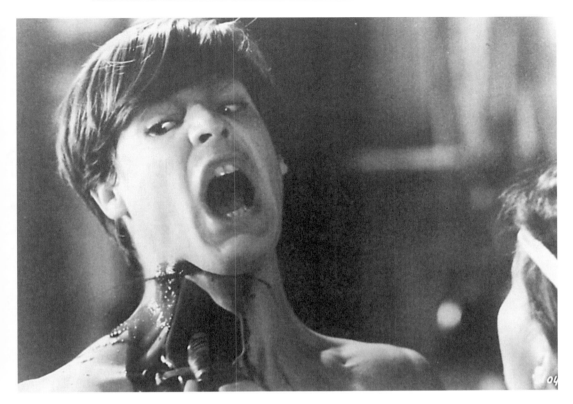

A sadistic stalker goes right for the jugular of Stefan in Dario Argento's typically gory *Opera* **(1987).**

and with whom he had worked previously on *Dawn of the Dead.*

After the less than spectacular box office take of *Friday the 13th Part VI: Jason Lives,* Frank Mancuso, Jr., was looking for a new angle to his series. He found it in the form of telekinetic teenager Tina Shepherd (Lar Park Lincoln), who inadvertently raises Jason from the dead with her supernatural powers and is forced to harness her little-understood ability in order to defeat him. *Friday the 13th Part VII: The New Blood* was shot over the course of six weeks in the woods of Alabama (interiors in Los Angeles) and was the first in the series to star Kane Hodder, the actor who has since become synonymous with the role of Jason. To direct, Mancuso chose John Carl Buechler, the special effects and makeup wiz whose 1986

film *Troll* he admired. Buechler took the assignment very seriously, but despite having the utmost respect for the horror genre he was never able to effectively mesh the supernatural aspects of the story with the standard slasher formula. *The New Blood* was released, quite appropriately, on Friday, May the 13th, 1988, and made a little over $19 million, about the same as the previous installment.

From the beginning, *A Nightmare on Elm Street 4: The Dream Master* was fraught with difficulties. Nobody was happy with the initial script, and with the Writers Guild on strike, help seemed long in coming. Because the story was such a mess, director Renny Harlin, whose subsequent career as an A-list director includes the blockbusters *Die Hard 2* (1990) and *Cliffhanger* (1993), chose to focus on

Top: Despite initial script problems, Freddy Krueger (Robert Englund) returns in *A Nightmare on Elm Street 4: The Dream Master* (1988), directed by Renny Harlin. Here he menaces Kristin (Tuesday Knight). *Bottom:* Never content to simply slay his victims, Freddy (Robert Englund) taunts a terrified Sheila (Toy Newkirk) in *A Nightmare on Elm Street 4: The Dream Master* (1988).

the special effects which he wanted to be more "surreal" and "bizarre" than terrifying. The task of creating his vision fell to John Carl Buechler's Magical Media Industries.[7] Despite its problems, *A Nightmare on Elm Street 4: The Dream Master*, released in August, 1988, was the most

successful installment of the series, earning over $49 million.

It was extremely surprising, then, when only one year later, *A Nightmare on Elm Street 5: The Dream Child*, by most accounts a far superior film, made only $22 million at the box office. While critics

Like father, like son? Not quite. Here, Freddy Krueger (Robert Englund) poses with a version of himself as a baby for *A Nightmare on Elm Street 5: The Dream Child* **(1989).**

praised Stephen Hopkins' direction, and David Miller returned to do the makeup for the fiend he helped create, audiences chose to stay away.

On October 21, 1988, almost exactly ten years after he escaped from Smith Grove Sanitarium, Michael Myers returned to Haddonfield. Comatose since the fiery inferno in which he supposedly perished in *Halloween II*, and oblivious to the debacle which was *Season of the Witch*, he awakes from his decade-long slumber after hearing that the Myers bloodline lives on in the form of a young niece, Jamie (Danielle Harris), the daughter of Laurie Strode (Jamie Lee Curtis, only shown through old photographs). *Halloween 4: The Return of Michael Myers*, directed by Dwight H. Little and scripted by Alan B. McElroy, who allegedly wrote the screenplay in 11 days to avoid the impending Writers Guild strike,

was filmed in Salt Lake City, Utah, for $5.5 million. It went on to gross $17 million and spent its first two weekends atop the box office charts. It had been nearly seven years since a true *Halloween* film and the series was being muscled out as a legitimate horror franchise by both the *Friday the 13th* and *A Nightmare on Elm Street* series which were producing sequels like clockwork. While absence may make the heart grow fonder, it doesn't necessarily make the product better, and *The Return of Michael Myers* is a rather tepid entry. Although it takes a cue from Carpenter's film and pares the gore down to a bare minimum, it never manages to create a fraction of the original's suspense. The film's high point is clearly the return not of Michael, but of Loomis, who survived the hospital fire himself and is both badly burned and quite insane, which allows Donald Pleasence ample opportunity to overact.

Rachel (Ellie Cornell) hangs on for dear life as Michael Myers slowly approaches in *Halloween 4: The Return of Michael Myers* (1988).

City. A lackluster and illogical ending in which Jason is sprayed with toxic waste and reverts to a naked child only adds to the disappointment. *Jason Takes Manhattan* took in only $14 million at the box office, making it the least successful of *Friday the 13th*'s sequels.

There were a lot of people who were, to say the least, unhappy with the way *Halloween 4: The Return of Michael Myers* ended. They found the idea of an adolescent girl continuing the work of the now deceased Michael Myers distasteful and ridiculous. In response to these complaints, after a brilliant credit sequence, *Halloween 5: The Revenge of Michael Myers* seeks to clarify some misconceptions which the previous film advanced. Michael Myers is not really dead, he found a hidden passageway in the mine and escaped by floating down the river; Jamie did not stab her stepmother to death, she simply injured her badly; and most importantly, she did not inherit her uncle's murderous tendencies. Instead, the now mute girl has developed a psychic bond with Michael and has been interned in Haddonfield's Childrens Clinic since the night of the murders.

Shooting for *The Revenge of Michael Myers* began on May 1, 1989. The film was rushed through post production to meet its October 13 release date. Like its predecessor, it was made cheaply, for less than $5 million, but this time only grossed approximately $11.5 million. There were some rumors of on-set clashes between director Dominique Othenin-Girard, who wanted a more graphic and visceral film, and both executive producer Moustapha

Friday the 13th Part VIII: Jason Takes Manhattan (1989) was a bad idea from the beginning, a perfect example of the type of half-baked high concept idea which Hollywood execs spend countless hours and dollars trying to come up with. Plopping Jason down in the middle of Manhattan was a crass gimmick, and most fans of the series held their collective breath, hoping for the best and expecting the worst. The film was a dismal failure. Jason doesn't cause unprecedented havoc in Midtown. Ironically, he blends in rather well with the other undesirables who director Rob Hedden seems to think are the only individuals who inhabit New York

Akkad and star Donald Pleasence. What resulted was the bloodiest and, some would say, most offensive of the *Halloween* films. The murder of Rachel (Ellie Cornell), the surviving star of *The Return of Michael Myers*, was less an homage to Janet Leigh's murder in *Psycho* than a prime example of why some people found the film so tasteless. But overall, *The Revenge of Michael Myers* is the same rehashing of the story we've all seen too many times; Michael chases a hysterical Jamie for a painfully long period of time while Loomis gives chase. The climax, which takes place in the cobweb-shrouded Myers house, finds Loomis capturing Michael in a carefully rigged chain net. He proceeds to beat him to uncertain death while a hysterical Jamie watches. With a quickly recovered Michael now in jail, and Jamie about to return to the institution, the saga of America's first boogeyman seems over. Then, just as the credits are about to tease

the bottom of the screen, a mysterious figure in black arrives at the holding cell, kills the guards and frees Michael.

The mystery of his identify would have to wait six years, until 1995, to be answered in *Halloween 6: The Curse of Michael Myers*, a film so bad and disrespectful to the series that it's a mystery how anyone could have even allowed it to be made. A complete mess in pre-production, throughout production and in post-production, the film is a prime example of the old adage that too many cooks (or in this case, clueless and careless film executives) don't just spoil the broth, they poison it. *The Curse of Michael Myers* is only a *Halloween* film in name, and despite the presence of Michael, it is an impenetrable jumble of random ideas and impossible coincidences which has something to do with a pregnant Jamie Lloyd (now played by J.C. Brandy, as if nobody would notice), an ancient runic symbol and some clandestine genetic research

Michael Myers' (George Wilbur) history is explored in Joe Chappelle's *Halloween 6: The Curse of Michael Myers* **(1995), easily the most disliked film of the** *Halloween* **series.**

at Michael's old home, the Smith Grove Sanitarium. *The Curse of Michael Myers*, which was universally detested, was Donald Pleasence's final film. He died shortly after shooting. This wonderful actor, an important fixture of the *Halloween* films, deserved better, as did the series for which he will be forever remembered.

With 1991's *Freddy's Dead: The Final Nightmare*—a title whose promised finality had lost some of its oomph after the joke which was *Friday the 13th—The Final Chapter*—the transformation of America's favorite boogeyman from evil incarnate into a bumbling blubbering buffoon was officially complete. The film was directed by the well-meaning Rachel Talalay, a member of the New Line family who had been involved with the series from its genesis, as production manager on *Freddy's Revenge*, line producer on *Dream Warriors* and producer of *The Dream Master*. Like a childhood fear which no longer has the power to frighten us, Freddy Krueger had

become both silly and quaint. Among the film's countless absurdities are a parody of *The Wizard of Oz* (1939) with Freddy as the Wicked Witch of the West, a video game in which Freddy has the power to control the film's characters and, most pointless of all, an unwelcomed cameo by Roseanne Barr and Tom Arnold. *Freddy's Dead* does makes an earnest attempt to explore Freddy's childhood at the hands of an abusive stepfather and, in the film's only effectively chilling scene, shows how Freddy killed his wife in front of their young daughter after she accidentally discovered his torture lair. But even these attempts at characterization feel more like filler until the hokey 3-D finale—a cautionary example of what happens when marketing is allowed to dictate a film's trajectory—which didn't surprise anybody who had already seen *Jaws 3* (1983). Somehow, *Freddy's Dead* grossed $34 million, proving only that there's no accounting for taste at a boogeyman's funeral.

In *Freddy's Dead* (1991), which delves into the life of Fred Krueger before he became everybody's favorite flambeed villain, a teenage Freddy (Tobe Sexton) puts an end to the beatings by his alcoholic father (Alice Cooper).

Jason Goes to Hell: The Final Friday was hotly anticipated, mostly due to the fact that Sean Cunningham had returned to produce. There hadn't been a *Friday the 13th* film since 1989's *Jason Takes Manhattan* and in that time Paramount had sold the rights to the series to New Line Cinema. *Jason Goes to Hell* was released on August 13, 1993, a few months after the thirteenth anniversary of the original *Friday the 13th*, and went on to gross nearly $16 million.

Directed by Adam Marcus, the film has the most complex plot of any of the *Friday the 13th* films. It begins with a lengthy prologue in which Jason is "killed" by an FBI SWAT team, but unlike the other installments, this time it is not Jason who returns from the dead; it is his spirit, who begins possessing people, forcing them to do his dastardly deeds. His quest is no longer just to knock off as many for-nicating teenagers as possible—which isn't to say he isn't up to his old tricks; there are murders aplenty—but to find his last remaining relative, for only through a Voorhees can he be reborn.

The film's most intriguing element, a shrewd marketing ploy, whetted the appetite of horror fans all over the world. In the last scene, Jason's hockey mask is lying in a forest clearing. Suddenly, from beneath the soft dirt, a hand shoots up. A gloved hand. Freddy Krueger's gloved hand. And pulls the mask into the bowels of hell as maniacal laughter plays over the scene. This final shock fueled the rumor that one day, now that New Line owns the rights to both series, the long awaited *Freddy vs. Jason* will become a reality. As this book goes to print, another *Friday the 13th* sequel, *Jason X*, is awaiting release. Supposedly, *Freddy vs. Jason* is next. The optimistic find this prospect a fitting end

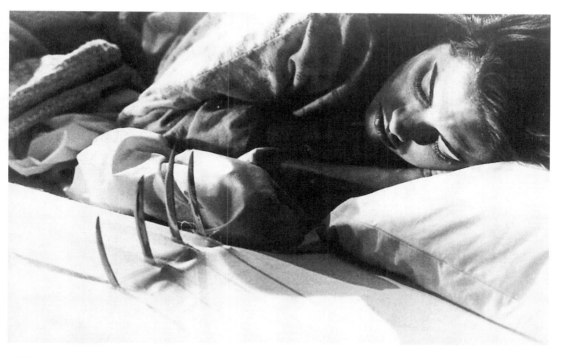

Using a novel concept—now Freddy can reach his victims in their waking state—Wes Craven returned for *Wes Craven's New Nightmare* (1994), the sixth installment of the *Nightmare on Elm Street* series. Here, Heather Langenkamp is about to say hello to an old friend.

to two of the proudest slasher franchises; opponents find it a crass joke, a post-modern repeat of what Universal did with their horror franchises in the 1940s with *Frankenstein Meets the Wolf Man* (1943), *House of Frankenstein* (1944) and *House of Dracula* (1945), films which seemed to think that if one monster was good, two or more would be much better. Needless to say, these cheap amalgams never were as popular as their predecessors.

Although Freddy Krueger was dead, he was far from unexploitable. Both Bob Shaye and Wes Craven were astute enough to realize that a conventional approach, no matter how original, to another *Nightmare on Elm Street* sequel would be nothing more than a crapshoot. The once fertile plains of cinematic horror had been left fallow by a blight of inferior sequels, hateful remakes and straight-to-video trash. It would take a lot to lure Craven—who, for a variety of reasons, had not been deeply involved with any *Nightmare* film since directing the original—back to the series which he created, if it could be done at all. Craven eventually did come back. In *Wes Craven's New Nightmare* he devised a scenario where the evil spirit of Freddy, which has been harnessed by the proliferation of the *Nightmare on Elm Street* films, is released into reality to stalk Heather Langenkamp. The kicker is that the only way to stop Freddy is to make another *Nightmare* film. Along with Langenkamp, John Saxon, Robert Englund, Bob Shaye, Sara Risher and others do double duty, playing themselves along with their cinematic alter egos.

Wes Craven's New Nightmare was released on October 14, 1994, and grossed $18 million. It was a gutsy and compelling

Some things never change. Freddy revisits the old "tongue-through-the-phone" gag he got Nancy (Heather Langenkamp) with in the original *A Nightmare on Elm Street.* **A decade later, in** *Wes Craven's New Nightmare* **(1994), it has lost none of its effect.**

concept, geared towards students of cinema as much as towards fans of the series. But a concept, no matter how brilliant, can only go so far. By the middle of the film, *New Nightmare* had devolved into the standard Freddy vs. whomever in special effects—driven combat. Critical reaction to *New Nightmare* was generally positive, for critics tend to champion those films which embrace reflexivity and attempt to tear down the proverbial fourth wall between the audience and the medium. Popular opinion, however, was sharply divided. Some fans felt Craven had destroyed the essence of his creation by tampering with the internal logic of the series, while others praised what they considered to be a brave attempt to reinvent the franchise.

By the mid 1990s, it was generally a forgone conclusion that the only way the slasher film would contain to endure was through sequels, some rather innovative and laudable, most absolutely dreadful. Those of *Halloween*, *Friday the 13th*, *A Nightmare on Elm Street* and *The Texas Chainsaw Massacre* could continue to exist on name alone, still able to pull down marginal profits as long as they kept their budgets to a minimum. New and original slasher films, however, were consigned to video, unable to scare up any national distribution or exhibition.

Then, in 1996, Dimension Films, a subsidiary of Miramax, released a film which broke all the rules, shattered box office records and once again made the slasher film viable, not just as an economic model of production, but as a genre which seemed to reconnect with its larger-than-imagined audience.

CHAPTER 10

The Resurgence

In the spring of 1995, an unusual script was making the rounds in Hollywood. It was called *Scary Movie* and was written by an unknown screenwriter named Kevin Williamson. It was filled with teenagers in peril, brutal murders and a psychotic killer. It was the kind of script that 15 years before would have been quickly snatched up by an eager producer, but which recently, given the changing horror climate, would be lucky to even get a read from a development executive.

Strangely enough, *Scary Movie* began attracting a good deal of attention. There was something different about it. It seemed to walk a fine line between poking fun at the classic slasher films and paying homage to them. The dialogue was witty, self-referential and seemed to capture the authenticity of modern teenage jargon. The characters were well-drawn and three-dimensional, hip enough to understand the conventions of the slasher film and still young and naïve enough to ignore them. It was the first slasher script to actively acknowledge the films which came before it.[1] But most of all, *Scary Movie* was scary. Really scary. For all its clever references and self-consciousness, it was a script of raw and terrifying power. The kind of script which only comes along once in a great while.

Williamson grew up in New Bern, North Carolina, where he developed his love of horror movies at an early age. He cites viewing *Halloween* for the first time as one of the most important moments of his life and tells a comical story about how he became so frightened while watching *A Nightmare on Elm Street* in the theater that his leg cramped up and he couldn't move.

Williamson graduated from East Carolina University, where he studied film and theater. In 1987, he moved to New York City to pursue an acting career. Although he landed a few commercials and a bit part in the popular soap opera *Another World*, he ended up waiting tables like so many other aspiring actors. Frustrated with his inability to break into the business, Williamson returned to North Carolina four years later. In 1991, he moved to Los Angeles to continue his fledgling acting career and took a job as an assistant to a music video director in order to pay the bills. Still unhappy, Williamson borrowed money from a friend to enroll in a UCLA screenwriting class. During the ten-week course, he wrote a script for a black comedy called *Killing Mrs. Tingle*, which was inspired by a high school English teacher who had humiliated him. *Killing Mrs. Tingle* was optioned by

Interscope for a low six figures but languished in "development hell," leaving Williamson once again broke and unsure of his future.

While housesitting in Westwood as a favor to a friend who had lent him money, Williamson saw a Barbara Walters special about the Gainesville murders.[2] His imagination ran wild and he convinced himself that there was a maniac outside waiting to slaughter him. He then called a friend of his, David Blanchard, and kept him on the phone as he searched the house clutching a large butcher knife. Blanchard, like any good friend, tried to calm Williamson by listing all the possible psychopaths—Freddy, Michael, Jason—who could be lurking in the shadows, and the two soon found themselves quizzing each other about horror films.

Motivated by his housesitting horror, Williamson went to Palm Springs for the weekend, locked himself in a hotel room and hammered out a script. He wanted to create a story which not only terrified audiences, but paid tribute to the classic slasher films he loved as a kid. As further inspiration, he listened to the *Halloween* soundtrack while working. By the time he was finished, Williamson not only had a script, but a five-page treatment for the second and third installments of what he always conceived as a trilogy.

Williamson's agent then sent the script to various studios and producers. Remarkably, Universal, Paramount, Morgan Creek, Oliver Stone and Bob Weinstein were soon furiously bidding for it. When the smoke cleared, only Stone and Weinstein were left standing. Stone made a higher offer but Weinstein had recently

Not since *When a Stranger Calls* has the phone been an instrument of such terror. In this scene from Wes Craven's *Scream* (1996), the film responsible for reinventing the slasher genre, Sidney (Neve Campbell) and Tatum (Rose McGowan) receive a call from Ghostface.

formed Dimension Films, a "genre" division of Miramax, and knew how to market this type of film. More importantly, he was willing to make the film immediately. With the experience of *Killing Mrs. Tingle* still fresh in his mind, Williamson promptly sold *Scary Movie* to Dimension Films for $500,000.

After purchasing one of the hottest spec scripts in history, Weinstein now had to find a director for *Scary Movie*, whose title had been changed to *Scream* to avoid any confusion that it was either a comedy or parody. When you're looking for horror directors, especially ones with a distinctive vision, only a few names come to mind. Ironically, Wes Craven had recently been in discussion with Miramax about a remake of Robert Wise's classic 1963 film *The Haunting*, which many consider to be the greatest haunted house movie ever made. While Craven was interested in doing the remake, the parties were never able to figure out an acceptable way to update the story for modern audiences while retaining the quiet unspoken terror which made the original so effective. Eventually, Miramax let their option on the project expire.[3]

When Craven was first offered *Scream*, which now had Drew Barrymore attached, he turned it down. He was looking to distance himself from the types of films which until now had defined his career. He also didn't have the energy for a prolonged and contentious battle with the MPAA which was sure to follow if he filmed *Scream* to the letter. However, he had also been deeply affected by the first scene of Williamson's script and was intrigued at the prospect of reinventing a genre which he had played no small part in creating. He called Bob Weinstein back and accepted the job.

Production on the $15 million film began in the spring of 1996. Aside from Barrymore, the cast, which Craven calls "the best cast I've ever had a chance to direct," included other young and up-and-coming actors such as Neve Campbell, Courteney Cox, David Arquette, Skeet Ulrich, Rose McGowan, Matthew Lillard and Jamie Kennedy.

The film's first, and most famous scene, which Williamson describes as an homage to *When a Stranger Calls* (see Chapter 4), was shot over the course of five days at a private residence in the mountains of Sonoma. For this scene, in which Casey Becker (Drew Barrymore) is terrorized by a series of threatening phone calls, Williamson thought it would be important to get a known star for the role. This way, when she is killed at the beginning of the film, the audience understands that all bets are off. Barrymore is perfect as the fresh-faced Casey, but to insure a completely authentic performance, Craven reminded the animal lover of a story he had heard about a dog being burned by its owner. Needless to say, the story had the desired effect on Barrymore.

After the death of Casey and her boyfriend Steve (Kevin Patrick Walls), the story shifts to high schooler Sidney Prescott (Neve Campbell), living a nightmare of her own after her mother was raped and murdered a year ago. When an opportunistic TV reporter, Gale Weathers (Courteney Cox), who wrote a trashy book about the murder, returns to investigate the current slayings, the quaint town of Woodsboro—filmed in the quaint town of Healdsburg, California—is turned upside down. Also thrown into the mix is Deputy Dewey Riley (David Arquette), a bumbling but kind-hearted officer who tries to solve the murders.

After their high school principal, Mr. Himbry (Henry Winkler), is brutally murdered in school, the apparently unfazed teens decide to throw a huge party at Stu's (Matthew Lillard).[4]

The party scene was shot at a 200-acre

ranch in Tomales, California, in which, it was rumored, the previous owners had died earlier that year, adding an extra element of uneasiness for the cast and crew. As expected (by everyone except the carefree teens), the killer arrives at the party, uninvited, and begins trimming down the guest list. Eventually, when only Sidney is left, the killer reveals himself. It is Billy Loomis (Skeet Ulrich), Sidney's own boyfriend, whose father was having an affair with Sidney's mother. But that's not all. There's a second killer, Stu, a deranged kid who just wants to get in on the action. In a bloody, over-the-top climax, the deeply disturbed duo begins stabbing each other in an elaborate plan to frame Sidney's father, who they've captured and plan to kill shortly after. Ever resourceful, Sidney manages to escape, brains Stu with a television set and shoots Billy in the head.

As expected, the MPAA balked at the violence in *Scream*. They felt the effects designed by the famous KNB EFX were too graphic. It was the same ordeal Craven had gone through countless times before, but after a lengthy battle, *Scream* finally got its R rating.

Every successful slasher franchise has at least one common element—a colorful, if not personable, killer. From Leatherface's gruesome guise, to Michael's expressionless face, to Jason's iconic hockey mask, to Freddy's burned visage, the slasher film has never lacked for a popular villain. It can even be argued that the failure of, or lackluster response to, many prospective slasher series—*Prom Night*, for example, or *Silent Night, Deadly Night*—was a direct result of their inability to provide fans with an adequate killer. *Scream* takes no such chance. Ghostface, whose mask, according to Craven, was found in a house in which the produc-

tion was location scouting, is a striking, surreal and downright terrifying presence.[5]

A hyperbolic rendering of Edvard Munch's famous painting, his face is twisted in an exaggerated, almost mocking grin, as if reflecting the look of terror and surprise on his victims' faces. As expected, Ghostface was a huge hit. By the next Halloween, the costume could be found in any pharmacy.

Scream was released on December 20, 1996, at the height of the holiday season. It was the type of gutsy marketing decision for which the Weinsteins were well-known. But what happened next was so extraordinary, it even took them by surprise. Instead of providing an alternative

Down but not out, intrepid reporter Gale Weathers (Courteney Cox) takes matters into her own hands in *Scream* (1996).

to the traditional holiday blockbuster, *Scream* slowly became that blockbuster. During Christmas, when innocuous family fare reigns supreme, a horror movie, and a slasher no less, had become *the* movie to see. By the time its run ended in the spring of 1997, *Scream* had grossed over $100 million.

The success of *Scream* trickled down to all the principals involved in its production. For the Weinsteins, it was another unlikely winner in their string of low-budget mega-hits. But while other calculated gambles had brought them Oscars and prestige, *Scream* brought them something equally sought after in Hollywood—money, and lots of it. The grosses were so impressive, in fact, that rival companies—prompted by a combination of genuine astonishment and sour grapes—accused Miramax of inflating the numbers. What initially seemed like a petty rumor was given some credence when, a year later, after vehemently denying the accusations about *Scream*, the company admitted to overstating the opening weekend gross of *Scream 2*. Although Miramax attributed the mistake to a simple miscounting of screens on which the film was playing, their explanation had many Hollywood insiders rolling their eyes.

Williamson won a Saturn Award for his screenplay and instantly became the talk of the town. Never one to let a hot young talent get away, Miramax immediately signed him to a $20 million deal. They also offered Craven a lucrative two-picture deal on the condition that his next film be *Scream 2*. Craven accepted after securing a promise that after he would be allowed to make a non-horror film.

At the MTV Awards, *Scream* won Best Film, maybe the best barometer—more than box office grosses or opening weekend records—for measuring its appeal. It had tapped into an unexploited and fertile market, at the same time rein-venting and deconstructing the genre for a smart, jaded and appreciative audience, which, until now, no one really knew existed. *Scream* was the first postmodern slasher film, and with a gross of over $100 million, one thing was certain: It was not going to be the last.

On October 17, 1997, another teen slasher, *I Know What You Did Last Summer*, opened in theaters across the country. Critics immediately descended upon the film, calling it a cheap and vulgar imitation of *Scream*, much like they had done to *Friday the 13th*, nearly two decades before, in relation to *Halloween*. But to those who bothered to look, it was clear that *I Know What You Did Last Summer* was a much different film than *Scream*. Although both were written by Kevin Williamson, *Last Summer* was adapted from Lois Duncan's 1973 young adult novel of the same name. Whereas *Scream* relied heavily on its self-conscious references and its pop culture veneer, *Last Summer* was a throwback to the slasher films of the early '80s. While, like *Scream*, it employed the services of a group of young, sexy and almost impossibly good-looking actors, *Last Summer* played its horror straight. Those looking for a good old-fashioned slasher film were pleasantly surprised.

Williamson was approached about adapting Duncan's thriller by *Last Summer* producer Erik Feig. Although *Scream* was still in production, *Scary Movie* had already made the rounds in Hollywood and most industry executives were familiar with Williamson's work. One of the first problems the producers encountered was that *I Know What You Did Last Summer* is a cautionary morality tale, the kind of story that sells novels, not tickets, and Columbia Pictures naturally wanted a slasher. With Williamson now attached, they were certainly not about to squander their greatest resource.

Williamson was all too happy to

oblige. He wanted to make a film which hearkened back to the slashers of his youth and didn't rely solely on "self-aware pop culture references." For the sake of commercial appeal, he changed the setting, added a new back-story about the victim and created a completely new villain. As a tribute to Williamson's father, who had been a fisherman, *Last Summer*'s killer wears a full-length slicker and does his victims in with a large steel hook. Naturally, Duncan didn't take kindly to the changes to her work, but after selling off the rights, there was little she could do about the adaptation.

Scottish director Jim Gillespie was

In Jim Gillespie's 1997 adaptation of Lois Duncan's novel *I Know What You Did Last Summer,* four teens are stalked by a revenge-minded fisherman. In this scene, tempers flare between Ray (Freddie Prinze, Jr.) and Barry (Ryan Phillippe).

chosen to direct, based mainly on his impressive short film *Joyride*. Shooting on the $17 million production began on March 31, 1997, in Southport, North Carolina, a small fishing village 35 miles south of Wilmington. Out of the entire 50-day shoot, seven weeks were devoted to nights, which not only took a toll on the cast and crew, but on the villagers who were unaccustomed to such commotion in their quiet town. Still, according to Gillespie, the townspeople were fairly hospitable to the production. The film's pivotal scene was actually shot on the California coast, where the crew found the treacherous location needed for Reaper's Curve.

During their last Fourth of July together before heading off to college, four friends—Julie (Jennifer Love Hewitt), Helen (Sarah Michelle Gellar), Barry (Ryan Phillippe) and Ray (Freddie Prinze, Jr.), all of whom should know better— commit a cornucopia of teenage slasher foibles: sex, drinking and driving. On their way around a hairpin turn, Ray loses control of the car and crashes into a young man. With their futures flashing before their eyes, they make their second biggest mistake of the night—instead of contacting the authorities, they dump the body into the sea.

A year later, nothing has gone right for any of them. To make matters worse, the group begins receiving threatening letters from someone who knows what they did last summer. After some amateur sleuthing and the deaths of Helen and Barry, Julie unravels the mystery of the killer's identity. It is not David Egan (Jonathan Quint), the young man whom they thought they hit. It is Ben Willis (Muse Watson), a local fisherman whose daughter was killed the year before in a car accident in which David was driving. Willis had never forgiven David for her death, and had gone out that night to murder him but was run over by Ray before he

got the chance. Willis manages to trap his two remaining "killers," Julie and Ray, aboard a boat before meeting his grisly end at the hands of the industrious teens. This riveting boat scene was filmed on the Cape Fear River and couldn't be completed in a single night because the changing tides wreaked havoc with continuity.

Guilt-free, Julie returns to college for the fall semester and appears to be pulling off a happy long-distance relationship with Ray. Just as she is about to take a shower, she notices the ominous declaration etched in the fogged-up glass of the shower door: I Still Know. Before she can even begin to process the ramifications of this message, a body comes crashing through the glass.

I Know What You Did Last Summer originally ended with Julie receiving an e-mail with the message, "I Still Know," but somehow this cyber-threat lacked the visceral terror of the film's chosen ending. While Gillespie purposely tried to pare down *Last Summer*'s blood and gore, he was realistic enough to realize that his audience would not accept a subtle approach to the murders. In fact, *Last Summer*'s first killing, the brutal "hooking" of Max (Johnny Galecki), was put in after the preview because Gillespie didn't want to let down his fans.

I Know What You Did Last Summer grossed $72 million, proving that *Scream* was not a singular anomaly, but simply the initiator of a trend which had legs of its own. The only dark cloud was a lawsuit filed by Miramax, who contended that Columbia's promotion of the film—"From the creator of *Scream*"—was inaccurate because Craven, not Williamson, was *Scream*'s official creator.[6] Semantics aside, *I Know What You Did Last Summer* surpassed even the most optimistic projections. It was now a two-franchise race for the title of most profitable modern slasher. Unlike *Halloween*, *Friday the 13th* and

A Nightmare on Elm Street, which were never intended to spawn sequels, *Scream* was conceived as a trilogy from the beginning. *Scream 2*—known as *Scream Again* and *Scream Louder* at various stages—was rushed into production in June 1997, as *Scream* was still playing in theaters. All the surviving cast members from the original returned to reprise their roles. With a budget of approximately $24 million, *Scream 2* was a substantially more expensive production than the original, but even if it made only a quarter of its predecessor's take, it would still earn a profit.[7]

The secrecy around *Scream 2* reached national security-like proportions. Fueled by both legitimate paranoia and the Internet's sinister new role as a spoiler for upcoming films, cast members were forced to sign a confidentiality agreement which held them legally responsible for leaking information about the script. Many of the actors didn't even receive their lines until the night before shooting. In a move which prompted both chuckles and support from within the industry, some of the script was printed on a special type of paper which couldn't be copied or faxed.

In keeping with the series' self-conscious tone, *Scream 2* opens at a showing of *Stab*, the movie based on *The Woodsboro Murders*, Gale Weathers' best-selling book about the grisly events in *Scream*. During the film, which brings audience participation to levels which would even impress regular *Rocky Horror Picture Show* devotees, an unlucky couple (played by Omar Epps and Jada Pinkett) is murdered in a sequence which owes quite a bit to *He Knows You're Alone*.

With a new Ghostface on the loose, the film moves to Windsor College, a small Midwestern university where Sidney, now a budding actress, is trying to get on with her life. These scenes were actually shot over the course of a month at Agnes Scott College in Atlanta, a liberal arts school for women. Cotton Weary (Liev Schreiber), an innocent man whom Sidney had previously fingered as her mother's murderer, has been released from prison. When the murders begin again, Gale returns to get the scoop, followed by Dewey, who has come to protect Sidney.

The killer manages to go through Randy (Jamie Kennedy), Sidney's close friend from high school, her best friend and roommate (Elise Neal), her boyfriend (Jerry O'Connell) and a pair of inept police officers before trapping her in the university's theater. Again, there are *two* killers: Billy Loomis' mother (Laurie Metcalf), who has been masquerading as local reporter Debbie Salt, and Mickey (Timothy Olyphant), a twisted film student. This time it's Cotton who arrives to save the day, protecting the very girl who had him wrongly incarcerated.

Scream 2 was filled with even more cinematic references and in-jokes than its predecessor, although Craven freely admits than Williamson's attention was probably divided between the film and *Dawson's Creek*, a semi-autobiographical television show he was creating at the same time. As Cici (Sarah Michelle Gellar) stands (or rather sits) guard over her sorority house, she watches *Nosferatu* on television—a bit arty for the stereotypical airhead, but a welcome touch for film buffs. Craven also pays heed to his roots in a scene in Sidney's bedroom. Among the jeans and halter tops, a striped red and green sweater hangs from her door. Maybe a hand-me-down from a horribly burned dream-hopping maniac? Even Williamson gets in on the action as a talk show host who interviews Cotton.

Scream 2 was released on December 12, 1997, less than a year after *Scream* had first opened. In a little over a month, it reached the $100 million mark, almost unheard of for a sequel. With only two installments, the *Scream* series had already

Both David Arquette and Courteney Cox returned to the roles of Deputy Dewey Riley and unscrupulous reporter Gale Weathers for *Scream 2* (1997), Wes Craven's sequel to his surprise blockbuster.

grossed more than the entire *Halloween* franchise, and with *Scream 3* imminent, it was poised to easily overtake both the *Friday the 13th* and *A Nightmare on Elm Street* series. Where Williamson had once struggled with the decision to append the treatment for two sequels to his *Scary Movie* script, now, his only mistake seemed to be not attaching 20.

Even as *Scream* and *I Know What You Did Last Summer* were proving that there was an insatiable demand for slasher films, the old guard stayed dormant until August 1998, when the *Halloween* franchise shook off its cobwebs. Conveniently pretending that none of the films after *Halloween II* ever occurred, *Halloween: H₂0* brought Jamie Lee Curtis back to face her boogeyman brother Michael Myers. Directed by Steve Miner, *H₂0* finds Curtis—who has not only faked her death but has

changed her name from Laurie Strode to Keri Tate—as the headmistress of a posh boarding school. Permanently scarred from her ordeal 20 years ago, Laurie/Keri is a functional alcoholic, barely getting by and still suffering hallucinations of her pursuer, whose body, as we find out, was never recovered from the inferno at the end of *Halloween II*.

After the disaster of *The Curse of Michael Myers*, most people forgot, or chose not to care, that Dimension Films had bought the rights to the *Halloween* franchise in 1994. But Dimension had no intention of squandering their investment. Once they secured the services of Curtis, they tried to get Carpenter to return, but unfortunately the parties were never able to agree on a directing fee. Next, Weinstein tried to get Kevin Williamson to pen the screenplay. Although the scribe was too busy with *Dawson's Creek*, he agreed to write a 14-page treatment and received an executive producer credit for his troubles. In his place, Robert Zappia and Matt Greenberg took over scripting duties.

Halloween: H$_2$0 grossed $55 million, fairly close to what the original *Halloween* had made, although with a $17 million budget, it was much less profitable. Still, many felt that the film was the best *Halloween* since Carpenter's, handing Dimension two hit slasher series and virtually ensuring that Michael, while now headless thanks to Curtis, was not gone forever.

After producing *I Know What You Did Last Summer*, Neal Moritz, bestknown for hits such as *Juice* (1992) and *Volcano* (1997), had no desire to revisit the horror film, even though it was obvious such films were still in demand. But when manager-producer Gina Matthews and screenwriter Silvio Horta pitched him a project about college students who were being murdered based on urban legends, he knew the idea was too good to pass up. Horta was a young NYU Film School graduate who had recently moved to Los Angeles, and whose script, *Even Exchange*, had impressed Matthews. When Matthews met with Horta and heard about his idea for what would eventually become *Urban Legend*, she too recognized its potential.

Moritz and his colleague at Original Film, Brad Luff, then pitched the project to Mike Medavoy, chairman of Phoenix Pictures. A deal was quickly made and Horta began working on a script. When the time came to find a director, Moritz immediately thought of Jamie Blanks, a 26-year-old Australian who had desperately wanted to direct *I Know What You Did Last Summer*. Blanks was so anxious to impress Moritz that he had gone off

and shot a three-minute trailer for *Last Summer*. Unfortunately for him, by the time Moritz had a chance to view the trailer, Jim Gillespie had already been hired. Moritz had never forgotten about Blanks, however, and when he offered the self-admitted horrorphile the opportunity to helm *Urban Legend*, the young director eagerly accepted.

In addition to the young, good-looking cast which had become *de rigueur* for a contemporary slasher, *Urban Legend* is filled with horror veterans, from a typically frazzled Brad Dourif, stuttering his way through a brief role in a none-too-subtle homage to his turn as Billy Bibbit

Jamie Lee Curtis, once again face to face with her worst nightmare in Steve Miner's *Halloween: H$_2$0* (1998).

Apparently, Michelle (Natasha Gregson Wagner) never heard the old "killer in the back-seat" story. In Jamie Blank's *Urban Legend* (1998), these modern-day folktales serve as the inspiration for a series of copycat murders.

in *One Flew Over the Cuckoo's Nest* (1975), to a somewhat distinguished Robert Englund, who appears eternally grateful to be out of his Freddy costume.

Production on the ten-week shoot began on April 20, 1998, at the University of Toronto, which doubled for the film's Pendleton University. In the hallowed halls of academia, Natalie (Alicia Witt) is the only one who seems to realize that her friends are being killed in ways consistent with famous urban legends. Under Blanks' sure hand, we're treated to recreations of such favorites as "the killer in the backseat," "the dead roommate" and "the pet in the microwave." The film ends before Natalie is set to become the victim of the most gruesome urban legend of all, "the kidney thief."

Urban Legend opened on September 25, 1998. By the end of its run, it had made over $38 million. Historically, a gross this

large on a budget of only $14 million would have been cause for celebration—not to mention sequel after sequel—but in the era of *Scream* and *I Know What You Did Last Summer*, anything under $70 million wasn't even in the game. While Blanks certainly admired *Scream*, he had no desire to imitate it, and openly bemoans the fact that his film is endlessly compared to Craven's. As unbelievable as it would have seemed barely two years before, the slasher film was now being measured on the same scale as the Hollywood blockbuster. Worst of all, it was slowly becoming a victim of its own success.

Like clockwork, *I Still Know What You Did Last Summer*, the sequel to *I Know What You Did Last Summer*, was released on November 13, 1998. Producers insisted that the film was born out the audience's desire to find out what happened to the characters, although it's a safe bet that its

Taking his cue from a college dorm horror story, the killer leaves a sinister message in *Urban Legend* **(1998).**

projected gross didn't hurt in getting the production underway. *I Still Know* cost upwards of $24 million, expensive for a slasher film, but a relative bargain if the film made anywhere close to the original. The one element which *I Still Know* didn't have was Williamson—neither his talent nor his name. Instead, the producers settled on Trey Callaway, a creative director at a Los Angeles ad agency, to pen the film. Danny Cannon (*Judge Dredd* [1995]), a young British director, was hired ten weeks before filming began.

While part of *I Still Know* was shot at Sony Studios in Culver City, California, the majority of the film was lensed on location at the El Tecuan Marina Resort, an isolated vacation spot about two and a half hours south of Puerto Vallarta, Mexico. The resort had been badly damaged in an earthquake four years earlier. Now deserted, it was the perfect spot to built the film's Tower Bay. While there are certainly worse shoot destinations than a tropical paradise, the stifling humidity, frequent downpours and local insect population created a host of problems. Mosquito bites and scorpion stings were commonplace, lights and cameras were constantly breaking down due to the bugs and moisture and Cannon was even bitten by a brown recluse spider. Despite it all, he was still able to bring the film in on budget.

I Still Know What You Did Last Summer picks up the action where the original left off, with Julie now at college. It conveniently circumvents the previous film's ending, however, by explaining that ever since arriving on campus Julie has been plagued by horrible nightmares. Exhausted, paranoid and frustrated at her inability to put the tragedy behind her, her fortunes seem to change when her roommate and best friend, Karla (Brandy), wins an all-expense-paid trip for four to the Ba-hamas. Karla also invites her boyfriend Tyrell (Mekhi Phifer). Because Ray (again played by Freddie Prinze, Jr.) is unable to get away from Southport, she asks Will (Matthew Settle), a sweet classmate who has the hots for Julie.

When the four arrive at Tower Bay, they find the resort deserted. Apparently, someone forget to inform them that it was the first day of storm season. Determined to make the best of their vacation, the four settle in, unaware that another uninvited guest has arrived. It appears that Julie's paranoia was not unfounded, as Ben

Julie (Jennifer Love Hewitt) has some new friends (Brandy), but the same old foe who "still knows what she did last summer" (1999).

Willis, whose body was never found, has indeed tracked her down. In a surprise twist, Will, who is really Ben's son, ex-plains that he was behind the whole plot to lure Julie to the resort. Before the Willises can get their final revenge for last summer, Ray, who has been trying to get to Tower Bay throughout the entire film, arrives to save the day.

I Still Know What You Did Last Summer made almost $40 million at the box office. To show how far the slasher film had come, this number raised eyebrows not because of high it was, but because it was nowhere near the take of the original or either *Scream* film. While it may have lacked some of the surprise of *I Know What You Did Last Summer*, *I Still Know* is certainly not an in-ferior film. Jennifer Love Hewitt has never been better, Cannon's di-rection is seamless and inspired and, most importantly, the murder scenes are carried out with a good deal of flair and creativity. With no discernible cause for the drop-off, it begged the question: Had the slasher film again exhausted itself after only a few films and two real franchises?

The slasher traditionalists who thought their worst fears had been realized with *Psycho II* were in for a rude awakening when an unthink-able rumor which had been floating around Hollywood was substanti-ated—*Psycho* was being remade. If a sequel to *Psycho* had been blasphe-mous, then a remake was downright heretical. What's more, it was being done by idiosyncratic director Gus Van Sant, fresh off an Academy Award nomination for *Good Will Hunting* (1997) and the man behind such distinctive films as *Drugstore Cowboy* (1989), *My Own Private Idaho* (1991) and *To Die For* (1995).

What was most peculiar was that Van Sant, usually the most independent of directors, had no desire to leave his personal touch upon the film. He not only planned to use the exact shots which Hitchcock had used, but arranged for the same rigid 37-day shooting schedule. Although Van Sant spoke freely about his desire to take a classic film and remake it using an almost identical shooting script, nobody could really figure out what prompted him to undertake such a thankless task. Aside from the much publicized support of Joseph Stefano, the writer of the original screenplay, and a politically correct endorsement from Patricia Hitchcock O'-Connell, Hitchcock's daughter, Van Sant came under attack from fans, critics, historians and even many of his contemporaries, most of whom considered the project an act of sacrilege.

Undaunted, Van Sant forged ahead, seemingly immune to the criticism he met with every step of the way. He cast the film: Vince Vaughn as Norman Bates, Anne Heche as Marion Crane, Julianne Moore as Lila Crane and William H. Macy as Arbogast. He met with Stefano to discuss updating portions of the script to reflect modern sensibilities. He had a new house built because the original had been moved from the bluff overlooking the Bates Motel. He had Danny Elfman reinterpret Bernard Herrmann's legendary score. But the more he tried to keep things the same, the more different they appeared.

When the new *Psycho* was released on December 4, 1998, it was met with a collective "why?" It wasn't as if it was so bad, or offensive, or disrespectful, it was just unnecessary. The new *Psycho* proved that a film is so much more than the sum of its parts, it is an organic creation, and that which gives it life is as indefinable as it is elusive. No director, no matter how talented, can harvest the elements of a suc-

cessful film and expect to grow an equally impressive work. Nowhere was this more apparent than in the new film's shower scene. Van Sant's replication of what is considered the most terrifying sequence in the history of cinema, looked flat, boring and, worst of all, indifferent. *Psycho* barely made back its budget of $23 million. By all accounts, the experiment that should never have been conducted in the first place, had failed.

Dimension Films wasn't even remotely concerned by the lackluster showing of *I Still Know What You Did Last Summer*. They viewed *I Still Know* as Columbia's failure, not as being indicative of changing attitudes in the marketplace. In fact, Miramax was so confident in their franchise that Mark Gill, President of Miramax LA, said, "The *Scream* franchise has been to Miramax what the Federal Reserve is to the U.S. government, a license to print money," a statement which was not far from the truth.

With supposedly the last installment of the *Scream* trilogy getting underway, the focus shifted from how to make money to how to preserve the integrity of the series. While Craven returned to direct and, once again, all the surviving cast members signed back on, the man who was most responsible for the *Scream* phenomenon bowed out. Although Williamson wrote a treatment for *Scream 3* and received a producer credit, he was in the middle of directing *Teaching Mrs. Tingle* and simply didn't have the focus or energy to write the screenplay.[8] Ehren Kruger took over scripting duties and managed to deliver a draft which referenced Williamson's penchant for self-conscious dialogue while contributing its own brand of black humor.

Scream 3 takes the series' running joke of life imitating art and plays it to its fullest. The film opens with Cotton Weary, now hosting his own talk show,

100% Cotton, and his girlfriend (Kelly Rutherford) getting paid a visit by Ghost-face. Once again, the killer could be any-one and everyone. *Stab 3: Return to Woods-boro* is well into production and the recent murders have ground the film to a halt, much to chagrin of its director, Roman Bridger (Scott Foley).

Meanwhile, Sidney has become a vir-tual recluse. She lives alone in the hills of Northern California in a well-protected and isolated home where she works for a crisis counseling hot line. Content to live in seclusion, she is thrust out of her soli-tude and reunited with Dewey and Gale after being contacted by the killer. The rest of the film is a combination of industry in-jokes, frenetic murder sequences, red herrings and tongue-in-cheek cameos by the likes of Roger Corman, Carrie Fisher, Kevin Smith and even Wes Craven.

Bucking the trend of two killers per film, in *Scream 3* there is only one Ghost-face. It is Roman, taking the meaning of tyrannical director to new extremes. But it turns out Roman has more directing ex-perience than just *Stab 3*; it was he who initiated the entire killing spree from the beginning, all the way back to the original *Scream*. You see, Roman is Sidney's half-brother. A long time ago, Maureen Pres-cott, their mother, was an aspiring actress. During this time, she became pregnant with Roman, but years later, when Roman came calling, she refused to acknowledge him. As revenge, Roman filmed her ex-tracurricular activities with Billy Loomis' father and gave the tape to Billy, setting the events of the trilogy in motion.

It had been over two years since the last *Scream* film when *Scream 3* opened in the first week of February 2000. If there was apprehension due to the fact that *Scream 3* had, by far, the largest budget of any installment of the trilogy, it quickly vanished when the film took in $34.7 mil-lion in its first weekend, the biggest open-

ing on record in a January–April period. It steamrolled the competition, grossing $16.4 million in its second week and run-ning roughshod over its closest competi-tor, *The Beach*, Leonardo DiCaprio's *Ti-tanic* follow-up. Within ten days, *Scream 3* had grossed $57 million. Although it barely missed the critical $100 million mark, its success no doubt made it all the more difficult for Weinstein, Williamson and Craven to maintain, which they have to this day, that the *Scream* franchise is truly over.

Nowhere does history repeat itself more prominently—and more shame-lessly—than in the arena of the slasher film. Just as movies such as *Student Bod-ies*, *Pandemonium* and *Wacko* spoofed the likes of *When a Stranger Calls*, *Halloween* and *Friday the 13th*, *Scary Movie*, released in July 2000, did the same for the current crop of teen slashers. The film, directed by Keenen Ivory Wayans and co-written by and co-starring his brothers Shawn and Marlon, is an all-out parody of both *Scream* and *I Know What You Did Last Summer*, with bits of *The Blair Witch Project* (1999)and *The Sixth Sense* (1999) thrown in for good measure. To say the film is in poor taste assumes that it even has the slightest inkling of what taste is, for how else can you describe a film which features the only instance of death by fake penis in the history of cinema? But for those who never seem to tire of scatological humor, *Scary Movie* is a welcome treat. And, if truth be told, aside from the fact that it caters to the lowest common denominator, it is not entirely unfunny. After all, any film in which Carmen Electra is stabbed in the chest, only to have her silicon breast implant ripped out, has at least some sense of relevant satire.

In the first three days of its release, *Scary Movie* took in $42.5 million. Its final domestic take was an astounding $157 million, more than one and a half times

After her ordeal in both *Scream* and *Scream 2*, Sidney Prescott (Neve Campbell) now lives in virtual isolation, terrified that Ghostface may one day return. She doesn't have to wait long for her worst fear to be realized in Wes Craven's *Scream 3* (2000).

the gross of the most successful film it parodied. What was even more astonishing was that *Scary Movie* grossed well over $250 million worldwide, proving that H.L. Mencken's prophetic statement—no one ever went broke underestimating the taste of the American public—was equally true of cultures all around the globe.

While the success of *Urban Legend* dictated a sequel, none of the producers were eager to remake the same film. Instead, they made one far inferior to the original. Mike Medavoy came up with the idea to set *Urban Legends: Final Cut* (2000) at a film school, where the seniors are all vying for the prestigious (and fictitious) Hitchcock Award for best thesis film, an honor which virtually assures the winner a ticket to Hollywood. John Ottman, best-known for his work as both the composer and editor of *The Usual Sus-*

pects (1995), made his directorial debut. Although he does the best he can with a rather preposterous script, he lacks Jamie Blanks' mastery of the genre's conventions. *Urban Legends: Final Cut* made only $21.5 million, forcing rival producers to take a long hard look at the slasher film and speculate whether this was simply the result of a bad film or a harbinger of lean times to come.

By mid–2001, the slasher film had once again reached a crossroad. Critics pronounced that films in which much of the terror was left to the imagination, like *The Blair Witch Project*, which grossed $140 million, and *The Sixth Sense*, which grossed $293 million, heralded an end to the graphic violence of the slasher. To them, that the two forms of horror could exist in a symbiotic rather than antagonistic relationship seemed impossible.

There is reason to be both optimistic and pessimistic about the slasher film's future. *Cherry Falls* (2000), a highly anticipated slasher which was slated for theatrical release, was relegated to the USA Network. The film banks on the novel conceit of a killer targeting only virgins. Both fans and the producers of the film were furious about its fate, but when people actually saw it, most agreed that *Cherry Falls* was indeed an awful film. *Valentine* (2001), Jamie Blanks' sophomore slasher effect, was lambasted by critics and sputtered out of theaters after only a few weeks. Although the disastrous spoof *Shriek If You Know What I Did Last Friday the 13th* (2000), which also aired on USA, seemed to signify an end to slasher parodies, *Scary Movie 2* managed to pull in over $71 million. *Jason X*, the long-awaited tenth installment of the *Friday the 13th* series, is tentatively scheduled for an April 2002 release, while *Freddy vs. Jason* continues to languish in development purgatory at New Line. After lots of rumor and innuendo the problem-plagued *Halloween: Homecoming*—directed by Rick Rosenthal, who helmed *Halloween II*—is slated for a summer 2002 release. Although the Dimension team continues to deny rumors that a fourth *Scream* is in the works, gossip about a third *I Know What You Did Last Summer* continues to abound.

For over twenty years, the slasher film has mirrored the resilience of its indestructible killers. Down but never out, it has weathered periods of stagnation only to return with a vengeance. Love 'em or hate 'em, slasher films are here to stay. Their evolution from underground cinematic oddity to multimillion dollar franchise—despite countless efforts to eradicate, ban and defame them—is one of Hollywood's greatest success stories. For years they have skirted on the edge of mainstream cinema, teasing, tantalizing and tormenting those who can't understand how a film about an indestructible boogeyman who kills babysitters could go on to become the most successful independent film of its time. How the story of a drowned boy who returns years later to continue his psychotic mother's killing spree could spawn eight sequels, with none of them ever losing money. And how a film titled *The Texas Chainsaw Massacre* could ever wind up in the Museum of Modern Art.

Janet Maslin once wrote, in regard to slasher films, that "the only good thing to be said about them is that their future isn't bright."

She couldn't have been more wrong.

Notes

Chapter 1: *What Is a Slasher Film?*

1. As discussed later in this chapter, this voyeurism is used, almost exclusively, to titillate the audience, not the killer.

2. Although Baker was the first "official" Best Makeup winner, William Tuttle won an honorary Oscar in 1964 for his makeup on *The 7 Faces of Dr. Lao*. In 1968, John Chambers also won an honorary Oscar for his makeup work on *Planet of the Apes*.

3. Actually, in the last scene of *He Knows You're Alone*, it is assumed that the Final Girl is murdered when her jilted lover returns on the day of her wedding. However, this epilogue has no relevance to the main plot of the film and feels as if it was tacked on simply to provide one last jolt for audiences who had come to expect this type of "shock" ending.

4. This quote from Prof. Kawin was originally taken from a review of *The Funhouse* and *The Howling* published in *Film Quarterly*. I came across his review in *American Horrors*, a collection of essays on the modern American horror film, edited by Gregory A. Waller. The Ebert article to which Kawin refers is "Why Movie Audiences Aren't Safe Anymore" (*American Film*, March, 1981). I have not quoted directly from this article simply because I prefer Kawin's interpretation of it.

5. As any fan of the slasher film knows, in the original *Friday the 13th* it was Jason's mother, Pamela Voorhees, who was the killer. Jason doesn't inherit the mantle of summer camp slayer until *Friday the 13th Part 2*, and it is not until *Part 3* that he dons a hockey mask. In fact, in the first scene of Wes Craven's *Scream*, Drew Barrymore is slaughtered by a homicidal prank caller because she incorrectly identifies the killer in *Friday the 13th* as Jason.

6. While the original list contained 52 films, 74 different films appeared on the list at one time or another. Thirty-nine of them were successfully prosecuted under the Obscene Publications Act.

Chapter 2: *The Pre-History of the Slasher Film*

1. For one thing, Gein didn't wield a chain saw, and he was far from the hulking behemoth which Hooper made Leatherface. Nor did he live with an extended family of fellow cannibals; once his mother died, Gein lived alone, carrying out his gruesome crimes in the privacy of his farmhouse.

Chapter 3: Halloween — *The Night He Came Home*

1. This isn't exactly true. Towards the end of the film, Leatherface drops the chain saw on his leg. It bites into his flesh and draws blood. However, the chain saw is never shown explicitly slicing his victims.

2. According to Yablans, he drew the sketch for the graphic while Hill came up with the tagline, "The Night *He* Came Home."

3. Technically a sequel to *Escape from New York* (1981), *Escape from L.A.* is actually closer to a remake. In the original film, Snake

Plissken (Kurt Russell) ventures into an apocalyptic New York to rescue the President of
the United States. In *Escape from L.A.*, he must
venture into an apocalyptic Los Angeles to
rescue the president's daughter.

Chapter 4: Deadly Prank Calls, Driller Killers and an Angry Young Woman

1. In Italy, *Dawn of the Dead* was called
Zombi. Therefore, Fulci's film was titled *Zombi
2* in order to capitalize on *Dawn of the Dead*'s
appeal. For its American release, it was cor-
rectly retitled *Zombie*.

Chapter 5: Friday the 13th, Prom Night and a Head in the Fish Tank

1. According to Lynch, the inspiration
for this scene came from a similar game which
Robert Guza, Jr., who is credited with *Prom
Night*'s story, played as a child.

Chapter 6: Trains of Terror, Funhouses, Horrible Holidays and a Maniac

1. While Curtis did return to the slasher
film in 1981 with *Halloween II*, the film was really just a continuation of its predecessor. *Terror Train* was her last *original* slasher.
2. In an interview in *Hysteria*, a marvelous website devoted exclusively to slasher
films, Lieberman insists that he had never seen
The Texas Chainsaw Massacre or *The Hills Have
Eyes* before making *Just Before Dawn*, despite
the assertion of critics who said he drew heavily from both films.
3. As fans of the slasher film probably
know, Tom Savini has reputedly "disavowed"
Maniac. Critics of the film naturally hold his
comments as indisputable proof of *Maniac*'s
worthlessness. However, according to Lustig,
Savini's disdain for the film has been greatly
exaggerated. "Remember, Savini was lambasted for all this violence he had created in all
these movies, not only *Maniac* but other films
like *Friday the 13th*, so he came under fire and
I guess he started to disavow some of these
movies. But you know what, we all live and

learn. Big deal. I was pissed off at Tom at the
time for having said certain things, but I love
Tom, and what's the big deal, he doesn't care,
he might have made some comments at the
time that he regrets. We were kids. We said
stupid things when the press would ask us
questions... It's sort of like wrestling a little
bit. Sometimes I would add a little fuel to the
fire, meanwhile we would go out and have
drinks afterward... Sometimes it's fun to have
these feuds. It gives the genre press something
to write about."
4. As a consultant for Anchor Bay Entertainment, Lustig has been instrumental in
locating the rights to the films of these and
other foreign directors, and then overseeing the
painstaking process of restoring and re-releas-
ing them on both DVD and VHS.
5. Link was actually executive producer
of *Rabid*.
6. Despite that fact that *Poltergeist* was a
spectacular box office success and one of the
best haunted house movies ever made, it was
an unpleasant experience for Hooper. The director clashed with producer Steven Spielberg,
who was too busy with *E.T.* (1982) to direct
the film himself. While rumors continue to
abound that Spielberg took the film over and
ordered Hooper to make unwanted changes,
Hooper has publicly said that Spielberg never
usurped his authority. Spielberg even took out
advertisements in the trades thanking Hooper
for his contribution to the film. But *Poltergeist
was* a problematic collaboration. As John Mc-
Carty astutely writes in *The Fearmakers*,
"There's no doubt that with its overemphasis
on technical razzle-dazzle, suburban California rather than rural South atmosphere, and
repeated shots of characters being awed rather
than sawed, *Poltergeist* looks and sounds much
more like a Steven Spielberg film than a Tobe
Hooper one."

Chapter 7: Campus Killers, Slashing for Laughs and One Human Brain

1. *Chatterbox* was a bit more tasteful than
its previous title, *Lips*.
2. The subterranean caverns underneath
Garth Manor, the manor's rooftop and the
bedroom in which the monster bursts through
the floor were all built on stages.
3. Van Patten's father, actor Dick Van
Patten, was best-known for his "wholesome"
television persona. However, one of his earliest

film roles was in the camp classic *Psychomania* (1963), a far inferior film to *Hell Night*.

4. Freed maintains that the only two slasher films he had even heard of were *Friday the 13th* and *Prom Night*.

5. According to Avergon, Ward actually played the killer in the aquarium scene.

6. By this time, a female killer wasn't such a shock. It had already been done in previous slashers, most notably *Friday the 13th* and *Happy Birthday to Me*.

7. Accounts of this macabre contest vary. Doubters says that it was indisputably a model brain which was submerged in a jar of preserving fluid, while the believers insist that an actual human brain was used. Most likely, the specimen was not authentic.

8. In *Halloween II*, *Halloween*'s climactic scene is actually truncated. However, it continues with Dr. Loomis examining the ground where Michael fell and then screaming at a curious neighbor to call the police and tell the sheriff that "he" is still on the loose. When the poor guy tells Loomis he's been trick-or-treated to death and just wants to make sure this isn't a Halloween prank, the good doctor tells him he doesn't know what death is.

Chapter 8: *Prowlers, Spaghetti Slashers and the Joys of Summer Camp*

1. For the trivia hounds, *Friday the 13th Part 3* is the only film in the series in which the name of Jason is never mentioned.

2. Which is what most people thought, until 1992, when Jack Palance won a Best Supporting Actor Oscar for his role in the comedy *City Slickers* (1991). Three years later, in 1995, Martin Landau won the same award for his portrayal of Bela Lugosi in Tim Burton's *Ed Wood* (1994).

3. In truth, there is no reason to believe that Craven had ever heard of, much less seen, *The Slayer*. He has always maintained that *A Nightmare on Elm Street* was inspired by a series of articles he had seen in *The Los Angeles Times* (see Chapter 9). While the similarities between the two films are curious, they are obviously coincidental.

4. In *Psycho II*, Ms. Spool (Claudia Bryar) explains that the woman who Norman thought was his mother was actually his aunt. Ms. Spool had Norman out of wedlock and had

some mental "troubles" of her own. When she was put away, her sister, Mrs. Bates, took Norman in and became his mother. To further complicate the issue, in *Psycho III*, we learn that this was a lie. Mrs. Spool was not actually Norman's mother. She was his crazy aunt who was in love with Norman's father.

Chapter 9: *A Nightmare on Elm Street, Sequels Galore and the Decline of the Slasher Film*

1. Ironically, the writer of *Dreamscape*, Chuck Russell, directed *A Nightmare on Elm Street 3: Dream Warriors* and even collaborated with Craven on the screenplay of that film.

2. Shaye has always taken umbrage with this nickname, which tends to minimize the invaluable role which he played in the years before *Nightmare*, when he built New Line Cinema from the ground up and positioned it as a leader in the field of specialty releases. In *The Nightmare Never Ends*, he says, "*Nightmare* didn't build the company but catalyzed it. It gave us enough capital that we could make use of this franchise ourselves to do at least a second one. There was more room made to make additional profits with this particular copyright. Second of all, we could expand on our own business base and create our own distribution company."

3. As hated as this ending was, the paramedic is not exposed as the killer until the film's final scene. For almost the entire film, the audience is never given any reason to believe that the killer is anyone other than Jason.

4. The film to which Bach is referring is actually *And Then There Were None*. It was directed by René Clair and is based on Agatha Christie's classic novel of the same name, whose original title was *Ten Little Indians*.

5. In this scene, Nikki (Deborah Goodrich) tumbles into a well filled with the bodies of her slain friends.

6. Only once did an actor other than Robert Englund ever play Freddy. During the first week of production on *Freddy's Revenge*, Englund was unavailable so director Jack Sholder was forced to shoot the shower scene with an extra. In hindsight, even Sholder admits this was a mistake. If you look closely, it is fairly obvious that the actor playing Freddy is not Englund, for he possesses none of Englund's distinctive screen presence.

7. Yes, the same John Carl Buechler who, that same year, directed Friday *the 13th Part VII: The New Blood*.

Chapter 10: The Resurgence

1. Obviously I'm not counting slasher spoofs like *Student Bodies*, whose entire existence is based on acknowledging the films which came before them.

2. In August 1990, the "Gainesville Murders" captivated the nation. At the University of Florida, four young women and one man were found brutally murdered, their mutilated bodies displayed in grotesque positions. The killer was Daniel Rolling, a deeply disturbed man who had been abused as a child.

3. An $80 million special effects—laden remake of *The Haunting* was eventually made in 1999. It was produced by Dreamworks and directed by Jan de Bont. Although the film took in $91 million at the domestic box office, it was generally reviled by horror fans.

4. The death of Mr. Himbry was suggested by Bob Weinstein because of concern with a 30-minute stretch in the original script where no one was killed.

5. The genesis of the Ghostface mask has become a point of some contention. During his audio commentary on the *Scream* DVD, Craven says that the mask was found in a house at which the production was location scouting. He calls it an "off-the-shelf item which is available at any dime store around Halloween." However, in *Fangoria* #189, Fun World employee Brigitte Sleiertin, who designed the Ghostface mask, says that Craven contacted the company after visiting some friends and noticing that one of the kids had the mask.

6. Mostly likely, the suit was in response to an equally ludicrous lawsuit which Sony (Columbia's parent company) had brought against Miramax after the release of *Scream*. Sony claimed proprietary rights to the title because of its similarity to the title of their 1996 film *Screamers*.

7. An additional $15 to $20 million was spent on advertising.

8. *Killing Mrs. Tingle*, Williamson's first original screenplay, was eventually released as *Teaching Mrs. Tingle* in response to the national backlash against movie violence which followed the Columbine Massacre. If only the solution was so easy.

APPENDIX

Alternative Titles

Anthropophagus
The Anthropophagus Beast
Gomia, Terror en el Mar Egeo
The Grim Reaper
Man Beast
Man Eater
The Savage Island

The Bird with the Crystal Plumage
The Bird with the Glass Feathers
The Gallery Murders
Phantom of Terror
L'Uccello dalle Piume di Cristallo

Black Christmas
Silent Night, Evil Night
Stranger in the House

Black Sunday
La Maschera del Demonio
Revenge of the Vampire
The Demon's Mask
Mask of the Demon
House of Fright
The Hour When Dracula Comes

A Blade in the Dark
House of the Dark Stairway
La Casa con al Scala nel Buio

Blood and Black Lace
Sei Donne per l'Assassino
Fashion House of Death
Six Women for the Murderer

Bloodeaters
Toxic Zombies

Cannibal Ferox
Make Them Die Slowly

The Cat o' Nine Tails
Il Gatto a Nove Code

The Church
Demon Cathedral
La Chiesa

Combat Shock
American Nightmare

The Curse of Frankenstein
Birth of Frankenstein

Deathdream
Dead of Night
The Night Andy Came Home
The Night Walk
The Veteran

Deep Red
Dripping Deep Red
Profondo Rosso
The Hatchet Murders
The Sabre Tooth Tiger

Demons
Demoni

Demons 2
Demoni 2
Demons 2: The Nightmare Returns

Don't Go in the Woods ... Alone
Don't Go in the Woods

199

The Dorm That Dripped Blood
Pranks
Death Dorm

Eaten Alive
Death Trap
Horror Hotel Massacre
Starlight Slaughter
Legend of the Bayou

The Evil Eye
The Girl Who Knew Too Much
La Ragazza Che Sapeva Troppo

Fanatic
Die! Die! My Darling!

Four Flies on Grey Velvet
Quattro Mosche di Velluto Grigio
Four Patches of Grey Velvet

The Great Alligator
Alligators
Big Alligator River
Great Alligator River
The Big Caimano River
Il Fiume del Grande Caimano

Hatchet for the Honeymoon
An Axe for the Honeymoon
Blood Brides
Il Rosso Segno della Follia
The Red Sign of Madness
The Red Mark of Madness

Haunts
The Veil

He Knows You're Alone
Blood Wedding

Home Sweet Home
Slasher in the House

The Horrible Dr. Hichcock
The Terrible Secret of Dr. Hichcock
The Terror of Dr. Hichcock
Raptus
The Horrible Secret of Dr. Hichcock
The Frightening Secret of Dr. Hichcock
The Secret of Dr. Hichcock
L'Orribile Segreto del Dr. Hichcock

Horror of Dracula
Dracula

The House by the Lake
Death Weekend

The House on Sorority Row
House of Evil
Seven Sisters

The House on the Edge of the Park
La Casa Sperduta nel Parco

I Spit on Your Grave
Day of the Woman

Killer Party
The April Fool
Fool's Night

The Killing Hour
The Clairvoyant

Last House on Dead End Street
The Cuckoo Clocks of Hell
The Funhouse

Last House on the Left
Sex Crime of the Century
Krug and Company
Night of Vengeance

Macabro
Frozen Terror
Macabre

Mardi Gras Massacre
Crypt of Dark Secrets

Mark of the Devil
Austria 1700
Burn, Witch, Burn!
Hexen Bis aufs Blut Gequält
Satan

Ms. 45
Angel of Vengeance

Murder by Decree
Sherlock Holmes: Murder by Decree

The Mutilator
Fall Break

The New House on the Left
Last Stop on the Night Train
L'Ultimo Treno della Notte

The New York Ripper
Lo Squartatore di New York
The Ripper

Night of the Creeps
Homecoming Night

Night School
Terror Eyes

Nightmare
Nightmares in a Damaged Brain
Blood Splash

Nosferatu (1922)
Nosferatu: A Symphony of Horror
Nosferatu: A Symphony of Terror
Nosferatu: Eine Symphonie des Grauens
Nosferatu the Vampire
Terror of Dracula

Nosferatu (1979)
Nosferatu, the Vampyre
Nosferatu: Phantom der Nacht

Opera
Terror at the Opera

Phenomena
Creepers

The Prowler
Rosemary's Killer
The Graduation

Rabid
Rage

The Redeemer
Class Reunion Massacre
The Redeemer … Son of Satan!

The Sect
The Devil's Daughter
La Setta

Silent Night, Deadly Night
Slayride

Sisters
Blood Sisters

Slaughter High
April Fool's Day

Sleepaway Camp
Nightmare Vacation

Slumber Party Massacre
Sleepless Nights

Snuff
Slaughter

Taste of Fear
Scream of Fear

Tenebrae
Sotto gli Occhi dell'Assassino
Tenebre
Unsane

Terror Train
Train of Terror

The Texas Chainsaw Massacre: The Next Generation
The Return of the Texas Chainsaw Massacre

The Thing (1951)
The Thing from Another World

Twitch of the Death Nerve
Bay of Blood
Antefatto
Before the Fact
Bloodbath
Carnage
Chain Reaction
Ecologia del Delitto
The Ecology of a Crime
The Last House on the Left Part 2
Reazione a Catena

The Two Faces of Dr. Jekyll
House of Fright
Jekyll's Inferno

Visiting Hours
The Fright

The Wax Mask
Maschera di Cera
Gaston Leroux's The Wax Mask

Witchfinder General
Conqueror Worm
Matthew Hopkins: Witchfinder General

X-Ray
Hospital Massacre
Ward 13
Be My Valentine … or Else

You Better Watch Out
Christmas Evil
Terror in Toyland

Zombie
Zombie 2

Zombie Flesh Eaters
Island of the Living Dead

Zombie Lake
Lake of the Living Dead

Bibliography

Castle, William. *Step Right Up! I'm Gonna Scare the Pants Off America*. New York: Putnam, 1976.

    Memoirs from a life in the B-movie business by the P.T. Barnum of horror. At once, both riveting and touching. You'll finish this book in one night.

Clover, Carol J. *Men, Women, and Chain Saws: Gender in the Modern Horror Film*. Princeton, N.J.: Princeton University, 1992.

    Scholarly work which takes a gender-based reading of the slasher film. Despite its academic bent, Clover's fondness for these films creeps through.

Curry, Christopher Wayne. *A Taste of Blood: The Films of Herschell Gordon Lewis*. London: Creation, 1999.

    Exhaustive and meticulously researched study of "The Godfather of Gore" and his films. The breadth of Curry's knowledge surprised even Lewis himself.

Dika, Vera. *Games of Terror:* Halloween, Friday the 13th, *and the Films of the Stalker Cycle*. Rutherford, N.J.: Fairleigh Dickinson University, 1990.

    The first and, prior to this, the only full-length work devoted exclusively to the slasher film. Overly cerebral but at times quite brilliant in its analysis. However, it's a safe bet that none of the slasher films examined were as carefully constructed as Dika insinuates.

Fischer, Dennis. *Horror Film Directors, 1931–1990*. Jefferson, N.C.: McFarland, 1991.

    Impressive examination of most of the better-known directors of the horror film. Entries include biographical details, plot summaries and critical analyses.

Golden, Christopher, ed. *Cut! Horror Writers on Horror Film*. New York: Berkley, 1992.

    Intriguing idea: a compilation of essays about the horror film, written by famous (and some not so famous) horror writers. As in any work such as this, some entries are far stronger than others.

Gordon, Mel. *The Grand Guignol: Theater of Fear and Terror*. New York: Da Capo, 1997.

    Wonderfully engaging history of arguably the most macabre form of popular entertainment ever.

Hardy, Phil, ed. *The Encyclopedia of Horror Movies*. New York: Harper & Row, 1986.

    Set the standard for horror reference books. A smattering of errors doesn't detract from its reputation as the genre's definitive guide. While it's heavily weighted in favor of older films and foreign offerings, it also gives many obscure cult films their just due. Well-written with refreshingly keen insight.

Kaufman, Lloyd, and James Gunn. *All I Need to Know About Filmmaking I Learned from the Toxic Avenger*. New York: Berkley Boulevard, 1998.

    The autobiography of Troma founder Lloyd Kaufman might turn off some readers who don't find his wife's battle with breast cancer or musings on sex with a colostomy bag very funny.

Martin, Mick, and Marsha Porter. *Video Movie Guide*. New York: Ballantine, 1995.

Along with Leonard Maltin's, it's one of the most popular general interest video guides on the market.

Mayo, Mike. *VideoHound's Horror Show: 999 Hair-Raising, Hellish, and Humorous Movies*. Detroit: Visible Ink, 1998.

Overly broad video guide from Visible Ink's *VideoHound* series. Noteworthy for its quirky but thorough appendices.

McCarty, John. *The Fearmakers: The Screen's Directorial Masters of Suspense and Terror*. New York: St. Martin's, 1994.

Although well-versed in the genre's long history, McCarty was one of the first authors to give critical attention to contemporary horror films. *The Fearmakers* examines the genre's greatest modern directors.

_____. *The Modern Horror Film: 50 Contemporary Classics from* The Curse of Frankenstein *to* The Lair of the White Worm. Secaucus, N.J.: Citadel, 1990.

McCarty's bias towards Hammer is well-reflected in this highly subjective look at the 50 greatest modern (post–*The Curse of Frankenstein*) horror films.

_____. *Movie Psychos and Madmen: Film Psychopaths from Jekyll and Hyde to Hannibal Lecter*. Secaucus, N.J.: Citadel, 1993.

Delightful idiosyncratic cross-genre work which focuses on the on-screen psychopath. Chock-full of great info.

_____. *The Official Splatter Movie Guide*. New York: St. Martin's, 1989.

Slim, but witty and accurate, splatter movie guide.

_____. *The Sleaze Merchants: Adventures in Exploitation Filmmaking*. New York: St. Martin's, 1995.

A look at the men responsible for some of the sleaziest, most despicable, reprehensible and beloved films ever made. Alternates between brief bios of the directors and interviews. Fabulous introduction to the subject of exploitation films.

_____. *Splatter Movies: Breaking the Last Taboo of the Screen*. New York: St. Martin's, 1984.

Watershed book which brought attention to the much-maligned subgenre of the horror film. Interestingly enough, McCarty has never been a fan of the slasher film, and although he has nothing but praise for the splatter opuses of Romero, he is extremely disdainful towards *Halloween, Friday the 13th* and *Maniac*.

McDonagh, Maitland. *Broken Mirrors/Broken Minds: The Dark Dreams of Dario Argento*. Secaucus, N.J.: Citadel, 1994.

Adapted from McDonagh's master's thesis at Columbia University, this is the first full-length work devoted exclusively to Argento. Walks a fine line between academic and accessible. McDonagh has distinguished herself as one of the brightest writers working in the horror genre.

_____. *Filmmaking on the Fringe: The Good, the Bad, and the Deviant Directors*. Secaucus, N.J.: Citadel, 1995.

Interviews with various directors of horror and exploitation films, from the well-known like Sam Raimi and Wes Craven, to the obscure like Andy Sidaris and Ken Wiederhorn. An appendix contains the filmographies of other horror directors.

Newman, Kim, ed. *The BFI Companion to Horror*. London: Cassell, 1996.

Ambitious project which attempts to define every term even tangentially related to the horror genre. Falls short of its ultimate goal, but certainly contains some great bits and pieces.

Newman, Kim. *Nightmare Movies: A Critical Guide to Contemporary Horror Films*. New York: Harmony, 1988.

Poorly organized, this underappreciated look at modern horror has all the trappings of a major genre work. Newman is arguably the most knowledgeable contemporary horror author, and when he's "on" there's no one better. His only flaw: He's certainly no fan of the slasher.

O'Neill, James. *Terror on Tape: A Complete Guide to Over 2,000 Horror Movies on Video*. New York: Billboard, 1994.

Excellent, straightforward video guide. O'Neill doesn't overlook much.

Palmerini, Luca M., and Gaetano Mistretta. *Spaghetti Nightmares: Italian Fantasy-Horrors As Seen Through the Eyes of Their Protagonists*. Key West, Fla.: Fantasma, 1996.

Long overdue book which manages to interview almost every major living figure of spaghetti horror, from Argento and Nicolodi, to Deodato and Lenzi. Stellar work whose only flaw is its unwillingness to list a film's English title alongside its Italian one. Extremely frustrating for novices who are unlikely to know to which film the authors are referring.

The Phantom of the Movies. *The Phantom's Ultimate Video Guide.* New York: Dell, 1989.

Video guide to horror, sci-fi, action, cult, mystery and just plain odd films. Not bad.

Robb, Brian. J. *Scream & Nightmares: The Films of Wes Craven.* Woodstock, N.Y.: Overlook, 1998.

Well-written informative biography-filmography of the man behind *A Nightmare on Elm Street* and *Scream.* Contains some great photos from Craven's personal collection.

Schoell, William. *Stay Out of the Shower: 25 Years of Shocker Films Beginning with* Psycho. New York: Dembner, 1985.

Along with *Splatter Movies, Stay Out of the Shower* was one of the earliest works to devote a substantial amount of time to the slasher film. Like McCarty, Schoell ain't no fan. In fact, his attitude toward the subgenre is nothing short of loathing. This out-of-print book is hard to find but isn't half bad once you get into it.

_____, and James Spencer. *The Nightmare Never Ends: The Official History of Freddy Krueger and the* Nightmare on Elm Street *Films.* Secaucus, N.J.: Citadel, 1992.

A nostalgic and intriguing look back at the *Nightmare on Elm Street* series. Contains marvelous production and behind-the-scenes photos. Relatively short, but filled with juicy gossip about the series.

Spoto, Donald. *The Dark Side of Genius: The Life of Alfred Hitchcock.* New York: Ballantine, 1983.

Probably the most famous Hitchcock bio. If you're only going to read one book about the Master of Suspense, let this be it.

Stanley, John. *Creature Features: The Science Fiction, Fantasy, and Horror Movie Guide.* New York: Boulevard, 1997.

Opinions on this book are as different as night and day. Personally, I love it. While there are some glaring omissions, and more than a few errors, it's refreshing to read reviews by someone who actually has an affinity for the horror film. Not nearly as lacking as its detractors would have you believe.

Stell, John. *Psychos! Sickos! Sequels! Horror Films of the 1980s.* Baltimore: Midnight Marquee, 1998.

Stell makes no bones about the fact that he's more of a fan than an author. But like any true fan, he knows his stuff. At least his book is absent of the careless errors found all too often in some of the more academic works on the genre.

Taylor, Philip M. *Steven Spielberg: The Man, His Movies and Their Meaning.* New York: Continuum, 1992.

Slim biography which does an admirable job of condensing Spielberg's career without shortchanging any one aspect of it.

Timpone, Anthony. *Men, Makeup, and Monsters: Hollywood's Masters of Illusion and FX.* New York: St. Martin's, 1996.

A thankfully non-technical survey of horror's greatest makeup artists by the editor of *Fangoria.* If there's anybody qualified to write about this subject, it's Timpone, the man most responsible for turning these makeup men into stars in their own right. Like his magazine, his book appeals to all fans of the genre, casual and otherwise.

Twitchell, James B. *Dreadful Pleasures: An Anatomy of Modern Horror.* New York: Oxford University, 1985.

An often brilliant sometimes impenetrable work with examines the allure of the genre through a critical examination of different horror archetypes. Casual fans may want to steer clear while psych, soc, lit, and anthro students are sure to find it worthwhile.

Waller, Gregory A., ed. *American Horrors: Essays on the Modern American Horror Film.* Urbana: University of Illinois, 1987.

A series of academic essays on popular modern horror films. Most appeared first (at least in some form) in other sources, but it's nice to see them together in a single work.

Index